JENATSCH'S AXE

Changing Perspectives on Early Modern Europe

James B. Collins, Professor of History, Georgetown University
Mack P. Holt, Professor of History, George Mason University

(ISSN 1542–3905)

Changing Perspectives on Early Modern Europe brings forward the latest research on Europe during the transformation from the medieval to the modern world. The series publishes innovative scholarship on the full range of topical and geographic fields and includes works on cultural, economic, intellectual, political, religious, and social history.

Jenatsch's Axe

Social Boundaries, Identity, and Myth in the Era of the Thirty Years' War

Randolph C. Head

University of Rochester Press

First published 2008
Transferred to digital printing and reprinted in paperback 2016

University of Rochester Press
668 Mt. Hope Avenue, Rochester, NY 14620, USA
www.urpress.com
and Boydell & Brewer Limited
PO Box 9, Woodbridge, Suffolk IP12 3DF, UK
www.boydellandbrewer.com

Hardcover ISBN-13: 978-1-58046-276-1
Hardcover ISBN-10: 1-58046-276-6
Paperback ISBN-13: 978-1-58046-565-6
ISSN: 1542-3905

Library of Congress Cataloging-in-Publication Data

Head, Randolph Conrad.
   Jenatsch's axe : social boundaries, identity, and myth in the era of the Thirty Years' War / Randolph C. Head.
      p. cm.— (Changing perspectives on early modern Europe, ISSN 1542–3905 ; v. 9)
   Includes bibliographical references and index.
   ISBN-13: 978-1-58046-276-1 (hardcover : alk. paper)
   ISBN-10: 1-58046-276-6 (hardcover : alk. paper) 1. Jenatsch, Georg, 1596–1639. 2. Clergy—Switzerland—Graubünden—Biography. 3. Statesmen—Switzerland—Graubünden—Biography. I. Title.
   DQ498.54.J46H43 2008
   949.4'7303'092—dc22
   [B]

                                                                    2007043034

A catalogue record for this title is available from the British Library.

This publication is printed on acid-free paper.
Printed in the United States of America

George Jenatsch in 1636, near the end of his life. Modern copy by Paul Martig (1935) of a contemporary portrait now in private possession. By permission of the Rätisches Museum, Chur (I.15).

CONTENTS

Illustrations

ACKNOWLEDGMENTS

This book has been many years coming, and many friends and colleagues have helped it reach its readers. When I originally wrote about Graubünden in the sixteenth and early seventeenth centuries, I avoided the troublesome figure of George Jenatsch, surrounded as he clearly was with layer upon layer of myth, local pride, and romance. The two monumental biographies chronicling his life, by Ernst Haffter and Alexander Pfister, seemed to say as much as was needed about an adventurer who had little effect on the institutions and the political culture I was studying—though these works did provide me with many useful references. Some years later, it occurred to me that Jenatsch, himself a convert, might provide a useful avenue for researching confessional difference in this region, an impression that intensified when I reflected that he was a convert not only in religion, but in language, social estate, and other ways as well. Stimulated by my colleague Edmund "Terry" Burke III of the University of California-Santa Cruz and his students' work on social biography, I proposed a paper for the 1997 Sixteenth Century Studies Conference that took a social biography approach to Jenatsch. Shortly thereafter, I entered into correspondence with Marco Bellabarba of the Istituto Storico Italo-Germanico in Trent. Dr. Bellabarba generously included my paper on Jenatsch in the volume of essays he was editing, *Identità territoriali e cultura politica nella prima età moderna*. There things remained for some years, until encouragement from several colleagues in Graubünden, among them Reto Hänny and especially Jon Mathieu (a fellow Jenatschologist), led me to take up the project again.

Throughout my career, Dr. Georg Jäger in Chur has encouraged my work and helped in innumerable ways to support it. The foundation for historical and cultural research he founded, the *Verein für Bündner Kulturforschung* (whose Romansh name, *Istitut per la perscrutaziun della cultura Grischuna*, always makes me smile) has provided me with a research base in Switzerland, helped organize funding, and arranged housing, travel, and chances to present my work to local historians. The maps in this volume were produced by Peter Vetsch and funded by the *Verein*, with careful review and correction by Florian Hitz. The Rätisches Museum, Chur, was forthcoming and flexible in providing the images for the rest of the volume: thanks to Dr. Jürg Simonett, its director; to Arno Caluori for graphical assistance; and to Yves Mühleman for providing a tour of Jenatsch's clothing, which is currently in storage. Likewise, many other colleagues in Graubünden, including Martin Bundi, Silvio Färber, Albert Fischer, Silvio Margadant, and Immacolata

Saulle Hippenmeyer, have helped an American avoid mistakes obvious and subtle. The Staatsarchiv Graubünden, the Bündner Kantonsbibliothek, the Stadtarchiv Chur, and the episcopal archive in Chur have offered me generous access to their collections, while the Archäologisches Dienst Graubünden responded swiftly and carefully to requests for information. In Zurich, the Historical Seminar at the University of Zurich, particularly the chair of Prof. Dr. Roger Sablonier, repeatedly provided collegial support and a place to work. I am also deeply grateful to Regula Schmid-Keeling for reading and commenting on the entire manuscript, and to Hildegard Elisabeth Keller for her comments on Chapter 6. Additionally, I wish to acknowledge the staffs of the Staatsarchiv Zürich and the Zentralbibliothek Zürich.

In the United States, the Academic Senate of the University of California-Riverside has provided steady funding that helped cover research trips and expenses. At the Department of History, my research assistants David Marshall, Ansara Martino, and Michael Cox will all see traces of their work in this volume, while my colleagues on the faculty put up with repeated conversations about that fellow "murdered by a man dressed as a bear." Michael Drake, an advanced graduate student, helped prepare the index. My colleague Thomas Cogswell coached me on presentation, as well as embodying shameless enthusiasm for historical scholarship in everything he writes and says. Kay Edwards of the University of South Carolina read and commented on the entire manuscript; thanks also to Amy Nelson Burnett, Marc Forster, and Edward Muir. I am grateful to the anonymous readers at the University of Rochester Press for their thoughtful comments. Since I joined the faculty of the University of California, Prof. Thomas A. Brady Jr. from Berkeley has joined my graduate advisor, H. C. Erik Midelfort, as both a mentor and a friend. My deep thanks to both of them: their impending retirement will reshape the landscape of Reformation and early modern European studies in the United States.

Finally, my family has patiently borne my absences for research and my absorption in writing and thinking about this book for over a decade. When progress slowed, my partner, Chih-Cheng Tsai, gently but firmly reminded me to get back to work, as did my mother, Anita K. Head, to whom this volume is dedicated.

Prologue

Murder (Victim) in the Cathedral

On August 4, at 10:30 in the morning, a skull was found at a depth of one meter, covered with dirt and debris. Even the first superficial examination revealed a deep slicing wound to the left temple. A few black hairs still clung to the edges of the injury. This established with great likelihood that the grave of Jürg Jenatsch had been found.

—In the newspaper *Der Freie Rätier*, 1959

Only small windows light the interior of the ancient Catholic cathedral in the Swiss provincial city of Chur, which is often dark enough already in the shadow of a rising mountainside or under the region's rainy sky. Centuries of relative poverty during the Middle Ages, even as the rest of Europe raised stunning Gothic churches, prevented the bishops of Chur from carrying out the remodeling that might have opened up the heavy walls or raised the ceiling. Throughout its history, the cathedral crouched within a walled precinct above the alleys and tightly packed buildings of the small city that lay below, since the bishop and his parishioners were only rarely friends. In the 1300s and 1400s, the city struggled against the bishop's political authority, and in the 1500s, its citizens eagerly adopted the rapidly spreading Protestant Reformation and tried to expel the bishops entirely. Even in the 1990s, local Catholics laid siege to the episcopal quarter with a sit-in in order to protest the current bishop's policies. In the summer of 1959, in contrast, the bishop's relations with the city, the local canton of Graubünden, and the Swiss national government were calm, but the cathedral floor was in disarray for a different reason. A party of excavators was on the hunt for the buried remains of a well-known historical figure: George Jenatsch.[1] They had already removed the heavy flagstones from the floor in several areas and sunk multiple trenches as they searched for their quarry.

The archaeologists' problem was simple: Jenatsch was almost certainly buried somewhere under the floor of the cathedral, since several reports of his death and funeral in January 1639—320 years earlier—described the procession to the cathedral and the ceremonious interment of his freshly murdered corpse. Unfortunately, the commentators had neglected to say exactly *where* in the cathedral his grave was located, although an old rumor (first recorded nearly fifty years after he died) put the location near the cathedral's organ. Moreover, his was not the only burial under the floor: in the long centuries since the current building had risen above Chur, dozens if not hundreds of prominent men had found their last rest there, close to the holiness of the high altar and the hope of resurrection. How, then, to locate one particular skeleton?

Initial newspaper reports noted, "at first, the excavations uncovered the remains of a number of burials, none of which provided sure clues that it might constitute the sought-after skeleton."[2] Indeed, the excavators nearly took a wrong turn at one point, as they later admitted, when they provisionally identified a particular "strongly-built and tall man's skeleton"[3] as their target. Digging a little further, however, they encountered another grave that possessed the one crucial feature that all others lacked:

> Here, both the left and the right side of the skull revealed deep cutting wounds (the pieces of bone that had been sliced out still lay nearby, mixed with hair!), which resulted from the deadly axe-blows to which Jenatsch had succumbed on the murderous night of January 24, 1639.[4]

After all, everyone knew not only that Jenatsch had been murdered, but also that it was an axe that had killed him.

Placing an upside-down mason's bucket over the exposed skull to protect it, the researchers removed more flagstones, which involved bracing the cathedral's modern pews, so that they could uncover the entire burial. The remains they found quickly confirmed what the axe-damaged skull had promised: this skeleton really did belong to the seventeenth-century personage they sought. His face, once reconstructed, corresponded to the best surviving portrait, and just as the historical accounts claimed, he had been buried in the same clothes he died in, still caked with blood. The clothes, later analyzed and restored in loving detail, were ostentatiously luxurious, made of velvet and silk and lined with fur and gold brocade.[5] When he died, Jenatsch had been the most powerful man in the region, a ruthless social climber who wielded enormous power because of his success as a military entrepreneur. He was also a cunning diplomat who had collected rich rewards from the foreign powers that were struggling to gain control of the region's mountain passes for their armies. He had come a long way from his schoolboy poverty, when he had taken his meals at the public soup kitchen in Zurich.

The clothes in Jenatsch's grave revealed something else: in addition to the rosary in his hand and the Catholic medallions found by his side, he had died wearing a scapular—a square of cloth that devout Catholics carried against the skin of their chest—finely embroidered with Catholic symbols.[6] Naturally, to be buried in the cathedral, Jenatsch had to be a Catholic, especially in light of the bitterness that divided Catholics and Protestants in the 1630s. Unlike most of his contemporaries, however, Jenatsch was a convert. Born and raised a Reformed

Protestant, he had even become a Protestant pastor before turning to Catholicism in the 1630s. He had gained so many political and social advantages from his conversion that it was hard for either contemporaries or historians to believe that he had converted out of deep religious conviction. Finding the scapular hidden under the sumptuous jacket he was wearing at the drinking party that ended his life suggested that his Catholicism might have been more serious than such skeptics thought.

On the wall near the skeleton under the cathedral floor, Jenatsch's gravestone celebrated in sonorous Latin that this "Saul, now become Paul" had died in the faith. Yet neither the Latin tongue of the Church nor Chur's German dialect was Jenatsch's native tongue. As a boy, he had spoken Romansh Ladin, a dialect of the Rhaeto-Romance language that was spoken only along the crest of the Alps between Italy and the German lands. During his rise to prominence, Jenatsch also learned to write and speak in several of Europe's major languages, all of them useful for his stormy career: Latin as a pastor, Italian when he served in the armies of Venice, German in Zurich and with his German-speaking wife, and French when he served and then betrayed the French general in Graubünden in the early 1630s. Zoartz, Giorgio, Georgius, Jörg—these were all names he had used when it was to his advantage.[7]

All advantages had failed him on the night when the axe struck him down. Jenatsch's murder took place in the private room of a tavern in Chur, where he was drinking with several other colonels, accompanied by musicians. Around eleven in the evening that January 24, a group of masked revelers entered the tavern and asked permission to join the drinkers, who were celebrating Carnival. According to the murder investigation, the revelers found a ready welcome: "Certainly let them come," Jenatsch and his friends agreed, "since we are all here to have a good time."[8] The band of men quickly surged up the stairs to join Jenatsch and the colonels. Their leader—dressed in a bear costume—saluted Jenatsch and took his proffered hand. The seeming friendliness was a ruse, intended to bring Jenatsch into position for a shot from the bear's hidden pistol. When the shot only wounded him in the torso, the masked men all fell upon Jenatsch, who tried to defend himself with a large candlestick. His resistance was futile, and soon a terrible blow with an axe split his skull; the wound was undoubtedly fatal, according to the evidence from his grave.[9] After his body hit the floor, another blow with a war hammer crushed the other side of his head, "so that his brains sprayed out," as one account has it.[10]

Both the ritualistic details and the extreme violence of the killing suggest that more than merely political passions were at work. In fact, Jenatsch was himself a murderer with many enemies in Graubünden. Ever since his entry into the political arena, he had been associated with bloodshed, including the death under torture of a Catholic priest in 1618, a fatal duel with his own commanding officer in 1626, and the ruthless assassination of a rival in Chiavenna in 1636. Most visible among his many enemies was the family of Pompeius von Planta. Jenatsch had helped murder Pompeius in the castle of Rietberg in 1621, using an axe that left Planta's body pinned to the floor with its blade. Consequently, when Jenatsch fell to masked killers who used an axe, a rumor spread rapidly. It was Pompeius von Planta's son who had killed him, many believed, using the *very same axe* that had killed his father!

The breathless tone of the newspaper articles from 1959 raises one last mystery. Why did they praise this ruthless and violent man as a patriot and national hero? To understand the excitement when his body was unearthed in 1959, studying the historical record is not enough. Jenatsch's story was well known across Switzerland and Germany not because of his historical importance, but mainly because people had read a popular novel by Conrad Ferdinand Meyer, *Jürg Jenatsch*, first published in 1874. As another 1959 newspaper article put it:

> [Jenatsch's] grave is now discovered. Conrad Ferdinand Meyer erected his literary monument, but a second monument in stone is still lacking. Yet this great if controversial son of Graubünden deserves both, if only because of his passionate love of liberty and his fatherland.[11]

In reality, this characterization of Jenatsch as a patriot and liberator derived primarily from literary works written long after his death. This chameleon, who repeatedly changed his status, his religion, and his languages while alive, also managed to bridge the gap between villain and hero—and thus between history and myth—after he died. How this happened, and what it can tell us about both the society he lived in and about how we tell (historical) stories, are the subjects of this book.

INTRODUCTION

A typical, if old-fashioned, way to organize a biography is to write about a person's life and times. In fact, *Georg Jenatsch: His Life and Times* is the title, in German, of a massive study about Jenatsch published in 1936. After some background information about Jenatsch's family, the biography by Alexander Pfister begins with Jenatsch's birth and continues through childhood, school days, and events in his adulthood—concentrating on his rise to political influence—until it reaches his death.[1] A brief reflection on Jenatsch's larger significance wraps things up into a neat package, into a *story*. Like most biographies, Pfister's provides readers with a single protagonist whose life has a beginning, middle, and ending—and so much the better if it is a dramatic ending involving an axe and a man dressed as a bear. Conventional biography reflects the way we experience our own lives as a single, relatively coherent thread of experience. This way of thinking about individuals' lives also reflects deeper tendencies about how Western culture thinks about the past. After all, most history books lay out their story in chronological order, as do many novels.

The life of Jenatsch calls for a different approach. He spent his life in a world divided by tangled and overlapping political authorities, riven by religious and regional differences, and suffering from agricultural crisis and multiple plagues. Conflicts in Graubünden swirled him into the greater crisis of the Thirty Years' War that tore Europe apart from 1618 to 1648. Most often, it was the bold and the ruthless—people like Jenatsch—who succeeded during these years, as underlying social and cultural patterns shifted in response to the forces of change. Experiencing the trials of his time, struggling within the rigid roles dictated by his premodern society before eventually transcending them as a self-made man, Jenatsch transgressed the expectations of his contemporaries as often as he conformed to them. The strangeness of Jenatsch's life, including the wild brutality of specific episodes, provides clues about the sometimes invisible but always powerful social and cultural patterns he confronted.

Jenatsch is thus interesting exactly *because* he challenged conventional wisdom and conventional boundaries of his age. His life merits attention not because of its unity, but because it helps us see how people in seventeenth-century Europe built their identities and imagined their world. In a society torn by religious division and economic transformation—not unlike our own—Europeans during the

Thirty Years' War faced complex contradictions between expectations and reality. On the one hand, public culture across the continent propagated strong models for the identity and behavior of individuals and groups, expressed in the language of religious orthodoxy and social estate. On the other hand, the clash between competing Christian denominations together with the corrosive social consequences of widespread warfare after 1618 put all such models in doubt. One way to approach this contradiction is to look closely at how those caught in this vortex of unstable identities coped with the challenge. For such an analysis, someone like Jenatsch, who appears to have accepted the values of the crumbling old system even as he broke all of its rules, provides an excellent case study. Taking this approach to Jenatsch's life thus does echo the concern found in traditional biographies for the times as well as the life, though not from a traditional perspective.

Writing a biography that concentrates on disruptions and boundary crossing faces its own particular challenges, though, even if the incoherence that cuts through Jenatsch's story offers valuable opportunities for analysis. If rupture and contradiction predominate when we analyze who he was and what he did, we can no longer make our goal the reconstruction of his supposed character or his imagined destiny. Instead, we must thread together diverging insights and shifting perspectives to understand Jenatsch as he struggled and changed. Fortunately, Jenatsch's life has long attracted attention, and many narrators have already confronted the challenge of making sense of it. Past authors employed a wide diversity of approaches as they sought to place Jenatsch in the tumultuous era of the Thirty Years' War. Their shifting strategies suggest different ways to approach this difficult subject, while simultaneously revealing how different authors and eras understood individuals and their actions within larger contexts. Many earlier accounts relied on conventional motifs that were characteristic for each author's own time, such as religious loyalties, national patriotism, or models of individual character. Tracing how representations of Jenatsch have changed can thus help us understand the interpretive framework available to authors from various periods; it also raises the more general question of how historians (or anyone) make sense of other people and their lives.

It is particularly telling that almost every storyteller—that is, almost every chronicler, novelist, dramatist, historian, or filmmaker—who has described Jenatsch has chosen to highlight some of the same story-building elements. The axe provides the most visible example of this problem of representation: the deadly weapon that Jenatsch supposedly used on Pompeius von Planta in 1621 and that an anonymous killer in 1639 allegedly used on Jenatsch. Ever since the murder in the tavern in 1639, stories about Jenatsch inevitably include an axe, though for changing reasons. Even the archaeologists digging in the cathedral floor in 1959 depended on this famous axe, or at least on the marks it left on his skull, to identify Jenatsch's grave. The notion that Jenatsch was murdered with the same weapon that he used years before to butcher his rival has simply been too attractive to leave out.

The story of "the same axe" is also at least potentially true. Pompeius von Planta really was killed with an axe (although Jenatsch was probably not the man who wielded it), and so was Jenatsch himself. Whether the same axe was used in both murders is beyond proof or disproof, and mattered less to various narrators than the way the story connected the Jenatsch of 1621 to the Jenatsch of 1639, as a single character. For some authors, the axe motif captured Jenatsch's troublesome yet fascinating tendency toward violence, whereas others thought that it revealed him as a man who would do what was necessary—even if it was distasteful for its brutality—for a greater cause. From the perspective of many Protestant authors, for example, the murder of the Catholic ringleader Planta was evil, but it was also a necessary act whose horror found resolution in the retributive murder of Jenatsch. Both biographical and literary representations of Jenatsch often sought to portray such closure, with accounts balanced and loose ends tied up. In the end, though, Jenatsch's murder in 1639 represented anything but closure: his life had been full of loose ends, crossed boundaries, and identities taken up and dropped, and representations of him both before and after his death continued to clash over what his life and deeds meant.

The two convictions sketched above shape my analysis. The first is that Jenatsch's life, which visibly transgressed his culture's expectations, is more revealing in its discontinuities than in its coherence. Every time Jenatsch broke the rules, he made more visible the boundaries of ethnicity, religion, and social estate around him. The second is that representing such a chameleon poses its own challenges, as seen in the way different writers have struggled to bring order to his story. The themes, motifs, and catchy historical tidbits that earlier authors—and this book—rely on are themselves part of a historical record that reveals a great deal not only about the life and times of Jenatsch, but also about how societies ceaselessly revise their narratives of heroes and villains to fit new circumstances.

Each of these convictions also embodies a vision about how to write history, and each draws on current ideas in history and the human sciences. Much innovative thinking in the humanities over the last thirty years has emphasized rupture and discontinuity over unity and wholeness. Today's critical theory and post-structuralism argue that many things once treated as stable entities, including individual persons, are as much scholars' constructions founded on our cognitive attachment to coherence—or on hegemonic power structures—as they are part of some unchangeable nature of things demonstrated through factual evidence. Clearly, my attention to disjunction in analyzing George Jenatsch reflects impulses from such post-structuralist critique. But what then? Deconstructing the unity of another historical icon may be intriguing, but why should anyone be interested in the leftover shards of a life that was lived four centuries ago? I leave the postmodern agenda behind when I use Jenatsch's life as a tool for uncovering a past era's way of understanding human identity, rather than as a reminder that understanding a fixed past is impossible. Similarly, treating representations of Jenatsch as an unstable product of constant writing and rewriting—in short, as a textual rather than as a historical phenomenon—draws on the important insights of deconstruction as proposed most forcefully by Jacques Derrida. But whereas philosophers debate the consequences of treating all knowledge as texts subject to a free play of signifiers, I prefer, like many historians, to bracket the relationship of text and context in favor of going back to the stories I want to tell. Finally, some historians have recently began an intensified study of the relationship between history and memory. Research on this subject emphasizes that although formal history can help shape and transmit memories, it inevitably works with other modes of memory—from local traditions and folktales to dramas, motion pictures, and lately advertising—in the construction of the historical past. From this perspective, writing another book about Jenatsch only adds another voice to, rather than seizing control of, a trajectory of memory that has incorporated many elements over nearly four centuries.

These convictions shape the chapters that follow, which do not adhere to the traditional chronological approach except in the short overview found in chapter 1. Instead, chapters 2 through 5 each concentrate on a specific social boundary that George Jenatsch challenged, using evidence from every period of his life, while chapter 6 traces representations of Jenatsch from the 1610s to the present.

Chapter 2 addresses the regional and linguistic boundaries that defined Jenatsch's world as he grew up and that provided the arena for his later actions. How did Jenatsch's origins in the Engadine Valley high in the Alps, in the quirky "republic of Three Leagues" in Graubünden, and in the Holy Roman Empire of the German Nation shape his path? Ours is an age used to thinking in terms of nations or countries (though with some skepticism), but in the seventeenth century, nations as an axis of identity were only taking shape, and had to coexist with other ways of understanding human groups in the larger world. Additionally, Jenatsch's particular background required that he speak multiple languages from an early age, including the local Romansh language of the Engadine, German and Italian in various dialects, and Latin, which was still the language of learning and (to a declining extent) of faith. How did he use different languages as he moved, and did his use of any particular language generate another identity, akin to what we today call ethnicity?

Chapter 3 turns to religion. Jenatsch was born into the Swiss Reformed Protestant Church and became a pastor through rigorous training in Zurich's seminary and Basel's university. His teachers expected him not only to become a shepherd for Reformed flocks in Graubünden, but also to fight for a beleaguered faith in a religiously divided land. Yet Jenatsch soon abandoned his pastor's gown and eventually his faith, becoming a secular Catholic before he died. What boundaries separated these two related but antagonistic religious faiths, and what drove someone so totally committed to one faith to convert to its greatest rival? How did Jenatsch perceive this spiritual terrain, and how did he act on religious motives at different points in his life? His struggles echo the larger confrontation that transformed Europe in the same era, as the division of Western Christendom into multiple and hostile branches after the Protestant Reformation led to bitter conflict as well as new ways of thinking about religion and its place in human life.

Chapter 4 concentrates on a system of social status and identity that no longer resonates in modern life: social estate. Throughout the sixteenth and even seventeenth centuries, many Europeans continued to imagine that a properly ordered human society consisted of three distinct status groups: the clergy, the nobility, and the common people. Since Jenatsch came from the clerical estate, spent the bulk of his career as a common man, and was moving toward ennoblement when he died, his life can cast light on how these categories functioned in the ideology and in the reality of his era. As a pastor, as a soldier, and as a (potential) nobleman, Jenatsch invested himself in his roles, at least in public, as we can see from his letters as in his actions. Yet his successes also marked him as a newcomer, unwelcome among the more established military and noble families in his region: not only power politics and religion, but also wounded pride and offended status helped to motivate his bloody murder.

Finally, chapter 5 turns to the enduring role of identities based on kinship and blood ties, identities that remained profoundly connected to early modern understandings of the relationship between men and women. Graubünden was notoriously a region torn by clan violence, and the Engadine in particular suffered from long blood feuds that involved whole villages over generations. Although the biographers of the twentieth century chose to emphasize high politics in explaining how Jenatsch rose and died, the surviving evidence contains telling revelations about how honor, pride, and blood ties shaped his career just as much as diplomacy and official institutions. This chapter also addresses one striking feature of the historical record in Graubünden: to a remarkable degree, the documentary evidence contains almost no information about women. In contrast to this silencing, surprisingly, the nineteenth-century plays and dramas about Jenatsch gave women—often imaginary ones—pivotal roles in their narratives. Why should this be so, and what does it tell us about seventeenth-century gender identity as well as later preoccupations?

Particular historical episodes may appear in several of these chapters, interspersed among others that took place earlier or later. Rather than a thread, the reader will confront a tapestry—or perhaps a kaleidoscope, shifting each time we look at it—as the book progresses. Moreover, a particular moment in Jenatsch's life may be described quite differently in different contexts, depending on the issues under consideration. For example, the notorious Thusis tribunal of 1618, in which Jenatsch became a significant participant, will first appear in connection with the struggles that divided Catholics and Protestants in the 1610s (chapter 3) but will reappear with a different focus, such as social boundaries between clerics and laymen (chapter 4) or the best way to really insult someone in the seventeenth century (chapter 5). Different evidence will move to the forefront at different points in this book, connecting what happened to multiple trends.

Chapter 6 turns to representations of Jenatsch's life by looking at folktales, histories, novels, plays, and movies about Jenatsch that were crafted between 1639 and the present. Representations of Jenatsch fall into quite distinct periods. During the first two centuries after he died, they mostly emphasized the religious boundary that he violated by converting to Catholicism—with anger from Protestant authors, and satisfaction from Catholic ones. A later romantic period, in search of an underlying unity in Jenatsch's life, cast him simultaneously as a national hero and as a deeply flawed individual shaped by his essential character. Unlike the first period, authors during this phase found it impossible to talk about Jenatsch without including the women who had shaped this character—even if they had to invent the women involved. Finally, in a third period that peaked after World War II, novelists and historians lost their interest in both national heroism and unchangeable personal character. Far more tentative and far more willing to cast a harsh light on the man, authors from this third period gave up the search for coherence that had characterized the second. In each case, the form of representation that writers chose reflected a tension between the evidence they had and the political and social issues that mattered to them. At a deeper level, shifting representations also captured their understanding of what it meant to be a full person, and how to tell a human story.

Looking at multiple versions of Jenatsch's life also puts the pursuit of biography itself into question—not because biography is the same as fiction, but because changing ways of telling the story draw our attention to the relationship between the form a biographical narrative takes and the content it conveys. In many ways, this book shares the characteristics of the third period, since it is skeptical about unity of character and pays close attention to issues of representation, as well as to questions of fact. If we believe that biography, like history-writing more generally, takes part in ongoing conversations about memory and truth, rather than fixing a single truth, then we must practice it differently and apply it to different goals.

From this perspective, each period's way of telling Jenatsch's story reflects deeper cultural trends that can help us differentiate our complex present from equally complex but very different pasts. In a sense, each period has placed Jenatsch (as represented not only in scraps of paper that have survived from seventeeth-century Europe, but also in his memory as transmitted along multiple channels) in terms of the challenges people in that period faced and the discontinuities that disrupted their confidence. Yet Jenatsch is not diminished by such shifting representation: he was a real person whose actions, triumphs, and murder were the stuff of human experience providing raw material for memories that will continue to evolve.

Chapter 1

A Brief Life of George Jenatsch

Before we start taking apart identities and social boundaries during the European seventeenth century, we first need to put George Jenatsch's life together. What happened to him and around him during the tumultuous years from 1596 to 1639, and how did he experience these events? Answering such questions requires that we first look at the region and the time in which Jenatsch's life took place, and then recount the major events he participated in between his birth in 1596 and his murder by axe. Of course, even the simplest chronological list of events rests on assumptions about what the real turning points in a life were, for better or for worse. With a figure as ambivalent and complex as Jenatsch, trying to tell his story simply soon becomes quite complicated. Still, every story must start somewhere, and this one will begin with a place, a time, and a life.

Graubünden, the Three Leagues, and the Engadine

Jenatsch's life allows us to trace the boundaries of identity in early modern Europe in part because of the distinctive region where he lived, acted, and died. This region is known by several names, reflecting the diverse languages spoken by its inhabitants. All the common names reflect the region's political structure, though, and they all mean the same thing: the "Grey Leagues"—Graubünden in German, Grigioni in Italian, and Grischuns in Romansh. French speakers used their own version of the name, Grisons, which has also become the preferred version in England. Only in Latin did the region have a different name, "Rhaetia Prima." This name, too, reflected political conditions, though from a much earlier period when the Central Alps formed a province of the Roman Empire.

Jenatsch came from the very heart of the Alps, from a long, high east-west valley called the Engadine that nestles among the major Alpine ranges. This valley faced profoundly different political, social, and cultural worlds to the north and to the south. Across the southern passes lay Italy, which had been part of the ancient network of Mediterranean civilizations for over two thousand years before Jenatsch was born. Over the passes in the other direction, to the north, lay the German lands. Agriculture and especially cities came to Germany much later than to Italy: the oldest towns dated back only to the Roman era, and most were much

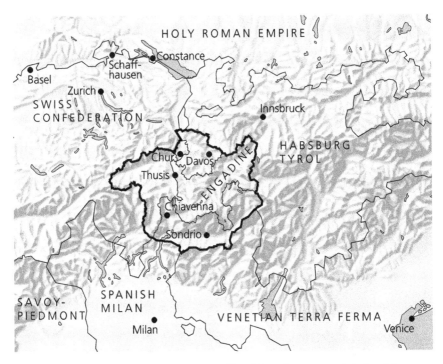

Map 1.1 Graubünden in regional context. The Three Leagues and their subject territories bordered on the Swiss Confederation, Habsburg Tyrol, the Venetian Terra Ferma, and Spanish Milan. Map designed by Peter Vetsch, Chur. Base Map: Schweizer Weltatlas 2006 © EDK. By permission of the Verein für Bündner Kulturforschung, Chur.

more recent, products of the flowering European civilization after the year 1000 C.E. Italians grew wheat, chestnuts, rice, and fruit in a sunny, dry climate; Germans tended oats, wheat, spelt, and rye during steady rains. Much of Graubünden itself, on the shoulders of Alpine peaks, lay at too high an altitude for any of these crops to thrive; the peasants in Jenatsch's Engadine therefore primarily raised cattle that grazed on mountain meadows in the summer before spending winters in stalls surrounded by deep snow.[1] Graubünden was economically as well as geographically and politically marginal—both because it sat at the margins of two different agrarian worlds, and even more so because the foundation of premodern life, agriculture, required serious adjustments because of the harsh terrain and climate of the mountains.

While geography and language patterns were important, its political system was what defined Graubünden. The structures that linked individuals, families, and communities into a larger system of political interaction gave Graubünden its identity as a specific region with its own historical traditions. During Jenatsch's life, outsiders would have described Graubünden as belonging to the Holy Roman Empire, and within the Empire to the Swiss Confederation and its allies. Before describing the exact political situation of Graubünden, however, one important difference from modern political systems must be noted. Today, a community's political affiliation usually depends primarily on its location, making borders extremely important. This fact helps explain why modern nations will argue, litigate, and even fight for years over seemingly trivial border disputes. In early modern Europe, in contrast, political space was layered in more complex ways. Political affiliation depended partly on location, of course, but it could also depend on a person's or a community's relationship with a particular lord. Both space *and* lordship defined political communities.[2] After about 1500, spatial boundaries began to predominate, slowly superseding older ties of lordship and dependence. In Graubünden around 1600, this process was by no means complete, since various lordly claims overlapped with the territorial boundaries that placed Graubünden within the Empire and linked it to the Swiss. The bishops of Chur, various monasteries and lordly families, and most important, the mighty Habsburg family, which ruled in Austria and reigned over the entire Holy Roman Empire, all had claims within Graubünden.

Viewed from the perspective of the local population, however, the space of Graubünden at the end of the Middle Ages was organized politically neither by national borders nor by lordships, but rather into communes and leagues. By the 1520s, Graubünden as a polity consisted of fifty-two individual "judicial communities" (*Comüns, Gerichtsgemeinden*), each of them a sworn association of the adult arms-bearing men who lived in a particular location. Most of these communities, which I will call communes in order to focus on their political and ideological character, included the population of a single mountain valley or a stretch of a larger river valley, although a few consisted of towns. Graubünden's only real city, Chur, also formed a single commune in this system. Some communes contained only one or two villages and only hundreds of inhabitants, whereas others comprised multiple villages (with their own local politics) and might have several thousand citizens.[3]

The fifty-two Bündner communes, in turn, formed three separate leagues that took shape during the 1400s. Like the individual communes, each league was an association created for a specific end, though the members of each league were communes, not individuals. The oldest league was the Grey League, which included most of western Graubünden and the upper Rhine valley. Its roots went back to the lordship of the Abbey of Disentis, and it grew as peasants began taking part in the struggles among local petty lords, helping them keep the peace or expand their influence. The largest of the three leagues was the League of the House of God (*Gotteshausbund, Chadé*), which included central and southern Graubünden, from Chur in the north to the Engadine and several valleys running toward Italy in the south. The bishop of Chur was the high lord for this league.

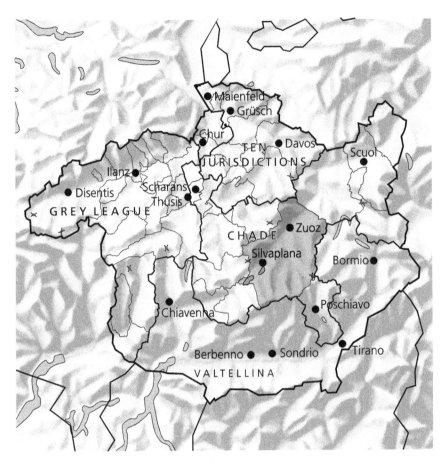

Map 1.2 The topography and politics of Graubünden. The shaded area is the Upper Engadine, Jenatsch's home community. Map designed by Peter Vetsch, Chur. Base Map: Schweizer Weltatlas 2006 © EDK. By permission of the Verein für Bündner Kulturforschung, Chur.

Indeed, its name reflects his pivotal role: the "House of God" not only referred to the cathedral that was the focus of Christian worship in the region, but also implied that the bishop was a kind of father to all the inhabitants, who lived, metaphorically, in his house and under his guidance. In reality, though, the league as a stable organization took shape because the local communes and their leaders sought to limit the bishop's power, or at least to domesticate his authority for their own interests. Jenatsch's family came from the mountain heart of this league. The third league, the League of the Ten Jurisdictions (*Zehngerichtenbund*), was the newest and smallest, consisting of ten communes in the northwestern corner of

Graubünden.[4] By 1500, eight of these communes had fallen under the personal lordship of the powerful Habsburg family; as this was happening, the communes banded together to preserve the privileges they had received from their earlier lords. Jenatsch eventually became a citizen of Davos, the largest commune in the Ten Jurisdictions.

The Three Leagues thus had separate origins, but they began working together almost as soon as they came into existence. By the late 1400s, delegates from all three met regularly to discuss shared problems, a fact mirrored in a complex and growing body of formal agreements and treaties among them and their neighbors. During the chaos of the Italian Wars in the late 1400s, the Leagues began intervening in the Italian Alpine valleys to their south; by 1512, they had made themselves lords over the northern Italian territory known as the Valtellina.[5] Ruling over subjects made the Leagues' union closer and encouraged them to craft a comprehensive letter of alliance, called the *Bundesbrief*, in 1525. By doing so, the Three Leagues took their final form as a single, though internally fragmented, political entity. The *Bundesbrief* called for regular meetings of the representatives of the fifty-two communes in Chur, Davos, and Ilanz, the main towns of each league, whenever they had business in common. The most frequent reason for meetings was to negotiate with foreign powers interested in using Graubünden's strategic passes.

Acquisition of a subject domain to rule over had important consequences for the Three Leagues.[6] Shared lordship over the Valtellina strengthened internal ties among the Leagues, although the temptation to exploit their new subjects also created new tensions and resentments. In particular, the custom that soon emerged of appointing judges and magistrates for two-year rotating terms in the Valtellina provoked constant strife. Individual communes soon claimed the right to appoint someone to these offices and did not hesitate to sell the offices to the highest bidders. The rising cost of purchasing an office meant that officeholders used their terms mostly to earn back their investment, and as much more as they could. The resulting corruption and incompetence triggered repeated conflicts both in the Valtellina and in Graubünden.

Graubünden's new acquisition had even more fatal consequences after the Protestant Reformation. The Bündner had seized the Valtellina in 1512, taking over as lords from the temporarily weakened Dukes of Milan. When the Protestant movement swept through Graubünden shortly thereafter, however, the Valtellina population remained almost entirely Catholic. Later in the 1500s, as the Catholic Counter-Reformation became more forceful, local resentment over the religious coercion and political corruption that characterized Bündner rule grew.[7] Additionally, the Valtellina was strategically located across crucial European lines of communication; possession of the Valtellina therefore drew Graubünden into large-scale politics in often unwelcome ways. Outside powers—especially Venice, France, Austria, and Spain—cajoled, bribed, and threatened the Three Leagues in order to gain access to the Valtellina's passes, or to deny access to their rivals.

Spain in particular also saw itself as the protector of the Valtellina Catholics, ruled by a majority-Protestant state, and frequently used religious affairs to justify intervening in the valley's and the Leagues' politics. The resulting struggles peaked during the Thirty Years' War from 1618 to 1648—that is, during Jenatsch's life.[8]

While local politics within Graubünden provide one context for understanding Jenatsch, we also need to understand that this bottom-up system coexisted with other, older forms of legitimate political authority. Each of these corresponded to alternative ways of dividing political space. What were these other political spaces? The largest and most encompassing was the Holy Roman Empire, that vast and ramshackle polity that stretched, in theory at least, from south of Rome to the Danish border and from Belgium to Bohemia. Headed by an elected emperor, the Empire provided a system of feudal and imperial law for its inhabitants, though it lacked much in the way of state apparatus or coercive power. It was imperial law, in fact, as it grew and mutated during the Middle Ages, that authorized the relative autonomy of the many states within the Empire, including large, centrally governed principalities, independent city-states, and confederations like Switzerland and Graubünden.

Imperial authority was multilayered and eternally contested, and its applicability to Graubünden remained uncertain. At one level, the Holy Roman Emperors claimed to be universal emperors, appointed by God to wield the "secular sword" over all humankind, just as the popes in Rome wielded the "spiritual sword." As such, everyone, or at least every Catholic Christian, was subject to the emperor, according to the Empire's propagandists. Other rulers in Europe, especially the kings of France, Spain, and England, ignored such claims or insisted that every king was "emperor in his own realm." At a more pragmatic level, however, the Holy Roman Empire really did provide a framework of government for a relatively well-recognized set of territories that comprised most of modern Germany, Switzerland, and Austria, along with much of the Low Countries and bits of other modern states. These lands had once included most of Italy, but by Jenatsch's day, imperial claims to Italy were entirely fictitious, brought into play only as cover for political maneuvers based on the real power of the major players, which included the Spanish branch of the Habsburg family, the popes, and France. Imperial authority in Switzerland was equally tenuous, since the confederation enjoyed exemption from most new imperial law and policies after 1499, when the Swiss had handily defeated an effort by the Habsburg family to reincorporate them into the family's control.[9]

Belonging to the Empire was both more and less important for Graubünden than for Switzerland. On the one hand, none of the towns and valleys that made up the Three Leagues of Graubünden possessed the status of "imperial liberty" (*Reichsfreiheit*), that is, legal privileges that freed them from all lords except the emperor. Since the emperors had little real governing power, being subject only to the emperor was equivalent to being subject to no one at all. Most members of the Swiss Confederation claimed such imperial liberty, and thus could largely ignore imperial politics, whereas most of Graubünden was under local lords, such as the bishop of Chur and the Habsburgs themselves, who were very much part of the larger imperial structure.[10] Being part of the Empire meant less in Graubünden, on the other hand, for a different reason. Throughout the 1500s and 1600s, all emperors were members of the Habsburg family. The same family also ruled as personal lords over substantial parts of Graubünden, and they were Graubünden's most powerful neighbors. The line between imperial authority and Habsburg lordly authority therefore often blurred, especially during the war years from 1620 to 1639, exactly when Jenatsch was most active. In effect, the Empire in Graubünden *was* the Habsburgs, whose close ties to the region made them a powerful threat to local autonomy. Therefore, it was less the Empire as an abstract whole, and more the one crucial family, the Habsburgs, that most affected affairs in Graubünden. Even though the Bündner lacked Swiss-style imperial liberty, their military capacity and strategic location usually forced the Habsburgs to negotiate with them as a separate nation, not as subjects. This relationship was firmly fixed in the Hereditary Alliance (*Erbeinung*) of 1518, after which relations between the Three Leagues and their Habsburg lords and emperors became a matter for diplomacy, not for law.

Even this brief sketch suggests why observers since the 1600s have called the Holy Roman Empire a "political monstrosity."[11] How significant was an emperor who dealt with his subjects through diplomacy or through imperial law that was nearly powerless because of extensive local privileges and growing princely power? Yet the Empire, along with foreign powers, the Leagues, and the local communes, did remain a critical part of political identity in Germany and in Graubünden. Showing how this complex political fabric applied to Jenatsch therefore reveals how things actually worked. Technically, Jenatsch was an imperial subject through his subjection to the bishop of Chur, who was lord over the Upper Engadine where Jenatsch's family originated. The bishop's subjects were mostly free people, rather than serfs, so Jenatsch owed neither the token payment (typically, a chicken at Easter) that signified personal unfreedom nor the death duties that serfs paid their lords. His status as imperial and episcopal subject was in reality far less important than his citizenship in his home commune and in his league, the House of God or *Chadé*. Later in his life, he became a citizen of Davos in the Ten Jurisdictions as well. As a citizen of the Leagues, he was bound by the law of the Leagues as a whole and the laws of his communes of citizenship, despite the fact that the emperor and the bishop were technically his lords. The law of the Engadine existed in carefully codified statutes that regulated every aspect of local life, while the treaties and traditions of the Three Leagues shaped the political process that took place when communal delegates assembled in Chur or Ilanz to set policy and regulate conflicts. Subject and citizen at the same time, Jenatsch learned to move with ease through this complex and tangled network of political authority and legitimacy.[12]

Just as was the case for politics, social life in the Three Leagues mixed aristocratic and democratic features. In principle, every citizen of a member commune was a free man, equal to any other—but again, reality was more complex. In many communes, a single family or two or three powerful clans monopolized access to land, trade, or the valuable mountain meadows, the alps, that give the mountain range its name. Indeed, a few families managed to put down roots in multiple communes: above all, the great kinship networks of the Planta (originally from Jenatsch's Upper Engadine) and the Salis (originally from the Val Bregaglia nearby) stood out for their wealth and ubiquity in the public affairs of the Three Leagues. These local magnates may not have been prominent compared to Europe's great aristocratic families, but in local terms, they stood out from their neighbors and most often represented the Leagues to the outside world. The Planta and Salis families consisted of multiple lines, often at odds with one another, but equally likely to support their cousins and fellow clansmen when the situation was right. Overall, more of the Salis than the Planta had converted from Catholicism to the new Reformed Church, and in general the Salis were more likely to favor connections with Venice and France, while the Planta leaned more toward Spain and Austria in their foreign ties. Both families had several branches that had received ennoblement at one time or another, and contemporaries certainly thought of them all as nobles, generally referring to them as "von Planta" and "von Salis" in German. Yet their noble status brought them no official political prerogatives, and in practice, they mixed and married freely with a larger group of twenty to thirty leading families who competed for public office and generally managed the Three Leagues' affairs.[13] Jenatsch's career became intimately entangled with these two clans in particular.

Two great shocks transformed the Holy Roman Empire and its politics in the 1500s, although one played a much more direct role in Jenatsch's experience. The first resulted from the massive Ottoman Turkish assault on the Empire's southeastern flank that began around 1500. Since their core territories lay in the Ottomans' path, the imperial family, the Habsburgs, faced the brunt of these attacks, which swept as far north as Budapest and Vienna in the early 1500s. To counter the Turks, the Habsburgs desperately needed financial and military support from their German subjects, which meant that those subjects gained greater leverage over imperial policy than had previously been the case. Without Turkish pressure, for example, it is hard to imagine that the nascent Protestant movement and its urban and princely protectors could have resisted the combined force of papal and imperial condemnation as they did.[14]

The second shock, of course, was the Protestant Reformation itself. Beginning as one theologian's protest over dogma and the existing church's interpretation of its own power, the Reformation unleashed a broad movement supported by a diverse, unstable coalition of actors that ranged from learned professors and spiritually engaged laypeople to rebellious peasants and ambitious princes eager to seize the church's wealth.[15] After a generation of struggle and insecurity in

Germany and across Europe that began with Martin Luther's protest in 1517, the Holy Roman Empire reached a workable compromise in the Religious Peace of Augsburg, signed in 1555. The compromise allowed every sovereign prince or town in the Empire to choose whether to follow Catholic tradition or the new church organized by Luther in Saxony. The treaty therefore ensured that at least two faiths would survive within the Empire. By excluding the growing Reformed or Calvinist movement, however—which included many of Switzerland's cantons— as well as a wide range of more radical spiritual views, the Peace of Augsburg did not provide a lasting solution to religious difference. Instead, the major positions within Latin Christianity—the Catholic, Lutheran, and Calvinist/Reformed—each struggled to bolster itself through teaching, organizing, and making international alliances.

In Switzerland and Graubünden, too, Catholics and Reformed Protestants continued to live and wrangle side by side, bolstered by local agreements in 1526 (Graubünden) and 1531 (Switzerland) that provided a basic framework for religious coexistence.[16] Thus, the religious situation in these regions differed from the rest of Europe in some important respects. Unlike France or England, Switzerland lacked a strong central government that could demand unity in religious affairs. Even compared to the rest of the Holy Roman Empire, which had at least a nominal monarch as well as powerful regional princes, the fact that Graubünden and Switzerland were confederations ensured that no single ruler could enforce uniformity of religion. Rather, from the outset, the tensions between those who adhered to the old faith and those who supported the emerging new religious movements became a political problem, one that could generate conflict, even civil war, but that also could provoke creative responses and new institutions and perspectives.

Even if imperfect, the religious peace in Switzerland after 1531 and in Germany after 1555 was stable enough to spare these lands a vicious civil war like the one that took place in France in the late 1500s. Protestants and Catholics in Germany and Switzerland seemed to be able to get along next to one another, if not together, tolerably well until the early 1600s. Nevertheless, the rival confessions each hardened their boundaries and marshaled their resources for what activists on all sides understood as a war against the devil. After 1608, negotiation among the three confessions halted, and in 1618, a war broke out that, because it inextricably entwined religious conviction and political ambition, turned out to be nearly impossible to end. Raging across Germany—and Graubünden—from 1618 to 1648, the Thirty Years' War had cataclysmic consequences for the regions it devastated and the people whose lives it transformed. Many suffered deprivation and death, although a few, including George Jenatsch, thrived in the unstable and difficult conditions of the war years.[17]

On top of the devastation that religion and politics wrought across central Europe after 1600, nature itself seemed to be at war against the region's inhabitants. About the time that Jenatsch was born, central Europe faced a wave of colder winters and wetter summers that experts now call the Little Ice Age. The effects were particularly devastating in mountain regions. Cold weather and increased snowfall meant that the crucial Alpine meadows only emerged from the snow late in the spring, which limited the number of cattle that could graze on them. When combined with damp, cool summers, these changes also made it harder to grow cereal crops on the valley floors where Graubünden's villages were located. As a result, high-altitude settlements that had flourished during the warmer period before 1550 shrank, and many were eventually abandoned. The peasants had less grain of their own and less butter and meat from their cattle to export. Hungry people and animals became vulnerable to diseases, a problem exacerbated when foreign soldiers, carrying diseases fatal to humans and to animals, marched through on their way to Europe's battlefields or invaded on behalf of the rival great powers. No wonder Swiss and Bündner mountain boys sought careers in the armies crossing Europe or moved to the lowlands of Switzerland where war profiteering supported agricultural expansion, especially in horses, a high-value military commodity.[18]

Our protagonist thus faced a physical and human landscape full of barriers and rifts. The harsh physical terrain found an echo in the tangled organization of political power in the region, and in the linguistic and religious differences that separated village from village and valley from valley. Suffering from economic crisis and unpredictable waves of epidemic disease, the inhabitants responded sometimes by making bold choices, and sometimes by retreating to reactionary visions of a golden past. Such conditions favored those who were simultaneously flexible and ruthless, persuasive and unscrupulous. Jenatsch, for one, thrived in this complex world, leveraging the order of life around him even as he undermined its foundations.

George Jenatsch: A Biographical Chronicle

We do not know exactly where or when George Jenatsch was born. The year was almost certainly 1596, and one unreliable source suggests a date of January 19.[19] His father Israel spent part of 1596 as pastor in Silvaplana and St. Moritz in the Upper Engadine, and part as pastor in the valley of Schams just north across the Alps. George may have been born in either location. In any event, his family soon returned to Silvaplana, where Jenatsch spent his childhood years. Consequently, we can be certain that Ladin Romansh was his mother tongue, specifically the Puter dialect of Ladin spoken throughout the Upper Engadine. He had five siblings that we know of, although two died in infancy.[20] The Jenatsch family remained citizens of Samedan, another nearby Upper Engadine village. There, they ranked among the more important local families, well respected for their traditional vocation as pastors and notaries. They had nowhere near the wealth of

Figure 1.1 The village of Silvaplana, where Jenatsch grew up. Etching by Caspar Ulrich Huber, printed in Jakob Frey, *Das Schweizerland in Bild und Wort* (Basel: C. Krüsi, 1867). By permission of the Rätisches Museum, Chur (H 1962, 230).

mighty clans like the Salis and Planta, though, and they stood behind them in status and influence as well.[21]

Jenatsch's father Israel and his grandfather Andreas had left their high valley as young men, studying at Swiss Protestant universities to prepare themselves for a career in the church. It was no surprise, therefore, that young George took the same path and departed for preparatory Latin school in Zurich in 1610, when he was fourteen. He spent the next five years in Zurich as a student, learning Latin and theology in school, as well as Zurich's German dialect in the streets. Jenatsch seems to have been a very bright student when he set his mind to work, but as he grew older, various distractions pulled him away from school. When he started his education, he benefited from a public fellowship from the Zurich authorities, who gave him a pass to the municipal soup kitchen and a modest stipend. His teachers, meanwhile, praised him at first for his eloquence and rapid progress. This was soon to change.

Although training Reformed pastors was the primary goal of the Zurich school, not all students held themselves to the high standards that the city council expected. In 1606, the council responded to complaints from the city's clergy and teachers with a set of strict rules about student behavior. Drinking was one problem:

> Since a miserable drunken life has become extremely common among the students, we have ordered that no student should go to a guildhall or wine-house in the evening or for a nightcap, nor should they gather in secret with other students to abandon themselves to wine.[22]

Sex posed another issue:

> All and every one of the studying boys who pursue daughters or maids, and who have to marry these when they become pregnant after extended fornication and misbehavior, shall be expelled according to the old school rules, and shall be rejected from church service.[23]

Bündner students like Jenatsch seem to have been particularly troublesome. In 1613, therefore, the school directors decided to stop supporting those students from Graubünden "who were not diligent in their studies or not inclined to be used in service of the churches."[24]

Jenatsch lost his scholarship to another student that same year, although the authorities did not record why Jenatsch deserved this punishment. Could it have been drinking or fornication? Another incident, this one involving fighting in 1615, nearly got him expelled from the school entirely. Without a scholarship, he supported himself after 1613 as the tutor for the sons of Giovanni Baptista de Salis, a powerful local magnate in Graubünden. Jenatsch was proud enough to wrangle with his new employer, too, as some early letters reveal, but he kept his position in Zurich, and then for a year at the university in Basel. He spent his year in Basel, from June 1616 to mid-1617, tutoring the Salis boys and completing his studies to be a pastor. In Basel, too, Jenatsch rubbed some people the wrong way, leading to complaints to his employer. He had supporters as well, though—most important, the young gentlemen he was tutoring. As one of the Salis boys put it in a letter to his father, "They won't be able to come up with anything against [Jenatsch] except his pride, and that because he does not easily live according to the advice of others."[25] The connections Jenatsch made at this time with various young men from powerful Bündner families—above all with the Salis clan—helped ease his path into the political scene when he returned to Graubünden itself.

The Reformed Synod in Graubünden, the organ of the local Reformed Church, was eager to employ well-trained pastors, especially young ones willing to take the poorly paid positions available in the mountain villages of Graubünden. When Jenatsch appeared before the synod on July 3, 1617, therefore, he quickly completed the theological examination that was required, swore an oath to uphold the synod's articles, and was appointed pastor in the village of Scharans, a relatively prosperous hamlet in the Domleschg Valley. Scharans had not renewed the contract of Jenatsch's predecessor, and the village needed a new pastor.[26]

Figure 1.2 Jenatsch's parish church in Scharans from 1617 to 1619. Watercolor by Felix Meyer showing the church ca. 1901. By permission of the Rätisches Museum, Chur (H 1965, 572).

Jenatsch's examination and appointment were simply routine business at the synod's July meeting.

Much more important to the gathered pastors was a raging debate over which foreign alliance, if any, the pastors would support from their pulpits. Graubünden had been tearing itself apart over this issue since the early 1600s, as Venetian, French, and Spanish ambassadors with bags of cash for bribes circulated among the communes, seeking to buy their votes. Partisans on all sides stopped at nothing to undermine their opponents, leading a series of partisan assemblies and kangaroo courts dominated by one faction or another. The synod, too, was divided: the clergy disagreed not only because of the genuinely divergent interests of the communes they served, but also about the proper tactics they, as clerics, ought to employ.[27] By 1617, a cautious and moderate group of older pastors in the synod faced a group of young activists who urged the church to engage aggressively in the current disputes. Jenatsch soon found his way into this activist cluster.

We know little about Jenatsch's activities in Scharans. One key connection he made was with the local military captain, Giacomo Ruinelli, who was also a translator for the sly Venetian ambassador Giovanni Baptista Padavino.[28] At the time, this friendship helped ease Jenatsch into the pro-Venetian faction in Graubünden, something his ties to Giovanni Baptista de Salis and his sons made even easier. Indeed, it is tempting to speculate that he obtained the plum position in Scharans because of his good connections with the Salis and the Venetian faction. Later, after leaving the clergy, Jenatsch worked for Ruinelli as a soldier as well, rising through the ranks partly under Ruinelli's command. It was therefore doubly shocking when Jenatsch killed Ruinelli in a duel in 1627.

The political scene in Graubünden was turbulent and violent when Jenatsch began working in Scharans, as political divisions and religious zeal drove ambitious men to extreme solutions. One increasingly important tactic in the intensifying struggles was the calling of mass political assemblies, a political event unique to Graubünden in this period, and possible only because of its federal structure and the autonomy of the individual communes that made up the Three Leagues. Graubünden's armed adult males, who made up the citizenry, felt that the future of the Leagues rightly lay in their own hands. It was therefore easy to appeal to them to assemble in order to take control of a political process that was obviously corrupt and dysfunctional. Usually, the leaders of one faction would appeal to communes where their own personal or financial influence guaranteed a sympathetic hearing; once these communes had voted to raise their banners—giving these impromptu assemblies their Swiss-German name, *Fähnlilupf* (banner-raising)— other communes across the Leagues would rush to join the action, lest they be left out of any decisions.

Such gatherings took place in 1565, 1572, 1585, and 1607. These assemblies, often consisting of several thousand armed men gathered in some central location in Graubünden, resisted all outside control. They sometimes began by following their instigators' wishes and establishing a penal court (*Strafgericht*) to "punish" the guilty—that is, they destroyed factional opponents by citing them before a popular court and imposing enormous fines, torture, or even execution. The courts' judges typically did their work surrounded by dozens or hundreds of "guardians," soldiers appointed by the communes to oversee who was accused and who was spared. More often, however, these wild assemblies surged out of control, turning the *Strafgericht* against the leaders of all factions. For a powerful politician in Graubünden, calling for a *Fähnlilupf* therefore meant playing with fire. If he could keep the movement under his guidance, it became a powerful weapon against his rivals, whereas an assembly that slipped out of control inevitably endangered everyone in the political class.[29]

In 1616, the Spanish and French factions, working together, had stage-managed just such an assembly in Chur. The assembled troops compliantly established a court that viciously pursued the Venetian faction. Rather than accepting this court's verdicts, however, the leaders of the Venetian faction decided to establish a counter-assembly that could cashier the verdicts of the Chur court and initiate new prosecutions more amenable to their own agenda. This counter-assembly and second court met at Thusis, a small but centrally located town just across the valley from Jenatsch's parish in Scharans. This proximity and his own connections let Jenatsch become an important political actor for the first time, even though he was only in his early twenties. In March 1618, as planning for the counter-assembly began, Jenatsch joined several more experienced activists from the synod in a secret meeting with Hercules von Salis, leader of the Venetian faction. There, they resolved to use the upcoming synod meeting in Bergün—a village that had been punished harshly by the Chur court of 1616[30]—to launch a new *Fähnlilupf* that would begin in the Protestant communes of the Engadine.

The conspirators' plans succeeded splendidly. Jenatsch himself traveled to Samedan in the Upper Engadine, where he was a citizen, and urged the more cautious pastors there to stir up the movement. He went on to the Lower Engadine, where the population hated the lordly power asserted there by Rudolf von Planta, who was also head of the Spanish faction in Graubünden. Urged on by the pastors and their allies in the Salis faction, the movement exploded into action at the end of July; by early August, nearly every commune in Graubünden had sent a troop of soldiers carrying its banner to Thusis, though the pro-Salis and pro-Venetian communes sent far more men than the others. The assembled soldier-citizens immediately passed a set of articles intended to "reform the Fatherland," whose thrust is captured in one provision:

> What should be punished? A majority was reached to punish anyone who had acted against the independence [of the Leagues], who got mixed up with princes, who acted against our *Bundesbrief,* or who committed high crimes in any other way.[31]

Figure 1.3 Thusis with the Via Mala Gorge. The tumultuous assembly at which Jenatsch acted as a clerical overseer took place in the village, right. Etching by Friedrich Lose, ca. 1825. By permission of the Rätisches Museum, Chur (H 1965, 294).

In reality, the court concentrated on the leaders of the Spanish faction, who prudently left the country to avoid capture. Later on, some Venetian factional leaders were charged as well, though they had plenty of time to escape. Another target did not get away, however. At the very beginning of the *Fähnlilupf,* a flying band of communal militiamen from the Engadine had swept down into the Three Leagues' mostly Catholic subject territory, the Valtellina, and captured Nicolò Rusca, the Catholic archpriest of Sondrio.

Normally, Protestant or Catholic clergymen had little to do with the operation of such courts, and clerics had often condemned them as lawless and chaotic. At Thusis in 1618, this changed. Since the pastors had been instrumental in raising the communes in the first place, the assembled men (or the magnates behind the scenes) decided to appoint a board of "clerical overseers" who would guarantee that the court acted uprightly. Although several Catholic priests and moderate Protestants were invited to join, only nine pastors from the activist wing of the synod actually served on this novel oversight committee. Among them was George Jenatsch. Under the pastors' eyes, the judges began trying the accused, first among them the priest Rusca (in person), and the leaders of the pro-Spanish faction, Rudolf and Pompeius von Planta (in absentia). Although Rusca had been acquitted of the same charges—some of which went back thirty years—at an earlier trial, he was nevertheless tortured repeatedly until he died. This judicial murder caused enormous outrage among Catholics in the Valtellina and Graubünden; it also drew the young pastor Jenatsch into the public eye because of his role as one of the overseers.[32]

After the Thusis Tribunal shut down, having run out of support and money without ever capturing its most powerful enemies, a series of further uprisings and tribunals continued until 1620. Two major factions—divided between Protestant and Catholic, pro-Venetian and pro-Spanish, Salis and Planta—struggled to shift the angry population in their direction. Wild swings of political fortune destabilized the Three Leagues as the communes vacillated between their divided leaders. Jenatsch himself, along with the other spiritual overseers, was repeatedly called before hostile courts, although he never obeyed any of these summons.[33] He also faced great criticism from his own partisans. Amidst the chaos, the Reformed Synod, now firmly controlled by its moderate members, disciplined the activists who had caused so much trouble, Jenatsch among them. In 1619, the synod sentenced him to a six-month suspension from his clerical office.[34]

Before and during this suspension from the pastorate, Jenatsch traveled ceaselessly around Graubünden, often accompanying his new best friend, the violent young pastor Blasius Alexander (or as he was known in Romansh, Plisch Lisander). The two young pastors were involved in the beating of a Catholic sexton in the Valtellina late in 1618, followed by confrontations with Protestant moderates in the Lower Engadine early in 1619. After they were suspended from their positions as pastors, their exile was made more pleasant by the substantial cash contributions they collected from the Venetian ambassador to Graubünden, who used every means possible to keep alive the Venetian faction's interests.[35] Jenatsch also got married in 1620 to Anna Buol, the daughter of an established Protestant politician and mercenary captain in the German-speaking commune of Davos.[36] Public condemnation neither slowed his meteoric rise nor deprived him of all of his friends.

When Jenatsch's suspension as pastor ended in 1620, he moved to the much less desirable and indeed dangerous position as pastor of Berbenno in the Valtellina, since his old parish in Scharans had not renewed his contract. In Berbenno, Jenatsch found himself at the frontlines of religious conflict, since his new congregation was located in the Three Leagues' Italian-speaking subject territory to the south. Only a few Valtellina families had converted to the new faith: in Berbenno, Protestants probably consisted of fewer than a dozen people, though the laws of their Bündner lords ensured that this small flock had equal access to the same church used by the hundreds of Catholics in the village. This habit of sharing churches with hostile rival congregations was common in Swiss regions of mixed religious adherence, and it caused frequent difficulties wherever it took place.[37] Thus, even the most agreeable Protestant pastor would have found Berbenno a difficult assignment; for someone with Jenatsch's fiery temperament, provocation and violence were almost certain to result.

Jenatsch took his new wife with him to his new position in Berbenno early in 1620, but he scarcely had time to settle, or to make the village unsettled, before he was thrown out. We know nothing of what happened to him personally while he was there, since no record of his actions survives. Rather, a general uprising by the Catholics in the Valtellina lay behind his flight. Working with secret agents sent by the Spanish and Milanese, the Catholic Valtellina aristocrats engineered a mass uprising in July 1620 that drove out the Bündner governors. The revolt also triggered the massacre of several hundred local Protestants, probably including many of Jenatsch's little congregation in Berbenno. The revolt and massacre came to be known among Catholic partisans as the *Sacro Macello*, the "holy slaughter," since it entirely eliminated Protestant worship from the Valtellina. For the next nineteen years, local aristocrats governed the Valtellina under the protection of Spain and Austria, although the valley's population had to survive repeated invasions and counterinvasions before its ultimate return under the sovereignty of the Three Leagues in 1639.

Warned just before the massacre, Jenatsch, his wife, and a few members of his congregation fled directly into the mountains above Berbenno and over the passes to his native Engadine. At this point, in July 1620, his career as a pastor was over for good. Instead, after leaving his wife with her family in Davos in the Ten Jurisdictions, Jenatsch joined the military campaign to retake the Valtellina. Supported by contingents from Zurich and Bern, Bündner troops surged southward over the mountains in the hope of quick revenge. After a few chaotic battles, however, the professional Spanish army that guarded the Valtellina and its strategic passes drove them back in disarray.[38]

Worse was to come. Seeing the impotence of the catastrophically divided Bündner regime, the Austrian and Spanish governments soon marched troops into Graubünden itself and occupied much of the Three Leagues. Many Catholics and moderates already hated Jenatsch as one of the spiritual overseers who had brought about Rusca's death; now he became a hunted man, because the pro-Spanish party in Graubünden finally had the means to enforce its will. By October of 1620, Jenatsch had fled Graubünden entirely for the safety of Zurich, where he joined a growing band of Protestant and pro-Salis refugees. Unlike many of their fellow Bündner, who lived in poverty and depended on the charity of the Zurich authorities, Jenatsch and his friend Alexander continued to collect money from the Venetian ambassador in Zurich. They used the funds to return repeatedly to Graubünden, hoping to raise an insurgency against the occupying troops and the dominant pro-Spanish faction, usually at risk of their own lives, but with little success.

In effect, Jenatsch and Alexander became an activist team, using their connections from their days as pastors to encourage the pro-Venetian and Protestant factions in Graubünden and to raise resistance wherever they could. By early 1621, as the shock of the Valtellina massacre and the invasion that followed began to fade, the remnants of these factions gathered into a more coherent resistance movement. Much of the Three Leagues' territory was firmly in the hands of their enemies, and the heads of the pro-Spanish party, who had rushed back from their recent exile, were busy cementing their control. A Catholic Swiss regiment also supported the pro-Spanish faction militarily, although it was balanced by a Protestant regiment from Zurich that took up quarters right outside Graubünden to the west. Only a few corners of Graubünden itself, including the Protestant core of the Ten Jurisdictions, provided safe havens for planning and mounting an insurgency. At the center of this effort stood the Salis family branch in the village of Grüsch, led by the sons of the recently deceased Hercules von Salis. Grüsch lay above a defensible gorge near the sheltering presence of the Zurich regiment on the border. The combination of refugees and Salis retainers there provided the core for bands of insurgents who began swooping out to intervene at critical moments. For example, a band headed by young Kasimir von Salis rescued Andreas Schenni of Rheinwald as Catholic troops were taking him to trial in Ilanz, while Jenatsch and Alexander themselves had to be rescued once by the Zurich colonel Johann Jakob Steiner.[39]

The growing resistance movement that Jenatsch and Blasius supported—now calling themselves "the goodhearted"—lacked the money and troops to mount an outright offensive against its enemies unless the Venetian Senate or the Protestant Swiss towns were willing to finance one. Indeed, their greater fear was that the pro-Spanish forces in Graubünden, headed by Rudolf von Planta and his brother Pompeius, would soon be able to burn them out of Grüsch itself. The "goodhearted" therefore turned to assassination and sabotage as the best way to carry out their struggle. Their first target was Pompeius von Planta, who lived in Rietberg Castle, not far from Jenatsch's old parish in Scharans. On the evening of February 24, 1621, a group of nineteen men on horseback departed from Grüsch. The Salis family left this dangerous expedition to their lesser supporters, including Jenatsch and Blasius Alexander. Avoiding enemy patrols near Chur, the men took little-used paths on the mountainside and rested for a few hours at an isolated farmstead. They arrived at Rietberg the morning after Ash Wednesday around five o'clock in the morning. Their victim was preparing to ride out, and his servant had already opened the castle gate, which allowed the assassins to burst in. They chased down Planta, still in his nightgown, and brought him to bay in the residential rooms of the castle. Despite his pleas, the leaders of the band struck him down with multiple blows, after which the assassins "tore his heart and organs from his chest"—this from a congratulatory first-person report about the murder—and left their victim pinned to the floor with one of the axes that had killed him.[40] A hostile pamphlet that appeared soon after Planta's death blamed the young pastors in particular for the crime, claiming that they had "washed their hands in the fallen gentleman's blood" before leaving the scene.[41]

Figure 1.4 Rietberg Castle, where Pompeius von Planta was murdered in 1621. Lithograph by Heinrich Kraneck, 1837, printed in *Die alten Ritterburgen und Bergschlösser in Hohen Rhätien* (Chur: Benedict, 1837). By permission of the Rätisches Museum, Chur (H 1968, 135).

Although various authorities in the Three Leagues expressed their horror at such tactics, Jenatsch and Alexander were soon on the move again. This time, they crossed the Alps from Grüsch into the Lower Engadine with a troop of sixty insurgents. There, they murdered Fortunat von Planta in a church, as well as several village magistrates who had supported the Planta faction in the region; rumor even had it that they had killed Daniel von Planta's wife after Planta had managed to escape. Even their political allies found this kind of action reckless. A Venetian agent in Zurich described this raid as "against every rule of politics," and its perpetrators as

> mostly desperate men, who have lost their houses, goods and liberty, and who have received tremendous harm from the other party. In particular, the Hohenbalcken brothers, filled with the idea of vendettas, are continuing their vendetta: inclined to die, they first want to soak themselves in the blood of the other party.[42]

Factional politics and blood revenge made for an explosive combination, only exacerbated by the external powers that supported the partisans in Graubünden.

The insurgents' tactics brought them success in the short term. The pro-Spanish party was thrown into disarray by Pompeius von Planta's death, whereas the Lower Engadine communes raised their banners again to drive out the Austrians in a brief reversal of fortune. With Jenatsch acting entirely as a soldier now, the uprising swept across Graubünden, once again forcing the Planta and their allies into exile. A column headed by Jenatsch was so close behind the Catholic Swiss regiment that had been occupying the Grey League that its commander had to leave his boots behind, not to mention his booty. Jenatsch publicly ridiculed the captain, a certain von Beroldingen from the canton of Uri, by circulating a song that began:

> Beroldingen follows the honorable course,
> He steals the cow and leaves the horse;
> But now his plan has all gone wrong,
> He couldn't even keep the cow for long.[43]

Jenatsch and Alexander immediately headed a new delegation from Graubünden to Zurich and the other Swiss Protestant towns, seeking to raise money in support of their movement. Clearly, Jenatsch was moving upward in politics much faster than he had as a pastor. The bitter hostility and polarization of the era is revealed by the fact that despite their participation in the notorious murder of Pompeius von Planta, Jenatsch and Alexander each received a special bonus of two hundred gulden out of the loans that the Protestant Swiss cities raised for the Bündner. The gift came with praise for their actions as "William Tells" who rescued Graubünden from "the tyranny of disloyal children of the land."[44] Back in Graubünden, though, their actions were less popular; the authorities only handed out the two hundred–gulden bonuses on the condition that no public money be used to repay them.

The reprieve from foreign pressure that the insurgent band in Grüsch created was short-lived. As the Thirty Years' War heated up across the rest of the German lands, Graubünden's passes became ever more valuable for the Habsburg monarchies in Spain and Austria, who had no intention of letting them return to the control of the unstable Protestant-leaning government of the Three Leagues. Moreover, even though the official government of the Leagues sought to negotiate with the Austrians, Jenatsch and other hotheads working for the Salis faction were preparing a new invasion of the Valtellina to recover the lost valley by force. In reality, though, even if Jenatsch and Alexander's terrorist raids struck fear into the hearts of their rivals, such methods undermined any hope of creating an effective Bündner army.[45] The force that the Three Leagues finally raised consisted of some eight thousand under-equipped and demoralized men, whose attempted invasion of the Valtellina in October of 1621 quickly turned into a fiasco. Not only did they fail to capture the town of Bormio, but they also triggered a Spanish counterattack from the south, coordinated with Austrian troops from the east, that swept back over Graubünden. The invading force met little resistance, and the victorious Austrians now completely dismembered the Three Leagues. Parts of the *Chadé* and most of the Ten Jurisdictions were declared to be Habsburg subject territory, and were immediately subjected to a forced return to Catholicism. The remaining two leagues had to give up the Valtellina, acknowledge the lordly rights of the bishop in Chur, and allow the practice of the Catholic religion in every church.[46] Most devastatingly, Spain and Austria received the right to send troops through the region without limitation. In addition to the burdens of quartering and looting that the people of Graubünden had to suffer, this brought the plague into the region, where it spread death and misery across the mountain valleys.

Jenatsch himself barely escaped Graubünden alive. Because Austrian troops blocked the main routes toward the safe haven of Switzerland, the group of partisans he was fleeing with had to take the rough path over the Panix Pass in early November of 1621, with heavy snow already falling. Pursued through a blizzard by hostile Catholic villagers, his party lost their way. Bonaventura Toutsch, another activist pastor, slid to his death, while Blasius Alexander was caught by the peasants when he refused to leave behind an Austrian warhorse he had stolen. Taken as a prisoner to Austrian Innsbruck, Alexander was executed for treason and heresy in 1622. Jenatsch made it across the pass and soon joined some 1,500 Bündner refugees in Zurich. The Austrian general in Graubünden, Baldiron, immediately demanded that Zurich extradite fifty-three leaders of these exiles, including Jenatsch, so that they could be tried for their crimes. Although Zurich delayed, the city's leaders made it clear to those sought by the Austrians that they could not count on the city for protection. Austrian armies were winning stunning victories across the Holy Roman Empire during this phase of the Thirty Years' War, and a small power like Zurich could not risk offending the triumphant imperialists.

For the next nine years, until the fall of 1631, Jenatsch spent much of his time outside of Graubünden. Moving permanently beyond his former estate as a pastor, he participated in the great military and political enterprise of the Thirty Years' War, though always with an eye to affairs in his homeland. When conditions improved for his party in Graubünden, he sped home to fight the various occupations and protectorates that dominated the Three Leagues in these years. In April 1622, for example, a popular rebellion in the Ten Jurisdictions drove out the Austrian garrisons. Jenatsch rushed back from the German Protestant army where he had been fighting, arriving just in time to lead a company of men against an overwhelming Austrian force that crushed local resistance in August. He retreated to Zurich, where he kept raising funds and buying weapons to carry on his fight. When a French-funded army invaded Graubünden again in October 1624, Jenatsch was one of the captains leading the successful troops, and by the time the army was disbanded in 1627, he was a lieutenant colonel.[47] As a man who could manage the political and financial as well as battlefield requirements of early modern warfare, Jenatsch rose quickly in these troubled times.

Figure 1.5 War in Chur, 1624. Note the rabbit accompanying the fleeing soldier. The couplets below read: "It is more fitting for a soldier to leave his life in battle than to escape healthy because fright made him take flight." Printed in Daniel Meisner, *Sciographica cosmica, dasz ist: Newes emblematisches Büchlein . . .* (Nuremberg: P. Fürst, 1642). By permission of the Rätisches Museum, Chur (H 1976, 210).

By the early 1630s, Jenatsch was no longer the young firebrand who risked his life trying to destroy his enemies. Instead, he had become a major player in the tangled politics of Graubünden. As long as war raged across Europe, Graubünden faced both the brutal violence and the webs of intrigue that characterized this conflict as a whole, helpless to withdraw because of its claims to the strategic passes that linked Austria to friendly territory in Milan, and Venice to troops and trade from Germany and France. Jenatsch remade himself during the war years by taking advantage of every opportunity he could. His activities varied constantly as the alliances shifted and the luck of battle swayed, but they always fit one of three major patterns. First, he was constantly active as a military recruiter. Much of his recruiting—which was highly profitable for him personally—involved raising troops by enlisting Swiss boys from regions untouched by the war. Other times he raised troops in Graubünden for service to outside powers like Venice or for deployment within the Three Leagues when the chances for restoration looked good. His second dimension of activity was as a soldier. The most profitable troops for him were often the ones who served in his own company, or later in his own regiment. His growing wealth and experience brought with it a steady rise in rank within the mercenary forces that did most of the fighting in Graubünden and across Europe. Sometimes the foreign powers, such as France, paid Jenatsch to fight within Graubünden with the men he raised, but he was equally willing to take his troops elsewhere when the situation demanded it. The third dimension of his activity during the 1620s was as a political leader intent on restoring both the autonomy of the Three Leagues and the Leagues' control over the Valtellina. Jenatsch shared these goals with most of the Bündner elite, even though there were tremendous disagreements about the best way to proceed and about which allies to trust. Whether they sought a Habsburg, French, or Swiss alignment, almost all of the Bündner magnates saw the recovery of the Valtellina as the ultimate goal of their efforts, as did Jenatsch.

We will investigate specific incidents from Jenatsch's turbulent middle life in the chapters that follow. At times, he found himself acting as sober political mediator, particularly between Catholics and Protestants, since the latter were willing to trust an ex-pastor. At other times he found himself bound by the violent code of honor of a seventeenth-century soldier, as when a minor incident exploded into a duel in which he killed his old friend and mentor Ruinelli. More than once, moreover, it appeared that his missteps might end Jenatsch's career. For example, late in 1629 he offended his commanding officer in Venetian service so seriously that the all-powerful Council of Ten imprisoned him for several months. Only the turn of politics set him free again, once the French sought to enlist Venice's help to seize control of the Three Leagues.[48]

The most publicly visible years of Jenatsch's life were from 1631 to 1639, when he first stood side by side with the French generals sent to secure the crucial passes for France, then betrayed the French cause by negotiating a lasting settlement for Graubünden with Austria and Spain. These were the most dramatic years of the entire Thirty Years' War across Europe, as King Gustavus Adolfus of Sweden brought hope to the Protestant cause before dying on the battlefield of Lützen. Gustavus Adolfus's great rival, the Austrian field marshal Albrecht von Wallenstein, saved the Habsburg cause and nearly established a new kingdom of his own before the Habsburg emperor had him murdered in 1634. In the subsequent stalemate, the rival power blocs struggled for advantage in theaters from the Atlantic to the Balkans, among which the Valtellina with its strategic passes and tangled politics remained pivotal.

A crucial figure on the French side was Henri de Rohan, a high nobleman and a Protestant who had led the French Calvinists, known as Huguenots, in a series of uprisings that had culminated in a royal siege of the Huguenot stronghold of La Rochelle. Although Rohan faced exile after his final defeat in 1629, the canny French minister, Cardinal Richelieu, offered him the chance to continue serving the French crown and thus perhaps to regain royal favor. As an experienced general and as a convinced Calvinist, Rohan was the perfect agent to represent French interests to the Swiss and Bündner Protestants. Accordingly, Rohan arrived in Chur late in 1631 to begin building up a French army in the region. A first attempt in 1632 failed as the tides of war and money undermined French efforts. Not until his Habsburg rivals had decisively defeated the Protestant Swedes at Nördlingen in 1634 did Richelieu make the Valtellina a high priority for French resources; the "Spanish Road" was providing crucial troops to the Habsburg forces in Germany and had to be blocked.[49]

It took until early 1635 to get all the French and Bündner troops in place for a campaign against the Spanish-occupied Valtellina. In the meantime, Jenatsch had carried out one of the most visible shifts in his identity: in January 1635, he publicly converted to Catholicism. At the time, he claimed to have secretly planned his conversion ever since his imprisonment in Venice, when he had begun rereading the Bible and church fathers. In the short term, Jenatsch's conversion had little effect on his situation, though it may have made him a more palatable negotiating partner both for Du Landé, the French lieutenant general, and for the Spanish and Austrians, since the religious situation in Graubünden and the Valtellina remained a key sticking point.[50] His former colleagues in the Rhaetian Reformed Synod attacked his conversion and his politics in a series of public letters, to which Jenatsch penned forceful replies.[51] The real action in 1635, though, was military. In a brilliant campaign from April to November, Rohan's forces defeated two Habsburg armies and took possession of the Valtellina. Now colonel of his own regiment, Jenatsch fought in most of the key engagements, earning Rohan's trust and respect through his courage and good judgment.

The new military situation led to new rounds of negotiations in a three-cornered round among the Habsburgs, the French, and—caught in between—the Bündner.[52] For the Habsburg negotiators in Vienna and Milan, as for the French in Paris, the key issue was control of the military road from Italy to Germany (for the Habsburgs) or from France to Venice (for the French). The Bündner elites, in contrast, wanted to regain control of the Valtellina with its lucrative offices and rich properties that they had lost. The Bündner were too weak by themselves to make any demands on either side, however. In particular, since Austria and Spanish Milan lay right next to Graubünden and provided important markets for its cattle products and transport services, the Bündner were in a poor position to exert pressure on these powerful neighbors. Only when the French were occupying the Valtellina did the Bündner have any trumps—namely, the ability to expel the French. Like his peers in Graubünden, Jenatsch had long since recognized this and had repeatedly shown himself willing to negotiate with the Spanish and Austrians.[53] Rohan's victories, therefore, ironically set the stage for Jenatsch's betrayal of the French. It was in this complex situation, laden with intrigue and crosscutting interests, that Jenatsch rose to true prominence. During 1636, he managed to retain Rohan's confidence by advising him both politically and militarily even as he became a leading figure in the negotiations with the Spanish and Austrians. A cabal of the most powerful men from all factions inside the Three Leagues formed a secret conspiracy, the "Chain League" (*Kettenbund*), in which they swore to work together to expel the French and regain the Valtellina on good terms.

While the *Kettenbund* leaders spent months in negotiations, both openly and in secret, Rohan desperately tried to secure two things from Richelieu in France: money to pay the mercenaries in his army, and a favorable treaty from his superiors that could forestall the Bündner plotting. In the end, it was a very narrow miss for Rohan: a signed treaty with favorable terms, along with a large down payment on the military debts, reached Chur from Paris only days after the Bündner troops had thrown off their French commanders and taken Rohan hostage.

Rohan's final actions in Graubünden cemented his reputation there as the "good duke," a living contrast to the apostate traitor Jenatsch, as far as the Protestant clergy were concerned. Isolated in Chur away from his troops, Rohan signed an agreement to withdraw his army in an orderly way; more surprisingly, he kept his word even when he had the means to break it. His battle-hardened French veterans had to retreat via Chur, where his lieutenant Du Landé urged Rohan to have the troops seize the city and resume the war. Whether out of exhaustion or out of his personal sense of honor, Rohan refused. His actions came at great personal cost, since he thus gave up any chance of regaining favor with Cardinal Richelieu and King Louis XIII. Rohan spent the rest of his life in exile and died in 1639. Jenatsch, meanwhile, enjoyed a few years of true power. As the pivotal figure who had brought about the realignment that promised to restore the Valtellina—something that was once again delayed by endless negotiation over details—he seized the opportunity both to cement his personal power within the Three Leagues and to gain the credentials, including a title of nobility, that could expand his options in the larger world of war outside. Some evidence suggests that he planned to leave Graubünden entirely once ennobled, though we will never know. The assassin's axe struck him down in January 1639.

*   *   *

Even this brief narrative of our subject's life, crammed with facts and events, reveals how much Jenatsch changed from his youth as a bright, if wild, divinity student to his high point as a clever, deceptive, and prudent military commander and politician. The fact that he was struck down at the height of his influence makes the story more thrilling. In the following chapters, specific aspects of his experience and identity will come into focus, one by one: What did national and ethnic identities mean in the seventeenth century? Where did Jenatsch stand in relation to his God? And how was social status measured and articulated in such turbulent times? To begin answering these questions, we must start back at the beginning again, with a young boy from an obscure mountain valley.

Chapter 2

"Georgius Jenatius, Engadino-Rhetus"

Mapping Identity among Region, Nation, and Language

When George Jenatsch was fourteen, he and his father left the mountains to bring him to school in Zurich, a regional metropolis and the center of the Swiss Reformed Church. In the registration book of the Schola Tigurina, the institute in Zurich for future Reformed pastors, Jenatsch signed his name as "Georgius Jenatius, Engadino-Rhetus." These four words open up a whole series of puzzles that can advance our investigation into how Jenatsch moved through identities and crossed boundaries over the course of his life. The first two words are his name, of course, but translated into Latin, which was only one of the languages he used during his lifetime. The words "Engadino-Rhetus," meanwhile, located Jenatsch in both physical and cultural space. The Engadine was his native soil: the valley where his family had originated and where he spent his youth, where a good part of his military career took place, and where he eventually struggled to bring some peace and cooperation among hostile religious factions. The Engadine also provided a base for the two great Bündner families, the Planta and the Salis, whose ambitions Jenatsch crossed and whose primacy he challenged. But by naming himself not just an Engadiner, but also "Rhetus," a Rhaetian, young Jenatsch also placed himself in a larger political and historical frame. Rhetus was the hero who had supposedly lent his name to the ancient Roman province of Rhaetia, which Bündner historians of the sixteenth century firmly connected to their own political system, the Republic of the Three Leagues.

At first glance, then, Jenatsch's youthful signature made several obvious statements about his identity. By naming himself in Latin, he claimed the status of an educated man, while the description he chose identified him regionally with the Engadine and nationally with the Three Leagues. Such linkages among language, region, and nation seem quite natural to us today. After all, one of the first questions we ask today when we meet an interesting stranger is "where are you from?" In the modern world of nation-states, the answer to this question tells us not only about a person's roots in a particular place, but also, we assume, about the person's likely ethnic background, language, and even religious convictions.

Given the enormous importance of national identity in today's world, historians have looked back to earlier periods to discover the roots of this particular form of identity—and found that things did not fit together so neatly in the seventeenth or earlier centuries. National identity in the modern sense rests on the conviction that a certain territory, a certain language, and a specific ruler or state share a natural bond that ties them together, creating a single community among people otherwise divided in various ways. Modern nations of this kind have a long prehistory in Europe, dating to the aftermath of the Roman Empire's fall, but took on much greater importance as various European states consolidated their internal control and their external prestige, a process that accelerated after 1500 and reached a peak in the 1800s. Nation-*states*—a kind of "imagined community" that claimed to transcend other identities—began to take clear shape in Europe by the 1700s, drawing away from older forms of political association such as the multi-faceted Holy Roman Empire in the German lands and beyond, or the complex confederations that emerged in Switzerland and the Netherlands.[1] Their emergence accelerated after the French Revolution with its intense popular patriotism, and gained reinforcement in the theories of Romantic writers who emphasized authentic national character.

Some of the ingredients for this new way of understanding the relationship between states and nations were much older, of course. People had long recognized that separate communities with different languages existed in western Europe. Since the early Middle Ages, moreover, they had described such groups using the Latin word *natio*, referring to the shared birth that allowed communities to continue from generation to generation.[2] One early use of the word *natio* occurred at Europe's medieval universities. Students often wandered from university to university during their studies, and when they arrived at a new college town far from home, they normally signed themselves into one of the "nations" they found there. These nations were student associations based on language and region, and corresponded more closely to what we might call ethnicities than they did to any modern nation-state. Indeed, the nations a student would find varied from university to university, depending on where most of the students came from. In northern Europe, they often included the German, French, and English nations. Students fit into these as best they could, which meant that Spaniards might belong to the French nation, whereas the Danes might fit into the English nation, for example.[3] Academic life took place in Latin, in any case, meaning that the students' mother tongues were more relevant in the tavern than in the classroom. All Western Christians, meanwhile, including the students preparing for careers as priests, lawyers, or doctors, were also viewed as members of the *corpus christianum*, the "body of Christians." This provided a shared identity that was more important, at least in theory, than any specific linguistic or cultural subgroup.

To this medieval sense of ethnic division, the Renaissance added a second, powerful element: the search for historical roots that could glorify specific regions and their political structures—that is to say, specific nations—around Europe. This happened in part because of growing political divisions in western Europe, which made the fiction of a single "Roman" empire headed by a "Holy Roman Emperor" less and less plausible. Once the king of France's lawyers declared in the early 1300s that every king was "an emperor in his kingdom," it was not long before historical and literary expressions of Frenchness accelerated, for example.[4] A second impulse that drove the search for national origins came from the Renaissance itself. One goal of the intellectuals who promoted the Renaissance movement was to restore the authority of historical perspectives through a rebirth of literature and history from Roman times. Since most of these intellectuals, from Dante to Machiavelli, were also fervent supporters of their home cities' independence, they quickly discovered that historical reconstruction could easily justify modern self-government. In Florence, for example, the city's chancellor around 1400 wrote learned treatises that argued the city had been founded by the Etruscans, not the Romans—meaning that it had been free before it fell to the Roman barbarians and should therefore be free again from Roman (that is, papal or imperial) control in his time.[5]

Looking more closely at our Engadino-Rhaetian Jenatsch, though, we will see that nations were still highly uncertain entities in the seventeenth century. Most Europeans probably felt that humans were naturally organized into groups defined by blood, culture, and tradition, and that such groups had connections with particular political systems. As modern states took shape after 1500 as political entities, their continued attachment to older ideas of nation thus helped produce our modern *nation*-states. Still, too much of Europe—notably its heartland from the Italian peninsula across the Alps to the German plains and the mouths of the Rhine—operated under more complex realities in which local loyalties, traditional ties, and broad commitments to "nations" and to Christendom did not line up into a straightforward hierarchy of political identity. Jenatsch was an Engadiner and a Bündner, but his life took place in a fluid world composed of wildly diverse political units that ranged from national kingdoms and homogenous principalities to city-states and voluntary confederations.

Notably, neither Graubünden, the Swiss Confederation, nor the Holy Roman Empire fit the modern description of a nation-state, since each had connections with multiple nations in the seventeenth-century sense. Linguistic and cultural frontiers surrounded the Engadine, which conducted its own affairs in multiple languages as well. In such a world, even the most fervent patriotism—and Jenatsch, from his own words, was a fervent patriot—meant something quite different than it does today. This chapter is thus dedicated to unpacking the complexities of Jenatsch's national, ethnic, and linguistic identities. Each of these categories implied boundaries and significant differences, whose meaning in the seventeenth century it will be our goal to illuminate.

Jenatsch's Engadine: A Cosmopolitan Periphery

George Jenatsch's family had been notaries and pastors in the Upper Engadine Valley for a long time. His parents and grandparents lived, worked, and died in a high Alpine valley that was, paradoxically, both remote and cosmopolitan at the same time. By asserting his identity as an Engadiner in Zurich, the young Jenatsch expressed his attachment both to the place and to the lively political and intellectual traditions that marked the Engadine, to its human geography as well as to the physical geography that set it apart from the rest of Europe.

Physically, the Engadine is a relatively wide, long valley running from west to east among the ridges of the high Alps. The region's highest peaks lie just to the south, culminating in the Piz Bernina at over 13,000 feet in altitude. A second chain of daunting mountains runs just to the north. In the mind of most early modern Europeans, mountainous regions like the Engadine were barbarous and dangerous, yet the Engadine, at the very heart of the mountains, is a surprisingly gentle place.[6] Located at the headwaters of the Inn River, the valley slopes only slightly: from its highest point at the Maloja Pass (5,915 feet), the Upper Engadine runs broad and nearly level to its lowest village, Zuoz (5,740 feet), over twenty miles away. Below Zuoz, the valley narrows and the Inn begins to cut a steeper path, dropping to about four thousand feet over the next twenty miles before leaving the territory of early modern Graubünden (and modern Switzerland) for the Austrian lands and ultimately the Black Sea. Numerous mountain passes connect the Engadine to the German-speaking north and the Italian-speaking south, but the primary language of the valley itself during the seventeenth century was neither. Instead, its inhabitants, including the young Jenatsch, spoke the Puter Ladin dialect of Romansh. This language descended independently from the vulgar Latin of the soldiers who had claimed Rhaetia for the Roman Empire some 1,500 years earlier.

Although known for its relatively sunny climate—the valley is today home to winter and summer resorts like St. Moritz—the high altitude and the long winters of the Engadine limited grain production even where the ground was flat enough and dry enough to plow and plant. Consequently, the valley always depended on imports of basic grains, mostly from the south, which it paid for by exporting cattle and dairy products, especially butter and lard.[7] The villagers of the Engadine thus depended on trade to survive. Additional trade and people from afar came through the region because of its central location. Although the most important Alpine passes lay to the west (the Gotthard, San Bernardino, Splügen, and Septimer) and the east (the Brenner), a substantial number of traders chose the classic Engadine passes (Julier and Maloja) to find their way from south to north or vice versa. Other merchants, along with messengers and soldiers, followed the Engadine from east to west since the valley's length connected two major outposts of the far-flung territories ruled by the Habsburg family, Milan and Innsbruck. Meanwhile, travelers headed from Germany toward Venice and the Adriatic could climb out of the Lower Engadine near Zernez via the Ofenpass on the way

Figure 2.1 Map of the Upper Engadine Valley in 1707. Silvaplana is near the center of the map. Printed in Johann Jakob Scheuchzer, *Ouresiphoítes helveticus, sive Itinera per Helvetiae alpinas regiones* (Leiden: Pieter van der Aa, 1723). By permission of the Rätisches Museum, Chur (H 1975, 1755).

Figure 2.2 The Engadine, looking southwest from above Silvaplana. Lithograph by
Heinrich Jakob Burger-Hofer and Johann Jakob Hofer, 1882. By permission of the
Rätisches Museum, Chur (H 1963, 100).

to Trent and the city of lagoons. Its location amidst the mountains thus put the
Engadine astride several major arteries of trade and diplomacy. Curious Engadiners could observe and talk with travelers from every corner of Europe.

The population of the Upper and Lower Engadine, consisting of perhaps eleven
thousand people during Jenatsch's lifetime, concentrated into densely packed villages during the later Middle Ages.[8] By the 1600s, many lived in a classic "Engadine
house" built of stone, with a large arched gate leading to stables on the ground floor.
Typically, the whitewashed houses were decorated with sgraffito etchings and had
pious sayings painted on their outside walls. On the second floor, a wood-paneled
living room or *stüva* with a large, tiled oven formed the center of domestic life. These
villages were not merely a gathering of houses; they were also rigorously organized
communities, part of a nested set of communal political institutions that regulated
every aspect of daily life, from access to land and pastures to churchgoing and all
kinds of quarrels. Most villages consisted of quarters, which were in fact economic
partnerships that managed the rights to the all-important summer pastures on the
mountain slopes above. Each village family owned not only its cows, but also pre-
ciously guarded allocations to pasture its private animals in collectively managed
herds. The hired herdsmen kept meticulous records, carved into long, square sticks
that kept track of the quantity and quality of each cow's milk. At the end of every
summer, each owner received a share of the butter and cheese produced in the huts
high above the valley, precisely calibrated to his cows' productivity.[9]

Figure 2.3 A typical Engadine house in the village of Guarda. Watercolor by Hans Jenny, 1923. By permission of the Rätisches Museum, Chur (H 1996, 687).

While much of each family's economic life was regulated by village quarters, the villages as a whole provided the forum when the population faced larger issues. These included endless conflicts with neighboring villages about the boundaries of fields and pastures, arguments and feuds among the local population, and major crimes such as theft and murder. The villages of the Engadine, in turn, formed two major regional political communes (the Romansh name is *Comün*, the German *Gerichtsgemeinde*): the Upper and the Lower Engadine. Each of them was a proudly autonomous member of the League of the House of God (*Chadé, Gotteshausbund*) and the Republic of the Three Leagues. The "honorable magistrate, council and whole community of the Upper Engadine"[10]—Jenatsch's own community—was a major political player in the Three Leagues, not only because of the potency of its assembled militiamen, but also because it was home to major branches of the mighty Planta and Salis clans. The political life that took place in these larger communes was intense. Candidates for office used tactics ranging from providing food and drink to the assembled voters during elections to orchestrating brutal murders and mass riots during especially tense moments. Factions were built around kin groups, with the great families building networks among the more humble citizens. Effective organization and intimidation could ensure that the faction leaders gained the prestigious and profitable communal offices, which also allowed them to manage the commune's votes on critical decisions facing the Three Leagues.[11]

The Engadine's connections and the wealth and ambition of its leading families were visible in the way Engadiners reached out into the larger European worlds of learning and politics. Young men from the leading political, clerical, and notarial families began attending schools and universities outside the Engadine early in the 1500s, often bringing their knowledge back home. Perhaps the most notorious was Simon Lemnius from the neighboring Val Müstair, whose talents as a Latin poet led him through universities at Basel, Ingolstadt, and Wittenberg. In Wittenberg, the heart of the German Lutheran movement, he became entangled in a nasty literary dispute with Martin Luther himself in 1538, which cost him his academic career. After retreating to Graubünden, Lemnius got his revenge by publishing a book-length poem titled *Monachopornomachia*, which contained an obscene attack on the German reformer's life. Later, Lemnius became a poet-in-residence in Bologna, Italy, where he was eventually crowned poet laureate.[12] Other educated Engadiners who came home after more conventional academic careers used their education to create the first written version of the Romansh language. When George Jenatsch left Silvaplana in 1610 for Zurich, he was following a generations-old path that dozens of young Engadiners had already taken toward higher education.[13]

Within the tapestry of nested communal organizations in the Engadine, the members of the Jenatsch family were minor but not insignificant players. George's father and grandfather, who had both attended university, served as imperial notaries in Silvaplana as well as pastors. The notary played a crucial role in the organization of the Engadine, whose legal system was closer to that of Italy than

Germany. By putting his personal mark on a document and recording the trans-
action in his register, the notary had the power to make contracts, debts, and
property transfers binding. The position required a license from the emperor or
pope, bought with considerable trouble and expense and carefully passed from
generation to generation. It is thus no surprise that the Jenatsch family was well
established and respected, if not wealthy. In their home commune of Samedan,
for example, they occupied the fourth pew in the church, after the Salis, Scandol-
era, Planta, Polin, and Bifrun families.[14] The pastor's influence, like the notary's,
rested on his public functions. Not only could a pastor conduct essential rituals
and ceremonies and teach God's word, which in the Upper Engadine meant the
Reformed Protestant version of Latin Christianity, but from the pulpit he also
made important announcements and could speak out to the entire population
about current affairs. George Jenatsch's father and grandfather had served as pastors both within and outside the Engadine; given the customs of his time, it was
natural that George expected to follow their example.

By calling himself an Engadiner when he began school in Zurich in 1610,
Jenatsch signaled his attachment to his Engadine roots. His childhood language
and the traditions of his family in the tightly knit villages and communes of this
distinctive region caused him to feel a strong connection to the Engadine. He also
described himself as a Rhaetian, however, a term that reveals a different aspect of
how identities formed at this time. Rhaetia was what the Roman Empire had
called the large province that included the east-central Alps as well as the hill
country leading down the Danube River farther north. Rhaetia Prima was the
subdivision that included most of Graubünden. The Roman Empire in western
Europe had collapsed more than a thousand years before Jenatsch was born, however. Neither the borders, the people, nor the political system around 1600 bore
the slightest resemblance to Roman times. Why, then, did Jenatsch, like many
other Bündner of his era, think of himself in terms of this old Roman name?

This question needs to be answered on several levels that reveal how complex
political identities in this region and period were. For the specific term "Rhetus," we
first need to look more closely at how intellectuals played the game of nation formation after 1500. Recall the highly vocal intellectuals in Renaissance Italy, who
had connected the glory of the Roman Empire with the independence of their
own city-states, or, like Machiavelli, with the rebirth of Italian glory. Renaissance
humanists north of the Alps also began producing historical reconstructions in the
name of regional independence around 1500, with an extra edge after the Protestant Reformation gave them another motive to criticize Rome. Particularly in
Germanic Europe, antiquarians pored over Roman histories to find the names of
obscure tribes they could celebrate as their freedom-loving ancestors who had
struggled against the "Roman yoke."[15] The Swiss intellectual Aegidius Tschudi
(1505–1572), for example, spent his life collecting old documents about Swiss
history, including scattered bits of myth and speculation from Roman documents.
In his only published book, he claimed that Rhaetia, the old Roman province

currently occupied by the Three Leagues, derived its name from another Etruscan, Rhetus.[16] Rhetus, according to Tschudi, had been a ruler in Tuscany around 500 B.C.E. When the invading Gauls overran his lands, he led his people into exile across the Alps rather than accept occupation and slavery. His refuge, Tschudi claimed, had been the Bündner valley known as the Domleschg, or Tumilasca in Latin, which sounded vaguely Etruscan to Renaissance ears. There, surrounded by the "ringwalls" of the high mountains, Rhetus and his Tuscans had lived in peace, at least until the Romans invaded the region several hundred years later.

From the perspective of modern archaeology and classical studies, this story is full of holes, and there is little reason to think that it is true. For the educated young men of Graubünden after 1550, however, imbued with the humanist agenda of Latin and Roman history, the story was deeply satisfying. Above all, it helped them explain why they were "free"—that is, why their government did not depend on feudal lords and a king. In the 1580s, Durisch Chiampell, a Protestant pastor, folded the Rhetus story into his massive unpublished history of Graubünden, whose central theme was the loss and recovery of "Rhaetian liberty."[17] By the 1610s, the story circulated in popular songs, pamphlets, and doubtless by word of mouth, and in 1616, the Protestant Bündner politician Johann Guler published a history that made the connection explicit in its title: *Rhaetia: That Is, a Detailed and Truthful Description of the Three Honorable Grey Leagues and Other Rhaetian Peoples, Explaining Who They Are and Their Origins and Deeds.*[18]

For Protestants in particular, the story carried the extra bonus of revealing how Roman tyranny was a permanent threat. Ever since the days of the noble Tuscans, they claimed, the people of Graubünden had fought the Romans. Who could resist the stirring words of Fortunat Sprecher's 1616 poem "A Nice New Song In Honor of the Three Leagues," which began:

> I am old Rhetus, I come from Tuscany.
> To hang on to my freedom, and stay out of slavery,
> I left my fatherland behind, with all its fields and goods,
> Together with my warriors, we found this neighborhood.[19]

The story of Rhetus was not simply about a distant ancestor who had given his name to the region: it was a claim to liberty even at the expense of exile. As a young man beginning a temporary exile of his own—not the last of his life, by any means—Jenatsch showed with his 1610 signature that he had absorbed such claims about his homeland's liberty.

Patriotism, Seventeenth-Century-Style

As Jenatsch's double identification "Engadino-Rhetus" suggests, seventeenth-century patriotism always existed side by side with other profound attachments.

As a youth, Jenatsch set his Rhaetian national identity next to his local origins in the Engadine. Later in life, two other competing relationships would shape his course: first, his attachment to the Reformed Protestant cause, and afterward his extensive services to foreign states, particularly France and Venice. Jenatsch himself repeatedly spoke of the interests of his church or his foreign patrons as complementary to his service to his "fatherland," thus echoing the common view at this time.[20] His efforts to explain how he understood such competing loyalties are helpful: they illuminate his thinking and feelings about where his loyalties lay, though we must of course consider whom he was writing and what he wanted from them, as well.

Jenatsch's patriotic identity, hinted at in his schoolboy signature, became clearly visible during the brutal struggles that broke out in Graubünden after 1617. In one of his earliest surviving letters, Jenatsch implored his ally and patron Giacomo Ruinelli to bring a company of troops into the fray in the name of "the peril to our church, the peril to our fatherland, the peril to all good men."[21] Writing in 1619, as rival factions in Graubünden tore the republic's institutions apart, the young pastor put protection of church and of state side by side. Yet the rest of the letter reveals that at this point, Jenatsch cared most about his church and the cause of Protestant survival. His goal was to ensure that Graubünden remained a Protestant state: "We will stand and have decided to die: it is about Christ and his Church," Jenatsch explained.[22]

As he gained experience as a soldier and in politics, Jenatsch soon gave up this position. Long before his conversion to Catholicism, he began linking his fatherland to liberty rather than to religion.[23] This put him back in the mainstream of Bündner thinking at the time, and correlated well with his decision to leave the clergy. Later on, especially after he converted to to the Catholic faith, he kept religion and politics even more separate. In 1636, for example, he argued with Stephan Gabriel, once a fellow pastor and now his bitterest public critic, about the place of spiritual concerns in politics. Jenatsch responded directly to Gabriel in one of his letters. "I'm astonished that you claim to know more about the fatherland's good than all the faithful and single-minded patriots who have poured out their blood and property for the fatherland,"[24] Jenatsch wrote, clearly drawing a line between true patriots and the religiously motivated Gabriel. Indeed, by this time Jenatsch believed that the Reformation itself had caused much of the chaos and corruption that Graubünden had to endure. Here, he fit into an emerging European trend, which emphasized that even though religious uniformity was an important contributor to political stability, spiritual and worldly concerns were best kept separate. The origins of later theories about the separation of church and state lay in this movement, which grew precociously in Graubünden, a federal state made up of communities divided by religion.[25]

By the 1630s, then, Jenatsch saw his fatherland as separate from his church, and his patriotism therefore separate from his faith. As was typical in this era, his concern for "Rhaetian liberty" also never prevented him from serving foreign governments as his career flourished. At various times, he expressed direct loyalty to the king of France and to the state of Venice, often in letters that simultaneously foregrounded his concern for the liberty of his fatherland.[26] In 1624, for example, he signed an appeal to Louis XIII of France for help against the Spanish troops occupying the Valtellina. After bemoaning the miserable conditions in Graubünden, the signers exclaimed that "aside from God, we have no hope to be restored in our original liberty except through your Majesty's victorious arms . . . and for our part, we shall employ our lives and our blood for the increase of your Majesty's glory."[27] A dozen members of the Salis faction, including Jenatsch, signed the letter. Of course, the diplomatic language of the time required humble expressions of obedience and loyalty when writing to any king; we should not put too much weight on what was partly a formality. We find similar sentiments (but directed to Venice) in Jenatsch's letters reporting events to the Venetian ambassador in exactly the same period. Nevertheless, the very fact that a politically influential actor like Jenatsch perceived no conflict in serving various rulers as his career proceeded suggests that he did not feel the kind of exclusive attachment to one state that characterizes modern nationalism.

Indeed, men like Jenatsch routinely combined local political loyalties with service to foreign princes. Jenatsch always insisted that he was not simply a mercenary, since he worked only for those foreign rulers who supported his own agenda in Graubünden. He expressed the distinction clearly in a letter to the Bündner magistrates in 1628, when they were considering a new treaty with Spain:

> I may honor and respect the King of Spain as he deserves, since he is a most powerful European monarch, but to put it clearly, if our lands should find it good to ally with that king, I will retire in peace and depart to serve those princes to whom I feel obligated as a member of my fatherland, both because of our ancient alliances and because of the rivers of gold they have spent in defense of our liberty.[28]

When Jenatsch switched his loyalty to the Spanish-Austrian side in 1636, he followed the same pattern, claiming that only an alliance with Austria and Milan, Graubünden's two closest neighbors, could bring a lasting peace and the return of the occupied Valtellina. Not surprisingly, therefore, he showed no hesitation in accepting money and (as he hoped) noble honors from his new patrons.

In a particularly revealing letter written in 1629, Jenatsch defended his Venetian service against critics in Graubünden. By then, the pro-Spanish faction had seized power in Chur and passed a law punishing anyone who entered military service with Venice. In an angry letter no doubt intended for public circulation, Jenatsch rejected the magistrates' power to pass such a law.

> I would never have embraced an office in service to the most serene Republic of Venice if you, honored Sirs, were not trying in double-time to firmly unite our

country with the King of Spain and the House of Austria. You know full well that my enemies, faithful servants of those princes, once they have been made strong and the treaties accomplished . . . will revenge themselves on me.[29]

After praising once again the effort and money that France and Venice had provided to support the Three Leagues, Jenatsch marveled that those who supported Venice now faced the death penalty, whereas not a single Bündner who had slipped across the border to serve in Milan, on Spanish territory, faced any punishment at all. Moreover, Jenatsch insisted, the company of troops he had raised would be available for Graubünden if the "liberty of the fatherland" were ever at stake, no matter the expense. In addition, so he claimed, he had made sure that his company consisted entirely of foreigners in order to avoid offense to the Bündner magistrates.[30]

Still, the accusation that he was selling out had stung Jenatsch. Later in the same letter, he defended himself directly:

The goods that I have accumulated with God's help in our country, I obtained not through public offices in Rhaetia, but in the service of princes, [although] without harm, but rather with benefits for the fatherland. And it is not true that I left [Graubünden] just to satisfy the wishes of those who wanted me not just in Venice, but as far away as the Indies (if under very different circumstances!). [31]

Clearly, he wanted to be regarded as a patriot, and he was equally angry that anyone might think he had run away from his enemies. Rather, he left because the current magistrates had chosen to ally themselves with his enemies and the protectors of his enemies. It is noteworthy how firmly Jenatsch insisted here that his fatherland had benefited from his foreign service.

After his religious conversion and his orchestration of the peace with Austria and Spain in 1636, Jenatsch continued to deny that his new allies would influence his position on Graubünden's interests, especially with regard to the all-important Valtellina. In another letter to his frequent rival Stephan Gabriel, he wrote:

What has happened, what has made you see me in such a sinister light that you could think I would support the rebels [i.e., the local leaders in the Valtellina] and not my fatherland? Dear Jesus, what have I come to? Let me die if it is not true that the rebels hate me like a dog or snake![32]

Naturally, Jenatsch was most likely to voice patriotic feelings in such public letters aimed at his critics, and to deny that there was any conflict between his patriotism and serving the king of France or the archdukes of Austria. Still, if most of his peers had seen a fundamental conflict in serving another nation, Jenatsch would hardly have admitted his commitment to foreign rulers so boldly. He was a seventeenth-century patriot, not a modern nationalist.

Speaking Out: Living with Multiple Languages

Speaking out for his fatherland was something that Jenatsch felt he could do with pride, but what language did he speak out in? As much as anywhere in Europe, speaking out in Graubünden meant using different languages in different situations. Coming from the Engadine meant speaking Ladin Romansh, leadership in Graubünden meant using German and Italian, coping with the interested powers in the region added French, while educated discourse required Latin. We have evidence that Jenatsch used all of these languages during his career. How did he manage the linguistic boundaries that his situation produced? And how important was language to him and his contemporaries?

By the 1600s, most European states operated in a single, dominant language, though variants and dialects remained abundant at the local level. Parisian French, Castilian Spanish, and London English became national languages because they were the speech of strong monarchies based in stable capitals. For republics, it seemed even more obvious to political theorists at the time that sharing a common language strengthened ties of affection, thus promoting republican cooperation among civic elites. Republics, too, could thus trigger the process by which a language became formalized and standardized. The emergence of the modern Dutch language, for example, coincided with the establishment of an independent Dutch republican state after 1560, just as the triumph of Tuscan Italian was closely connected with the rise of a self-governing republic of Florence after 1300. In the Swiss Confederation, German was the language of the ruling cantons, and thus of politics and law, even though the confederates also ruled over subjects who spoke other languages.[33]

The language landscape in Europe also included certain high-status languages that educated individuals from every part of Europe could be expected to know. Throughout the Middle Ages and into the 1500s, Latin filled this role: as the language of the church and of all higher education, it allowed young men from the remotest corners of Europe to take up spiritual or diplomatic careers that often spanned multiple regions. During the Renaissance, Italian became the primary language of political diplomacy, though French began to supplant it during the 1600s. After the Reformation, moreover, Protestant clergy—following the Reformation's emphasis on God's word in the Bible—increased their efforts in school to learn Greek, and sometimes even Hebrew, so that they could be confident in their knowledge of scripture. A son of pastors and notaries anywhere in Europe therefore faced years of language study if he hoped to make his way upward in the world.

But Graubünden was unusual: not only were its relations with the larger European world carried out in multiple languages, so were its own internal affairs. In the northern and western parts of the Three Leagues, most of the population spoke Alemannic dialects of German. They had no trouble conversing with their Swiss neighbors to the west, but the Bavarian dialects to the northeast diverged strongly from their own idiom.[34] Those who learned to read and write used a version known as Alemannic or southern chancery German, which resembled the other major written forms of German well enough to ensure relatively easy communication across most of the Holy Roman Empire. In the southernmost valleys of Graubünden, those draining south toward Como, Milan, and the Po River, the people spoke Italian of the Lombard dialect. Since these dialects were virtually incomprehensible to someone who spoke only Tuscan or Venetian, literacy in these valleys also required learning a different form of Italian.

Across the middle of Graubünden, from the Lower Engadine to the upper Rhine, the local population spoke various dialects of Romansh, none of which had an established written form before the 1550s.[35] The first New Testament in Romansh was not printed until 1560, for example, using the Ladin of Jenatsch's Upper Engadine; secular printing began only well after 1600.[36] Local life, including government and legal affairs, took place in Romansh in much of Graubünden. Even though the communal statutes of the Engadine were written down in Latin, for example, the courts always operated in Romansh. Indeed, once the Engadiners had become used to seeing written Romansh, they promptly translated their statutes back into their spoken language. Most of the elite in the Romansh areas also spoke both German and Italian since they had to communicate with relatives and rivals from the German and Italian parts of Graubünden and beyond. The need to communicate thus drove many people to become multilingual.

The survival of a cache of family letters from the Engadine offers us a rare chance to see how people there used different languages in everyday life. Various members of one branch of the Salis family in Samedan—including not only adult men but children, women, and youths in school—wrote letters to one another between 1585 and 1615 that have survived to the present.[37] These letters reveal some clear patterns about who used which language, and under what circumstances. When the Salis men wrote to each other about local affairs in Graubünden, they used the locally dominant written languages, Italian and German. In a long series of letters back and forth between Johannes Baptista von Salis and his son Johann Friedrich, for example, they both switched back and forth between German and Italian, often within the same letter. Younger writers, however, followed a different pattern. Sent off to Zurich, Augsburg, and Basel to study, several of the Salis boys wrote home exclusively in Latin. After all, their father was spending money to support them while they studied, and they needed to demonstrate their progress. (One can also imagine their schoolmasters standing over them, demanding that they write home to demonstrate what a good job the teachers were doing!) Their father, in contrast, wrote back in whatever language suited him. Some of his letters are even trilingual, freely mixing Latin, German, and Romansh. Romansh was used in one other circumstance: when the Salis boys wrote home to women back in Samedan. This, as well as the snippets of Romansh that appeared in other letters, suggests that for Engadiners like the Salis, Romansh remained the language of the home and of family feelings. When one of the sons,

Friedrich, settled in Paris, he began writing his father in French. What remains truly impressive is how easily the members of this family, women as well as men, switched between German, Italian, and Latin. Educated Bündner, we may conclude, were routinely fluent in several languages—a conclusion that applies to Jenatsch as well.

Tracing Jenatsch's path, from the Romansh Engadine through German Zurich and service to France and Venice, highlights the fact that his own life frequently crossed the boundaries of language. If we look at him with modern eyes shaped by the nationalist idea that every country has its natural language, we might expect shifts in his linguistic environment to affect his sense of who he was. Yet as far as we can tell, different languages played at most a minor role in shaping Jenatsch's identity. Indeed, it is much easier to show how language has resonated in recent *interpretations* of Jenatsch's life than it is to show language difference affecting that life itself. Still, Jenatsch's early career certainly raises the issue of language use. The local dialect of his native Engadine became incomprehensible only a few miles from his home and was ridiculed for its barbarism by outsiders.[38] As the son of a minister, Jenatsch would have had close contact not only with spoken Ladin, but also with the Ladin Romansh catechism and New Testament translated by Jachiam Bifrun in the late sixteenth century. That Jenatsch could and sometimes needed to write in Romansh is certain. When he was mediating between the Capuchins and the Protestant villages of the Lower Engadine in the 1620s and early 1630s, for example, he wrote one letter in Romansh that has survived.[39]

As soon as Jenatsch left the immediate sphere of the Engadine, though, he needed other languages, which he quickly learned. His education both as a boy in Silvaplana and as a student in Zurich took place primarily in Latin, a language he needed to master as a clergyman. He also learned German, as we can see from two letters that he wrote to his employer Giovanni Baptista de Salis in 1614 and 1616.[40] The German is colloquial and fluent, though Jenatsch writes informally and with clear echoes of Swiss dialect.[41] Despite his father's efforts to get Jenatsch a tutor when he arrived in Zurich, Jenatsch's knowledge of Greek and Hebrew is far less certain, since no trace of either appears in his correspondence. Still, his contemporaries praised his extensive knowledge of languages both as a student and later in life, so it is possible that he mastered at least the rudiments of these classical tongues.[42] On the whole, though, his surviving correspondence strongly suggests that he was most comfortable writing in Italian. Of his surviving letters, about two-thirds are in Italian.[43] Although he studied in Zurich and Basel, served in a German army, and married a German-speaking woman, Jenatsch avoided the German language in his later letters.

In fact, Jenatsch's letters reveal a man who was not a fluid author in multiple languages. Particularly revealing is the nearly complete absence of jumping from language to language, or code-switching, within individual letters.[44] Again, the Salis correspondence, written by individuals from exactly the same region at the same time, provides a useful contrast since the Salis writers moved easily among

German, Italian, Romansh, and Latin.[45] Jenatsch was less flexible, and all the surviving documents suggest that when writing, he favored Italian—relatively similar to his native Romansh—above other languages that he used, though he was capable of writing fluently in German and Latin when the situation demanded it.

Jenatsch himself left us no commentary on how language skills shaped his career or identity. We know that some of his contemporaries, including one of the Salis boys, thought that if they wanted to get ahead in the world, they needed to know not just French, but French with a proper Parisian accent. Getting ahead also meant shedding any traces of Romansh. Thus, young Rudolf von Salis wrote to his father in 1586 that "for the sake of improving my crude habits, I willingly removed myself far from our people's words and conversation; and I have no doubt but that in this way, I am about to turn from their horrid and rude speech to polished and smooth oration."[46] Such cosmopolitan views were the opposite of nationalist linguistic pride; they rested on the long tradition of shared Latin literacy among elites, which attributed low status to vulgar languages like Romansh and even German. Engadiners from this period did not often express much pride in their peculiar language, though the occasional phrase inserted into letters suggests that they were aware of the tension between formal and everyday speech.[47] Jenatsch's own correspondence—in Italian when possible, in other languages when necessary—shows that his choice of language depended mostly on practical considerations.

A further clue to Jenatsch's linguistic consciousness comes from his signatures, more specifically from how they vary. The historian Norbert Furrer discovered at least twelve different ways that Jenatsch signed his letters. His signature ranged from the Romansh Zoartz Jenatz to the Latinized Georgius Jenatius. Furrer's key observation is that in Italian, Jenatsch always wrote his first name the same way: he was always Giorgio. When he signed his name in German, in contrast, he used Georg, Geörg, Görg, or Jörg without any pattern.[48] This suggests that his sense of himself was weaker when thinking in German, allowing him to write his name however seemed right at the moment, just as people at the time used multiple spellings for all sorts of words. This is not a surprising conclusion in light of the other evidence from his letters. Given that he never expressed any special pride in his Romansh and that he wrote most comfortably in Italian, the most we can conclude is that language did not form a key axis of Jenatsch's identity, even though his ability to use many languages was an important resource as he moved through life. Modern nationalism often assumes that language has a profound shaping force on individuals and groups, but this view was foreign to the seventeenth century. Jenatsch's school enrollment as "Engadino-Rhetus" certainly revealed a distinct *regional* identity, but little more.

In contrast, the mutations that Jenatsch's first name has undergone in subsequent centuries are revealing. In particular, the debate over a suitable title for Conrad Meyer's 1874 novel, and subsequent polemics, show how language and identity became entangled in the 1800s, long after Jenatsch was dead. A man called Georgius on his gravestone or Giorgio in his letters became "Jürg" at the wish of Meyer's German publisher. In fact, even that name was a compromise for Meyer, since the publisher initially suggested that rebaptizing Jenatsch with the distinctively North German name Jürgen might help anemic early sales of the book.[49] Both of Jenatsch's major biographers rejected this change and called their books *Georg Jenatsch*, choosing one modern German version of his first name. When the fourth edition of Alexander Pfister's biography appeared in 1984, however, the publishers once again intervened. This time, they changed the title to *Jörg Jenatsch*, another compromise, "taking account of the rootedness of the form 'Jörg' in popular consciousness."[50] Such a change, taking place thirteen years after Pfister's death, reveals how modern myths about Jenatsch have taken on linguistic contours that were largely absent from Jenatsch's own experience. We will scrutinize these myths in more detail in the final chapter of this book.

*   *   *

His sense of place and his understanding of language certainly shaped Jenatsch's identity. For all the fluidity he showed in practice, it seems likely he would have gladly accepted the designation he chose for himself as a boy, "Engadino-Rhetus," even at the end of his life. His attachment to his native land, as the term itself suggests, encompassed both the geographical space, with its mountains and crucial central location in Europe, and its political system, shaped by both real and imagined historical roots. Yet we must recognize equally that neither nationalism nor ethnicity in the modern sense would have made much sense to him. The same man who wrote fiery defenses of his patriotism—his love of his *patria*—throughout his life also had no qualms about serving the military and political interests of foreign rulers. Seventeenth-century loyalty to one's nation was not exclusive, but rather one attachment in a more complex system of identity. Nor would Jenatsch have connected his love of fatherland to his use of a particular language or his participation in a particular local culture. His native Romansh was not the language he favored in his correspondence, though he sprinkled occasional Romansh terms into letters to his countryman from the Engadine, Stephan Gabriel. Nowhere do we find the kind of sentimental loyalty to the external signs of a particular culture—food, clothing, housing styles—that became so important to the popular nationalism of the 1800s and 1900s. The local and the cosmopolitan have long been competing poles for elite European loyalties. Jenatsch's place on this spectrum, and his ability to move fluidly and adapt easily to different cultures, are typical for the seventeenth century, part of the European continuum even if characterized by instability and dynamism. The place of religion in European identity during Jenatsch's life raised greater challenges, as we shall see, because of the bitter divisions between Catholics and Protestants.

Chapter 3

From Religious Zealot to Convert

During his short career as a Reformed pastor, George Jenatsch acted as a zealous and intolerant advocate for the Calvinist cause. Rejecting the caution of his older peers among the pastors in the Three Leagues, he let religious passion shape his actions, including playing a role at the notorious Thusis trials of 1618. There, as one of the spiritual overseers intended to guarantee that the assembled militia "protected the fatherland and punished the guilty" (as they saw it), his role was close to that of an Old Testament prophet. Judge and shepherd simultaneously, he embodied the intertwined duality of religion and politics that had long character-ized European society. That duality faced a severe challenge after the great schism of the Protestant Reformation that began in 1517, though the old ideas persisted for generations. By the early 1600s, Europeans' ideas about religion and politics had become critically unstable, and would continue to fracture during the politi-cal and cultural crisis brought on by the Thirty Years' War.

During the course of that war, after what he described as five years of resisting his own inner voice, Jenatsch publicly announced his conversion to the Catholic faith.[1] Since he converted in the midst of high-level diplomatic maneuvering over the future of the Three Leagues, many of his contemporaries wondered about his motivations. After all, moving from one religion to another was one of the most visible changes in identity that a person living at this time could undertake. It transformed family life, home, and social connections for the convert, while leaving ruptures and anger among his former coreligionists. Converts became marked for special treatment, for better or for worse. When Jenatsch died, for example, his body was interred inside Chur's Catholic cathedral with high honor, something otherwise reserved for clergy-men, and his gravestone called him a promoter of sacred peace, despite his violent early career as an anti-Catholic activist. In contrast, his many enemies insisted that this "atheist" must have cynically assumed a Catholic façade because of his unbri-dled lust for political power (to be had with support from the ultra-Catholic Spanish), his craving for a noble title (only available from the Catholic Austrians), or his per-sonal greed (to be sated with the bribes he received for betraying the Protestant Duke of Rohan in 1637). We could thus ask, as his contemporaries did, was his conversion politically motivated, or did it reflect genuine conviction?

A more careful look suggests that putting the question this way would miss the shifting grounds of religious identity during Jenatsch's life. To deny that his conversion transformed his political situation is naive; to claim that he acted without spiritual reflection is to ignore the evidence. Since no one—not even a biographer—has privileged access to a person's private motivations, discovering how political and spiritual considerations weighed in shaping Jenatsch's conversion is extraordinarily difficult. Rather, both his own statements and the way he and his contemporaries acted before and after his conversion provide useful evidence for considering a different issue: what did religious conversion mean in Europe's profoundly Christian culture of this era, and how was that meaning changing? The tension between faith and interest, and between religion and politics, was at least as old as the separation between the Roman Church, headed by the pope, and the kings and nobility of Europe. Yet such tensions did not challenge the widely held conviction during the later medieval period that orthodoxy—that is, correct teaching and belief—was the defining feature and crowning achievement of western European societies. Until the Reformation divided the Christian majority itself, therefore, conversion from one Christian belief to another was inconceivable: a change could only be to, or from, the single true faith. Even the word "conversion" had a quite different meaning before 1500 than it does today, signifying primarily an inner turning toward God on the part of devout seekers after spiritual consolation, rather than a change of faith.[2]

By the early 1600s, the situation had changed in profound ways. When he was still a Calvinist pastor, Jenatsch embodied the spiritual ideals of pre-Reformation Christianity in his insistence on orthodoxy, even though his dogma was in conflict with that of the Roman Church. According to his own words and actions, only a truly Christian government had any right to rule Graubünden. When Jenatsch became Catholic in 1635, he did not simply change one dogma for another while retaining the conviction that orthodoxy was essential. Instead, his letters reveal a very different understanding of what religion was and what it demanded of the faithful. Peace, prudence, and respect for authority, rather than fervor, characterized his later view.

In the older way of seeing things, religion was not an identity as we think of it today—that is, an individual's way of locating him- or herself among groups sharing certain characteristics—but rather a prerequisite for becoming a full person socially, legally, and spiritually. One powerful strand of European thought throughout the Middle Ages accordingly defined people who were not orthodox as people "without religion," who were therefore somehow less than human. By the later 1500s, this orthodox understanding of humans, society, and God confronted profound challenges from an alternative position, one that had its own ancient roots, and that also has close ties to modern ideas about the individual and society. Resistance to the exclusive claims of traditional orthodoxy came from different directions and for different reasons, but maintained the fundamental conviction that humanity came before, rather than from, dogmatic precision. From this perspective, religion became one source of identity among many—a crucial identity, to be sure, but not a qualification for full personhood in the first place.[3]

We can capture this distinction in two emblematic passages from Jenatsch's own letters. As a young man in 1619, Jenatsch begged his Protestant patron Giacomo Ruinelli for support by writing that "the Church is in danger, the fatherland is in danger . . . it is a matter of Christ and His Church," thus connecting two things that were, in his view at the time, inextricably linked.[4] In 1638, older and transformed by the same forces transforming the larger culture, Jenatsch wrote to a Catholic ally that the best policy was "to live and let live" in religious affairs.[5] He followed this approach in his own relationships with his family, allies, and peers. Truly a convert, the boundary he had crossed was not only between the combating doctrines, but also between an orthodox and a tolerant worldview. A century earlier, such a conversion would have been nearly inconceivable; a century later, it was common.[6]

The shifting meaning of religion and of conversion in Jenatsch's own experience thus captures a larger shift underway across Europe at this time, which scholars describe with two technical terms: confessionalization and secularization. Confessionalization describes how western European Christians, who mostly imagined themselves as a single community before 1517, came to see themselves as belonging instead to one of the new, rival denominations or "confessions" (Catholic, Lutheran, Reformed/Calvinist, etc.). Although the schisms that gave rise to these distinct movements took place during the 1520s, and the new institutional churches had taken clear shape by 1540, many European laypeople continued to view themselves primarily as Christians without a confessional label. Although their clergy might claim that their respective churches were the only truly Christian ones, laypeople during this transitional generation often seemed less interested in demonizing Christian dissidents, and sometimes treated the rival confessions as equally valid. However, this changed by the 1570s: whether because of strenuous education campaigns by the new churches backed by coercion and persecution by Europe's confessional states, or because of other changes in culture and society, more and more western Europeans came to define themselves by their particular confession. Historians are still hotly debating how and why this shift took place, what its consequences were, and how long it lasted.[7]

Secularization was an equally profound process, but one that undermined the status of all confessions rather than raising sharper and more visible divisions between them. The outcome of secularization (if it ever took place, which some historians question) was less emphasis on the exclusive claims of any single Christian confession to be orthodox, coupled with tolerance, apathy, or a turn toward new sources of identity, such as the nation-state. Most historians agree that the second generation after the Protestant Reformation saw, if anything, a decline in secularism and an increase in confessional fervor among a broad cross-section of the European population; one rarely sees the term secularization applied to the period from 1550 to 1600. Sometime between 1600 and 1750, however, this trend reversed, leading to a decline in most Europeans' willingness to put their faith above other considerations. It is important to recognize that neither confessionalization nor secularization necessarily meant that people were becoming more or less spiritual: what these terms describe are shifting relationships between religious and other forms of identification and motivation, rather than the degree of religiosity itself.[8]

Such general terms are not well suited to describing the complex internal dynamics of a single community or a single individual, though. Some interesting recent research has therefore concentrated on these dynamics, leaving the question of larger trends aside. What such studies show most clearly is that at the level of communities or even particular individuals, such as Jenatsch, orthodoxy, confessions, and secular tolerance combined in unexpected and rapidly shifting ways. Transformation is therefore the key to this chapter, which follows Jenatsch's spiritual commitments from the young pastor's zeal to the seasoned soldier's prudence. Throughout this shift, religious duty and political ambition remained the key, eternally entangled moments. Faith was inevitably political, and politics was always informed by faith, even as the way each contributed to the boundaries that shaped society and self began to change.

The Militant: "The Church Is in Danger, the Fatherland Is in Danger"

George Jenatsch was born at a time when tension between Catholics and Protestants in Europe, including Switzerland and Graubünden, was reaching new peaks, and his early life coincided with a spiraling increase in religiously motivated political conflict across Europe that ultimately helped trigger the Thirty Years' War in 1618. His own short career as a militant pastor reached its climax in 1619, the same year that the armies began moving in Spain and Italy, in Bohemia and Germany. His position as a Reformed pastor in the Three Leagues exposed him to the full intensity and complexity of early modern religious politics and political religion. Unlike most of western Europe's confessional states with their state churches, the Three Leagues formed a confederation that formally included both Catholic and Protestant communities.[9] Consequently, religious polarization became deeply entangled with the republic's political affairs at every level. In this era, coexistence often produced not toleration, but heightened sensitivity to religious difference on the part of elites and an increasing temptation to demonize political rivals as spiritual threats. Yet the majority of people in cities or regions where more than one version of Christianity was practiced usually managed to live next to adherents of other faiths, to buy and sell from them, even to share in political duties and rights with them.[10] Similar conditions applied in Graubünden, where the Three Leagues thrived during most of the 1500s despite their division into a patchwork of Catholic and Protestant communes, not to mention a good number with mixed populations.

Rulers and especially clergymen on all sides were frequently shocked by such everyday accommodation and devoted great efforts to undermine it. Such side-by-side coexistence violated their fundamental understanding of religious faith as an exclusive path to salvation, defined by the authorized church and protected by secular rulers. To put it simply, for most European clergymen before 1600, religion was a word that had no plural. Religion was Christianity as revealed in the scriptures, interpreted by the Church Fathers, and administered by the true church, whether that church was Catholic or Lutheran or Reformed. Any deviation fell into a different category, meaning that its adherents became pagans, infidels, Jews (a special case), or worst of all, heretics. Bolstered by their conviction of rightness, most authorities across Europe, especially those in places where adherents of Catholicism, Lutheranism, and Calvinism lived near one another, set out to make the difference between truth and error more visible. Catechisms, schooling, and better-trained priests sought to make the flocks more aware of religious doctrine, while pamphlets, plays, and images portrayed the other camps as deceitful and dangerous.[11] Here again, Graubünden, even more than Switzerland, was exceptional. Despite loud clamors from the Reformed clergy in particular, the secular authorities in Graubünden were slow to apply the tools of political coercion to religious problems. By the late 1500s, however, the increasingly confessional culture surrounding them began to affect the way both magistrates and the common laity viewed confessional divisions.[12]

One event that reveals the hardening religious lines that divided the neighboring Swiss cantons was the 1586 signing of the so-called Golden League by seven Catholic cantons in Switzerland (out of thirteen in all). This treaty, sealed with the encouragement of the Spanish ambassador and the papal nuncio, contained the following clause:

> We have collectively deliberated and decided, and finally proclaimed, to persist in the true, old, undoubted Apostolic Roman Catholic and Christian faith, entirely, persistently, and firmly, to live and die within it (to which may God the Almighty always grant his grace); . . . and in addition, we the seven Catholic cantons promise to protect and preserve one another in the same aforementioned faith with all our power and ability, with our bodies and with our goods, against all those who might threaten us, with no exceptions; *nor should any older or newer alliance that had been made or might be made, hinder us in any way in this obligation.*[13]

Faced with religious disunity in the larger Swiss Confederation, the Catholic cantons here reasserted an older vision in which orthodoxy was more important than any secular consideration. By explicitly placing religious obligations above the Catholic cantons' alliances with the Protestant cantons, moreover, the agreement threatened the survival of the Swiss Confederation and consequently provoked loud protests from Zurich and Bern, the leaders of the Protestant bloc. In the following years, the Catholic cantons found themselves unable to act in accord with the Golden League's grand assertions. Rather, they continued to cooperate and to haggle with their Protestant confederates, sometimes conceding even on religious issues, and they shaped their foreign policy according to the demands of Europe-an shifts in military power, trade, and diplomacy, not just loyalty to the old faith. What the Golden League reveals, therefore, is the continued attractiveness of the traditional orthodox model. It embodied the same values that contemporaries caught up in the vicious religious and civil war in France kept repeating: one faith, one king, and one law.

Conviction about the inseparable connection between true religion and legiti-mate government was no less intense in Protestant Europe, at least among the clergy and those who accepted their guidance.[14] In Switzerland, the heads of the Reformed Church passed this view on to their pupils, both future pastors and fu-ture magistrates. For German-speaking Switzerland, the most important center was Zurich, where Ulrich Zwingli's successors as *antistes*, heads of the church, never stopped calling the magistrates to support the church in all their policies. It was to Zurich that young George Jenatsch traveled around 1610 as a Romansh-speaking fourteen-year-old in order to prepare himself for a career as a Protestant pastor.

Little evidence survives about the specific events that shaped Jenatsch's attach-ment to the Reformed cause, but the entire structure of his educational experi-ence was configured to make him a zealous and loyal supporter of his faith. Most obviously, he was a pastor's son and destined from an early age to become a pas-tor himself. Likewise, his move to Zurich as a young student, supported in part by prizes awarded to needy boys preparing for the ministry, revolved around his fu-ture calling as a pastor.[15] The school authorities in Zurich had high expectations for the boys they supported, and did not tolerate any distractions from the serious business of preparing religious and political agents for outlying areas such as Graubünden. In 1613, for example, they issued a mandate rejecting any students "either unsuited to studies or not possessed of the intention to serve the church."[16] Though Jenatsch did absorb the activist attitudes of the Zurich clergy, he evi-dently failed to conform fully to their agenda, since they cut off his public stipend shortly after passing the new regulations. Most likely, his pride and his escapades with nobly born Bündner youths had something to do with it.[17] To cover his ex-penses, Jenatsch tutored and supervised the young sons of Giovanni Baptista de Salis, a local magnate from Graubünden, as they studied in Zurich and later Basel. His lifelong complex relationship with Graubünden's most powerful fami-lies is foreshadowed in this employment, as are the complex tensions between per-sonal, political, and religious loyalty that tore at many men in this era.

In 1616, after brief studies at the university in Basel, Jenatsch returned to Graubünden. For the next four years, he confronted a distinctly seventeenth-century dilemma. On the one hand, he fought for his church and faith, demand-ing with increasing violence that it be given the place in public life that religious truth deserved; on the other hand, his struggle was shaped by the unavoidable fact that his was only one of the churches making such a claim, which could be en-forced only by enlisting political allies and deploying political measures. The resulting combination of fervor and anxiety—part of what historians have labeled confessionalism—peaked in the early 1600s, and signs of it appear everywhere in Jenatsch's career as a young pastor.[18] If adopted wholeheartedly, the confessional perspective saw the world engaged in a war between good and evil that allowed no quarter or moderation. Every victory was a victory for Christ, every defeat another triumph for the devil. By 1600, moreover, the lines separating the parties had become clear and rigid, and most doubters or champions of restraint had been silenced.[19] When news of the 1572 St. Bartholomew's Day massacre in France reached the Catholic capitals of Europe, bells were rung and masses were held to celebrate the death of thousands of Protestants. The victories of the Protestant champion Gustavus Adolfus of Sweden around 1630 produced equally ecstatic expressions of joy from Protestants across Europe. For those who saw themselves caught up in such a titanic conflict, spiritual and political means were merely parallel tracks to the same goal. When Jenatsch arrived back in Graubünden in 1616, this was his struggle.

The first evidence we have of Jenatsch's return is his admission, after oral examination, to the Rhaetian Synod. Headed by a senior pastor, the synod disciplined and supported individual pastors, represented the entire clergy to the political authorities in Graubünden, and provided the main pipeline for information and guidance between Graubünden and the center of the Swiss Reformed Church in Zurich. In the 1500s, one of the synod's main roles had also been to suppress "deviant" religious ideas *within* the Reformed Church, but by 1600, the growing pressure it felt from the Catholic Counter-Reformation meant that the synod's main focus was fighting Catholicism. Thus, while Jenatsch was examined on his knowledge of Reformed Christian doctrine before being admitted to the clergy on July 3, 1617, the qualities his seniors were most looking for included energy and zeal.[20] On these counts, there is every reason to believe they found Jenatsch more than satisfactory, since they appointed him to serve in the church at Scharans in the prosperous but religiously divided Domleschg Valley. His less promising colleagues often found themselves in impoverished mountain villages with tiny salaries and little support in the community.[21]

From 1617 to 1620, Jenatsch joined a group of younger confrontational pastors within the Rhaetian Synod. Although the more senior pastors shared this group's dedication to blocking the spread of Catholicism, they were more cautious about how to proceed, and they drew back from open participation in politics—with good reason, as it turned out. In the past, whenever pastors had publicly intervened in political struggles in the Three Leagues, not only their Catholic countrymen but even Protestant political leaders had objected, telling the pastors to see to their flocks and stop causing unrest. As late as 1615, for example, the actions of Chur pastor Georg Saluz and Malans pastor Johann à Porta during a dispute over who could use village churches caused the Assembly of the Three Leagues to admonish all clergymen to keep the peace and stay out of politics. The Bündner magnates also resented the Reformed clergy's preaching against corruption in the leagues, especially against the lucrative and highly dis-puted sale of public offices to the highest bidder. The faction heads, both Catholic and Protestant, found it objectionable that the pastors openly appealed to public opinion on this issue. Living in the villages and preaching every Sunday to their flocks, the clergy of Graubünden controlled one of the most important channels of communication between authorities and people. In the rough democracy of the Three Leagues, this made them potentially powerful rivals to the leading men.[22]

By 1616, a growing political crisis triggered renewed debates over how the pas-tors should promote their faith. The balance between the factions in the leagues depended in part on the main foreign powers that had an interest in the region's strategic passes. On one side were Habsburg Austria and Habsburg Spain, which also controlled most of northern Italy. Firmly Catholic and dependent on the "Spanish Road" that moved troops from Spain and Italy through the Alps to Ger-many and the Netherlands, these two powers supported helpful Graubünden leaders—usually Catholic but sometimes Protestant—with private pensions, while offering bribes to entire communities in the Three Leagues before important votes.[23] These powers also applied economic pressure by regulating the vital cattle and grain trade with Milan, and they made direct military threats from time to time, as when Spain built the infamous Fort Fuentes for its soldiers on Milan's bor-der with the leagues' territory in the Valtellina. On the other side were Venice and France, who shared an interest in closing the passes to Spain, and who both drew mercenary regiments from Graubünden itself. The most active and knowledge-able diplomatic agents in the Three Leagues came from Venice, which was after all a direct neighbor and trading partner. Spain was the most active and informed power on the other side, because of its control over Milan and its generous bribes.

In the early 1610s, a minor diplomatic revolution destabilized both the politi-cal and religious landscape in Graubünden. After the assassination of King Henri IV in 1610, France began improving its relations with Spain while repudiating its previous ally, Venice. This shift caused intense anxiety among the pro-Venetian magnates in Graubünden, especially the Salis family members who had tied their fortunes to Venice. Their concern was that the newly empowered Spanish-French faction, headed by Rudolf and Pompeius von Planta, would use its wealth and in-fluence to turn popular hostility against Venice and its supporters. Even more ter-rified were the Reformed pastors, who feared that Spanish influence would bring not just political servitude but also religious coercion. Rather than waiting for the worst, the pastors and magnates struck out against this new constellation. George Jenatsch, with his Salis connections and the passionate attachment to the Protes-tant cause he had absorbed in Zurich, soon moved to the center of the action.

Just over twenty years old and not from a powerful family, Jenatsch played only a minor role during the political maneuvering that preceded the tribunal of Thu-sis. When he became one of the spiritual overseers of the court of 1618, though, he laid the foundation for his later reputation. Jenatsch's rise to prominence began when he joined the activist pastors who met with a key Venetian-aligned magnate, Hercules von Salis, in March or April 1618. Also attending were three far more experienced men from the synod: Caspar Alexius, a senior scholar called back from Geneva to encourage the timid Rhaetian Protestants to become more aggressive; Bonaventura Toutsch, another pastor from the Engadine; and Blasius Alexander, who soon became Jenatsch's closest friend.[24] The secret meeting itself left no records, but when the entire synod held its April meeting in the mountain village of Bergün, the gathered pastors issued a remarkable call to action against the Spanish peril. Their intention was to trigger another uprising of the military companies across the Three Leagues. The communes had already risen in 1616 and 1617, and calling them up was a tried and true way for a single faction to break through "politics as usual," controlled by the local magnate families. This is exactly what happened again in 1618.

The 1618 synodal letter vividly illustrates the relationship between political action and religious faith that motivated Jenatsch at this time. The letter began by describing the pastors' efforts to improve "the miserable condition of our common beloved Fatherland" through appeals to the Assembly of the Leagues. Not only had their pleas been ignored, the authors complained, but they had also faced

> insults, threats, and open violence, yelled down or accused by many . . . they think they can tie our mouths shut by such means, so that we will remain silent about various matters and not reveal them to the common man. . . . In short, they treat us not like teachers, not like servants, not as fellow citizens, but as the most harmful creatures, as rebels, and the source of all evil, and they have (to our particular dishonor) forbidden us to speak about public affairs, something that every goatherd can do.[25]

And what had the synod been recommending? That both the damaging Spanish alliance as well as the pervasive Venetian bribes and gifts should be rejected "for the benefit of this state and mindful that God does not leave unpunished the rejection of His word and of the true religion."[26] The pastors even threatened to lay down their spiritual offices and leave Graubünden rather than continuing to endure the abuse and dangers they faced.

The synod's letter illustrates many features of religiously motivated activism in the early seventeenth century: its authors saw a world at war, filled with dangerous forces that required both public witness by the clergy and immediate action by the authorities. True religion was threatened, which God would not forgive, while those who stood up for it could expect to be silenced or worse. To correct this unfortunate state of affairs, the authors suggested not spiritual responses, but a clear *political* agenda, which they urged their fellow citizens to enact.[27] Even as the activist pastors were denouncing Venice's influence in the Graubünden, they worked closely with the pro-Venetian faction and the Salis clan to stir up further trouble. After the synod's meeting, Toutsch and Alexander returned to their parishes in the Lower Engadine and preached insurrection to their flocks, who rose up in June and marched on Chur. Stymied by the city's refusal to open its gates, the gathered men then retreated to the centrally located town of Thusis, where armed companies from most of the leagues' member communes soon joined them.[28]

The synod and one faction in the leagues had seized the moment. By rousing popular anger against local leaders, especially the pro-Spanish branch of the Planta family, and by promising an end to political corruption and foreign influence, the pastors had excited the population and were finally in a position to act, politically and religiously.[29] One of the first targets of the tumult was the Catholic archpriest of Sondrio, Nicolò Rusca, himself a vigorous fighter for the Catholic religious-political cause. Jenatsch and his friend Alexander joined an overnight raid into the Valtellina that brought Rusca and several other captives to Thusis. There, the assembled troops appointed a court to try their captives. The assembled men also expressed their support for the liberty of both official religions, for the expulsion of foreign ambassadors, and for the punishment of anyone who accepted foreign pensions. The assembly further decreed that three clerics from each league should have the right to attend all public assemblies at public cost. The troops immediately put this unprecedented measure into effect by appointing nine pastors, all from the activist wing of the synod, as the spiritual overseers of the penal court they set up.[30] One of those appointed was young George Jenatsch.

The spiritual overseers participated actively in the trials that followed, much to the dismay of the more cautious faction of the Reformed clergy. The fact that preaching from the pulpit had triggered the uprising already upset the senior pastors, as noted by chronicler Bartholomäus Anhorn, a member of the more cautious faction.[31] The synod even called a special meeting in Chur to dissuade any further unrest, without effect. Meanwhile, the presence of clergy as overseers at a secular court—however irregular the court—made the question of the proper relationship between the clergy and political life even more prominent than it had been before. Consequently, the way various players, including Jenatsch, responded allows us to analyze the competing visions they held.

First, we will examine how the court acted, and what role the overseers played in its procedures and decisions. Afterward, we will turn to the justifications that the activists offered both before and after their service on the court.[32] The chronicler Anhorn pinpointed the tribunal's targets: "Afterwards, weighty trials were held against all those who leaned towards the Spanish faction."[33] Greater detail, though colored by hostility, appears in the chronicle of Fortunat von Juvalta, a prominent moderate who himself faced minor charges before the court. Writing many years later with the benefit of hindsight, Juvalta claimed that the "pastor from Scharans"—Jenatsch—was one of the most influential spiritual overseers.[34] Although Juvalta may have been projecting Jenatsch's later prominence back to the wild days of 1618, he had good reason to know his man, since Scharans was in the district where Juvalta served as highest magistrate. Juvalta described the spiritual overseers' role in detail:

> The overseers composed the written accusations against those called before the tribunal. These were given to the public prosecutors, who laid them before the judges. The overseers initiated the hearings, heard the testimony of witnesses, and recorded the testimony; then they participated in reaching the verdicts. Almost everything happened at their nod, and if anything was done without their command, they declared it invalid.[35]

Even if the overseers' control was not quite as thorough as Juvalta portrayed it—other reports suggest that the overseers did not participate in reaching actual verdicts[36]—the court's treatment of the captured archpriest of Sondrio confirms how much the spiritual war against Catholicism drove its agenda. No doubt Rusca was a fervent and effective partisan for Catholicism in the Valtellina, and he may well have maintained friendly ties to Spanish Milan, but the charges he faced at Thusis were both old and vague. He was accused of having encouraged, more than twenty years earlier, the abduction of a Reformed pastor, Scipio Calandrinus, who was taken to Rome and later executed for heresy. In addition, the prosecutors claimed, Rusca had fomented rebellion in the Valtellina in 1606 and 1607 by telling his congregation that they should not fight against a Catholic ruler like the king of Spain.[37] Although an earlier court in Chur had found Rusca innocent of these crimes in 1608, he was nevertheless subjected to torture in Thusis. The first day he endured the strappado three times; on the second day, now wearing a hood, his torture resumed. When the ropes lowered him after his second hoisting, he was already dead. Under the supervision of the spiritual overseers, the Thusis Tribunal had liquidated a dangerous spiritual enemy by using the tools of political power and brute force.

Fortunately, the evidence allows us to look beyond actions, which are always subject to conflicting interpretations. Because the activity of the spiritual overseers caused considerable anger among laymen and more cautious clerics in Graubünden, the overseers themselves spoke out in defense of what they had done. One response went to their peers in the Reformed Synod, who had questioned their actions; the other, composed in cooperation with the lay participants in the Thusis Tribunal, was widely distributed in pamphlet form after 1618. These two responses were strikingly different.

Reprehended by the synod for "allowing themselves to be used in secular matters,"[38] the spiritual overseers rejected the charge. They began with a biblical argument:

> When God had chosen the people of Israel as his special people and property, and had given them their church and political laws, he provided them not just with ceremonies and church rituals, but also with laws that demanded good morals, upright discipline, and also how to manage judicial affairs.[39]

By comparing themselves to prophets in Israel, the overseers tried to provide a firm theological basis for their actions in Thusis. There, they claimed, they had only supervised the secular judges in order to ensure that no injustices occurred, since they were responsible to God for good morals and justice. Like many contemporaries who sought closer ties between secular and spiritual authority, they evoked Old Testament stories and God's relations with his chosen people to make their case. In this, the spiritual overseers were drawing on a rich and living tradition.[40]

In contrast to the spiritual overseers' response to their fellow pastors in the synod, the public defense of the Thusis Tribunal aggressively downplayed the religious dimension of its work. In a pamphlet that reached a wide international audience, since it was published not only in German and Italian, but also in French, Dutch, and even English, the anonymous authors argued that the Three Leagues' "spiritual and worldly liberty of conscience and self-government" had moved them to rise up and act. Not religious bigotry, but the upright wishes of the common man, who had the highest authority in the republic's "democratic" form of government, had forced them to act. They also pointed out that Catholics had sat among the tribunal's judges and that the tribunal had even asked Catholic clergymen to sit among the spiritual overseers, unfortunately in vain. Whereas everyone else in Graubünden sought to advance one or another worldly faction, the pamphlet praised the tribunal at Thusis as the "faction that protects God's word and honor."[41]

What explains the appearance of such wildly different defenses of the same event, the court at Thusis, from its spiritual overseers? Obviously, the different audiences that the overseers sought to persuade—Calvinist ministers in one case, international diplomats and local observers in the other—help explain some differences. Nevertheless, the fact that two such different tacks *could* be taken, and that the authors thought it necessary to take them both, once again highlights the tensions and uncertainties about politics and religion that characterized the period. Within the fold, calling it God's will to have clerics guiding politicians was persuasive, but to the larger world, it was necessary to deny exactly this motivation.

The inflammatory letter Jenatsch wrote in 1619, which we have already cited above, confirms that at this point he still firmly believed that pastors were called to act in the political world. He wrote the letter to his patron and friend Giacomo Ruinelli, who commanded the militia in Fürstenau, near Scharans. By May 1619, the Spanish faction had recovered from its setbacks at Thusis and was agitating for another uprising in order to set up a counter-tribunal, which eventually met in Chur. During the rush to assemble, each faction struggled to make sure that its partisans dominated the growing movement. Jenatsch therefore urged Ruinelli to lead the Fürstenauers down to Chur in defense of the pro-Protestant and pro-Venetian position:

> The decisive moment is right now: the church is threatened, our fatherland is
> threatened, all right-thinking men are threatened. . . . We shall stand, we are

determined to die, it is a matter of Christ and His church, our common cause, for which we shall have to render our accounts.

In short, it was time to support the truth and "resist the Devil's emissaries."[42] Jenatsch gave a similar reason for leaving his pastorate in Scharans around this time, though Juvalta later claimed he had been fired.[43]

Judging people's motives is always difficult, and trying to separate political from religious motives for Jenatsch's actions at Thusis would be a mistake, as their entanglement in this letter to Ruinelli illustrates. Religious differences were a powerful if complex reality in the early seventeenth century, which shaped the spiritual overseers' efforts to explain and defend their actions. Things were easier for the overseers' enemies. A number of bitter attacks subjected Jenatsch and his fellows to scathing criticism for two things: violating the standards of Christian and clerical behavior, and improperly entangling the spiritual with the political. In a sense, both defenses of and attacks on of political religion in these years benefited from the fact that no consensus existed about how politics and religion *should* relate to each other. However, even as Jenatsch's religiously motivated activism seemed to reach a high point—he was now twenty-three—it was also about to end. His actions during the years after 1619 launched him on a new career as a soldier, a partisan, and ultimately, a political force to be reckoned with.

From Pastor to Convert, 1620–1635

From 1619 to the 1630s, Jenatsch's engagement with politics and religion changed profoundly. During this period, he also learned to move in new ways through the violent world of Europe during the Thirty Years' War. Four moments capture his progression from activist Reformed pastor to conciliatory Catholic colonel. The first took place in 1619 and 1620, and ended with his departure from the clergy. The Reformed Synod briefly suspended Jenatsch's license as a pastor in 1619 because of his political actions; when he returned to service, they sent him to a much more challenging position in Berbenno in the Valtellina. His brief stay in Berbenno was cut short by the massive uprising by the Valtellina Catholics, the so-called *Sacro Macello* (Holy Slaughter) of July 1620. During his flight from Berbenno, Jenatsch decided to give up his clerical career and become a soldier. A second key moment in Jenatsch's shifting role and reputation came when he took part in the daring assassination of Pompeius von Planta in 1621, an act that vaulted him to prominence and may well have shaped his final fate. A third moment occurred later in the 1620s when Jenatsch, by now an established military leader, acted not as a fighter, but rather as a mediator of religious disputes of behalf of the political leadership of the Three Leagues and the French ambassador. Finally, in the mid-1630s, Jenatsch became a key figure in negotiating a possible return of the Valtellina from Spanish possession back to the leagues. The most difficult sticking point was religion. The Spanish and their Austrian allies were dead set against the restoration of Protestant worship in the Valtellina. Jenatsch himself was moving toward his eventual conversion to Catholicism during these negotiations, yet he had to represent the political interests of the Three Leagues as a whole while managing the religious sticking points. His success in these negotiations required flexibility, not rigidity. The details of these four moments allow us to see how his actions highlighted shifting religious boundaries as well as boundaries between religion and other sources of identity.

Jenatsch's participation in the Thusis Tribunal had required him to take a more active political role than most clergy approved of in this era. His decision shortly thereafter to join personally in the ongoing struggles between the factions that were ripping apart the Republic of the Three Leagues took him even further. Early in 1619, in fact, the synod suspended him from clerical office for six months, as punishment not only for his behavior in Thusis but also for the beating he and Blasius Alexander gave a Valtellina Catholic sexton early in 1619. Jenatsch also gave up or lost his position in Scharans at this time. When he returned to service, he became pastor for the small Reformed congregation in the Valtellina village of Berbenno, where a large and resentful Catholic majority surrounded his flock.[44] In any event, he spent little time in Berbenno, since he spent much of 1619 and early 1620 engaged in the tumults that led to two further mass assemblies in the republic, and also got married. His effectiveness is revealed by the sizeable Venetian cash contributions that he began collecting to support his work against Spanish and Austrian influence.[45]

Jenatsch's flight from Berbenno with his wife in 1620, barely escaping the local mobs that were hunting down every Protestant they could find, very visibly marked his movement from the spiritual to the worldly sphere. As the chronicler Anhorn put it in Jenatsch's obituary, this was the moment when he "laid down the toga or pastor's gown and took up the sword."[46] He never sought another parish after 1620, and he was soon excluded from the pastorate altogether because of his violent behavior.[47] From this moment onward, Jenatsch threw himself into politics and military action. After taking part in the first military efforts to retake the Valtellina from the Spanish troops that occupied it, he attached himself to the leadership of the Venetian faction, which clustered in the Salis-dominated village of Grüsch. There, a plan emerged to bring down the opposing party not by the popular uprisings, which had been ineffective, but by assassinating of its leaders and terrorizing its supporters with targeted violence. The first victim was Pompeius von Planta, the politically savvy younger brother of Rudolf von Planta and powerful partisan of the Spanish alliance. Pompeius's bloody murder with the infamous axe became an iconic moment for biographers and novelists captivated by Jenatsch.

Like every event in these troubled times, the assassination had religious as well as political overtones. The entanglement is most visible in the debate after the murder. Many, including those who cheered the elimination of Planta, nevertheless found it disturbing that two of the murderers had been clerics, "since one says, these are spiritual persons, and they should carry the spiritual sword, namely God's word, and let the secular magistrates carry the worldly sword."[48] But as the chronicler Anhorn reports:

> When they were criticized in this way, [Alexander and Jenatsch] answered: they had previously used the spiritual sword, but he, Planta, had driven them from the [clerical] estate, so that they had been forced to take on the secular estate . . . when the magistrates did not carry out their office, moreover, and true worship of God and the praiseworthy liberty of the Fatherland were in danger of destruction, then clerics could well carry out such excesses, and use the worldly sword.[49]

Their opponents put it more simply: a pamphlet about the murder circulated with the ironic title *The Bloody Meekness of the Calvinist Pastors!*[50]

Jenatsch spent much of the next few years in exile, while Austrian and Spanish troops stormed through the Three Leagues. He served briefly in the mercenary army of Ernst von Mansfeld in Germany, but most of his time was spent closer to home, plotting uprisings and finding the funds, troops, and allies to carry them out. Although everyone knew that he had once been a pastor, the catastrophic circumstances that hit the region—repeated invasions, humiliating concessions to Austrian and Spanish demands, the virtual dismemberment of the leagues, starvation, the plague—made his competence as a military leader and his persuasiveness as a propagandist and negotiator more important. The story of his rise to high military rank and surprising power within the leagues will occupy us elsewhere; here, keeping our eye on religious boundaries and the changing ways Jenatsch approached them, we will jump ahead to the later 1620s.

During the Austrian invasion of 1620–24, Catholic missionaries from the Capuchin Order had entered into the intensely Reformed Lower Engadine as part of the Austrian effort to convert the population to Catholicism. Indeed, as long as Austrian troops occupied the villages in the valley, the mission seemed to be having some success.[51] Most of their conversions evaporated, though, as soon as Austrian troops evacuated the area late in 1624 in the face of a French-led invasion. Many Protestant exiles came back to Graubünden behind the French troops, but the Capuchins remained, protected by French influence since the powerful Cardinal Richelieu wanted to remain on good terms with the papacy. The Capuchins even demanded and received continued access to the churches in the Lower Engadine villages and to the funds intended to support them, which greatly angered the local population.[52] In 1627, when the French in turn evacuated the region, the Reformed Engadiners finally took back their churches and excluded the Capuchins, although the monks remained in the villages to minister to their remaining local supporters. Into this context, Jenatsch came as a mediator. Still a Protestant and a former pastor, he enjoyed sufficient trust among the local population to gain concessions from them; at the same time, he was in the service of France, which wanted to avoid any Protestant gains in the region that Spain might use for propaganda elsewhere in Europe.[53]

Jenatsch thus found himself at the frontlines of an outright struggle between churches. On one side stood the Capuchin missionaries, ready to make great sacrifices for their small flocks, and unwilling to retreat an inch from their demand that only they were entitled to occupy all churches and collect all church revenue.[54] On the other side stood the Lower Engadine Protestants, enraged by the abuse and coercion they had endured under Austrian occupation, and demanding exclusive use of their churches for the Protestant majority. Tensions were high, and the mediation became a trial for Jenatsch. In one letter to a Catholic relative, he complained that:

> God knows I have done everything in my power to accommodate the Capuchin Fathers' affairs. . . . In Tschlins, where the women wanted to stone me, I had to tell them I wouldn't negotiate at all if they didn't make the women retreat.[55]

He struggled to persuade the Engadiners that, however just their demands, the international situation was still too dangerous to offend the Capuchins or Cardinal Richelieu. Simultaneously, he had to convince the local Capuchins and their powerful supporters that allowing Protestant religious services in the churches was absolutely essential to avoid both open violence as well as political disaffection among the population.

Jenatsch had to return to these issues repeatedly, negotiating directly with his former brothers from the synod, as compromise after compromise crashed into the rocks of confessional intransigence. He wrote despairingly in a 1626 letter,

> This will all nevertheless turn out to be vain, since no one wants to compromise without a thousand limitations that in the end would shape the outcome entirely to the taste of the person who offers the compromise.[56]

Six years later, in a rare Romansh letter, he was still pleading with the Protestants to be patient:

> I would have thought you might show this grace to his Excellency [the French Ambassador] . . . since you have only been asked to let the Fathers preach before you on Sunday mornings in the church; in the winter, you only hold services at ten in the morning, in any case.[57]

His moderation as he wrestled with the tangled affairs in the Lower Engadine thus demonstrates that his own understanding of religion had changed even before his conversion to Catholicism.

What stands out is that Jenatsch went to the Lower Engadine without taking sides for either party, in sharp contrast to his behavior from 1616 to 1621.

Although himself from the neighboring Upper Engadine and thus able to talk to the locals in Romansh, and although himself still a Protestant, he took on the mediation in order to preserve French support for the Three Leagues. His letters on the problem, which are numerous, constantly reflect his exasperation at the hotheads on *both* sides. For example, he wrote his in-law at the bishop of Chur's court, Johannes von Flugi, that there would never be rest in the village of Ramosch until a particularly demanding monk, Padre Donato, departed.[58] Shortly thereafter, he confirmed that he had finally persuaded the villagers to tolerate the monks.

> For the rest, they have promised me to live with the Fathers in a way that will give no just grounds for complaints; and if the Fathers would be willing to accept reasonable results, I think we've wrapped up the matter and have been able to accommodate them very well.[59]

What the people he was negotiating for still saw as life-and-death struggles, he now saw as tactical matters. This represented a profound shift in the kind of boundary that confession was for him. His shift away from the fervor of his youth foreshadowed a similar transformation all over Germany toward the end of the Thirty Years' War. Adherence to Catholic, Lutheran, or Calvinist doctrine by no means vanished as an important source of division in this era, but the power structure of Europe increasingly encompassed confessional conflict rather than being disrupted by it.

"Live and Let Live . . .": The Convert and Politician

Jenatsch himself converted to Catholicism in 1635. He later wrote that he began reconsidering his faith as early as 1628–29, when a period of imprisonment in Venice gave him the opportunity to read deeply in the Bible and Church Fathers.[60] St. Augustine became his favorite author and helped convince him to return to the old church—in striking contrast to Augustine's role in motivating Luther to break with the church a century before. What Jenatsch saw in Augustine and in the Catholic Church was certain authority, something that by the 1630s evidently appealed to him. The historian Jon Mathieu describes Jenatsch's shift toward Catholicism as a process of acculturation, as Jenatsch himself rose in social rank. "[Jenatsch] now supported the traditional hierarchy, which no doubt came easier to him in 1635 than it would have in 1620, since he had climbed astonishingly high on the social ladder in the intervening years."[61] Considering the broader context in this way avoids trapping Jenatsch's conversion in a sterile dichotomy between interest and conviction, as earlier biographies have done.[62]

Jenatsch certainly had very concrete political reasons for considering conversion, in particular to make him a more acceptable negotiating partner for the

Catholic Habsburgs over the return of the Valtellina. Nevertheless, such concrete reasons do not necessarily mean that his statements defending conversion in spiritual terms were cynical posturing. Jenatsch defended his move in a series of letters to his former peer in the synod, Stephan Gabriel, and these letters encourage a more nuanced view. Conversions often led to bitter accusations from the convert's former coreligionists, and conversion letters were often set pieces drafted for prominent converts by ghostwriters to trumpet the superiority of one faith. It is worth noting that our copies of Jenatsch's letters come not from Gabriel's papers or Jenatsch's, but from the archive of the *Congregatio de Propaganda Fide* in Rome. These were not the late-night musings of a willful colonel, we can be sure, but carefully vetted polemics intended for wide circulation.[63] Still, Jenatsch's particular polemics were too idiosyncratic to be mere boilerplate, since they contained detailed discussions of political and social issues in the Three Leagues as well as doctrinal exegesis.[64] Even the theological points Jenatsch made in the letters did not simply stage Catholic virtue against demonic Protestantism. He easily admitted, for example, that certain popes had not only sinned, but were no doubt already in hell.[65]

Nevertheless, his letters to Gabriel were not at all indifferent about key theological issues. For example, Jenatsch returned repeatedly to the issue of the "real presence" during communion. Whether Christ's body was truly present in the communion wine and bread during the central ritual of Christianity was one of the most prominent debates separating Catholics, Lutherans, and Calvinists in this era. In his conversion letters, Jenatsch portrayed the Calvinist view as both absurd and as a novelty that rejected clear traditions going back to the earliest days of the church. The issue of tradition on other issues, such as the use of images and the authority of the popes, also generated real heat in Jenatsch's letters.[66] As Mathieu points out, tradition looked quite different to a man who was a candidate for the nobility than it had to a young, impoverished minister two decades earlier in 1618. In one letter, Jenatsch introduced his argument for the real presence by noting that "without tradition, even the most mediocre heretic cannot be refuted." He added a personal note to the letter that gave emotional expression to the same idea: "Now, after great waves of doubt, my soul is at rest because my faith matches that in the custody of the universal Church."[67] Tellingly, he turned to politics later in the same letter by deploring "our confused democracy, if that is what it is."[68]

Jenatsch also assured Gabriel, a theological opponent who had been launching bitter spiritual attacks as well as working to block Jenatsch's political plans, that spiritual and secular affairs were separate things for him. Regarding the Capuchin monks who were causing so much conflict, for example, Jenatsch curtly insisted, "I do not discuss politics with them."[69] His proposal for the Lower Engadine was equally simple and equally distant from the enthusiasm and single-minded commitment of his youth. In one of the last letters he wrote, to the confessor of the Austrian archduchess of Tyrol, Jenatsch insisted that he was doing everything he could to support the Catholic faith. In the Lower Engadine, however, he indicated that "the most that we can do is to retain entrance and use of the churches for the Catholics there, for the rest contenting ourselves to live and let live."[70]

That we are dealing with a different Jenatsch is confirmed when we examine his behavior in other religious matters after 1635. He acted as anything but a religious zealot. Although he energetically defended his conversion to his former colleagues in the synod, he put no pressure on his wife to convert. He even allowed the Reformed ministers in Davos to baptize his two subsequent children.[71] As he put it in another of his letters to Gabriel,

> I live in [the Roman Catholic Church] in such a way that I do not want anyone to be deprived, either by law or by force, of the liberty of conscience: and my wife, children and friends are testimony to this.[72]

Just before Jenatsch's death, he did send his eldest son to the Capuchin monks for education, but his family remained Protestant after Jenatsch's conversion and after his death.

Jenatsch showed a similar pattern in his political positions. When negotiating the new relationship with Spain and Austria that was his great triumph, Jenatsch demanded complete freedom of worship in the Lower Engadine and Prättigau, where Austria was still the nominal lord over the republic's citizens. The matter was a key sticking point for the highly orthodox Habsburg government, and therefore required considerable tenacity on the part of Jenatsch and his two fellow negotiators. In August of 1637, he even wrote Stephan Gabriel to ask for political support for this position, specifically denying to Gabriel that his faith had any influence on his current negotiating position.[73] He was equally forthright with his Austrian correspondents, making it clear to them that freedom of worship within the Three Leagues was a precondition for any permanent diplomatic settlement. The ultimate treaty with Austria contained the protections he sought. Thus, his deeds matched his words. For the Valtellina, in contrast, he recognized from the outset that toleration of Protestantism was a lost cause, and he acted accordingly—for political reasons. We can thus conclude that Jenatsch had taken on a Catholic identity by converting, and that both his writing and his actions show that he took this identity seriously. As his behavior in the Engadine in the 1620s already suggested, however, his religious identity no longer demanded the older, exclusive way of understanding the place of religion in his life. His earlier ardor, born of the genuine possibility around 1610 that confessional activism would give his church the power to shape the state, had faded. Indeed, Jenatsch's main concerns in his last years were not about religion at all, but about moving into the nobility.

*   *   *

Confessional religion enjoyed great success in seizing the European imagination from the 1550s to the 1650s, thus making religious conversion one of the most visible ways an individual could change. Among all the multiple identities that people of that era typically possessed, religious ones were particularly loaded with significance. The duties of faith were proclaimed loudly from the pulpits and in a flood of books and pamphlets, whereas religious tolerance was denounced as an error even more dangerous and pernicious than heresy—as atheism and subversion. To convert from any of the officially sanctioned Christian faiths to another was a profoundly public and disruptive act, praised as a triumph or deplored as a catastrophe, but never treated as something private and personal. This does not mean, of course, that people's feelings about religion did not involve intensely personal convictions and attitudes, though these remain hidden except in extraordinary cases.

Even as public emphasis on the all-encompassing nature of religious adherence peaked, however, Jenatsch's career allows us to see how some individuals were slipping away from this model. Although his personal intentions remain obscure, Jenatsch's actions suggest that he underwent two conversions: from Reformed Protestant to Catholic, but also away from confessional attitudes toward a more secular understanding of faith's place in human life. Such a shift may have taken place more easily in the Three Leagues, one of the few European states that openly enshrined freedom of conscience, and even of worship, in its formal documents and public discourse. Yet, like all great cultural shifts in history, this change had less to do with formal debates or established laws, and more with the changing sensibilities of an entire society.

Chapter 4

"SOMETHING THAT EVERY GOATHERD CAN DO"

Pastor, Soldier, and Noble

The boundaries of identity that we have considered in Jenatsch's life so far—nationality, ethnicity, and religion—should feel quite familiar to modern readers, though they did not necessarily work the same way in the seventeenth century as they do today. Ethnicity and language did not yet possess the seemingly natural connection to political order that gives the modern nation-state much of its potency, yet Jenatsch's life illustrates that linguistic and local identity could unite some people and exclude others in a way that resembles more recent conflicts. Similarly, religious difference, including conflict between those for whom religion is central and those for whom it is not, continues to divide the modern world, nor do we find it any easier than Jenatsch's contemporaries to separate religiously inspired action from politics clothed in religious garb. This chapter, however, turns to a way of grouping people and establishing boundaries between them that differs in essential ways from modern patterns: social estate.

The idea that orderly human societies consist of three distinct estates, defined by their different contributions to the common good, coalesced within the European tradition during the tumultuous eleventh century, and it remained a potent ideology—even though far from a reality—during Jenatsch's era. As analyzed by historian Georges Duby, a group of thinkers active around the year 1000 proposed that three distinct estates defined most human relations (by "estate" they meant status or condition). The first estate consisted of the clergy, who contributed their prayers and led the community in its worship and service of God. In return, they deserved protection from the second estate and support from the third. The second estate consisted of the nobility, who risked their lives by fighting to defend the other two estates. Thus, military training and action were the key criteria for membership in this estate, which also deserved to be supported materially by the third estate. Members of the third estate, which included all other honorable people, labored in order to produce the food and goods needed to sustain the first two estates and themselves. Praying, fighting, and working: in this vision of human society, these functions defined every person's responsibility within an orderly, safe, and prosperous world.[1] Members of each estate had to possess particular virtues that suited them to their roles—piety and learning for the clergy, honor and courage for the nobility, and patience and obedience for the laborers—and were expected to follow the demands that their estate put upon them. From its beginnings, then, this European model of the three estates was a social *theory*, an attempt to understand and to shape both the underlying structure of society and the role that each individual human should play in it. Like many theories, this model of three estates implied that harmony would flower if people only understood and conformed to the roles that providence had assigned to them.

In reality, the theory of three estates was not a very good description of the society of eleventh-century Europe, and it was wholly inadequate to describe Jenatsch's world of the seventeenth century.[2] Nevertheless, it exercised surprising influence over both thinkers and ordinary people for many centuries. A quick glance at the model reveals that its original proponents had been clergymen, who put themselves first among the hierarchy of estates. The model's later appeal thus makes some sense in parts of Europe where the clergy and nobility, in a usually uneasy alliance, continued to monopolize political power and legitimacy. In contrast, its persistence seems especially paradoxical in the great belt of urban and communal societies that stretched from northern Italy to the Low Countries, which included the Swiss Confederation. Before looking at how Jenatsch's life spanned the three estates and how he himself manipulated the expectations of this tenacious theory, we must therefore investigate the genealogy and impact of European ideas about social estate a more closely.[3]

Understanding the Human World:
The Potent Myth of the Three Estates

Every human society seeks to understand itself. The varied ways that people live call out for explanation, which priests, poets, and intellectuals have worked to provide. In the European tradition, God's revealed will and the order of nature formed the cornerstones for intensely debated and constantly evolving theories of the world and humankind's place in it. The theory of the three estates captured one facet of this ongoing conversation, proposing how society was (or should be), and helping every person understand (or contest) his or her own position and responsibilities within that arrangement. Like all theories of human order, the vision of estates included expectations about human nature and statements about justice and fairness in human affairs. It is because these elements differed in fundamental ways from modern Western theories that the model of the three estates requires a conscious effort to understand today.

We may start by observing that virtually all modern Western social theories rest on the assumption that societies are made up of individuals. This is not something that engages only philosophers and sociologists, nor is it just a matter for laws and institutions. Rather, a widespread and shared sense of who we are takes for granted that human individuals are equal in principle, whereas the many differences that separate them are secondary. It is individuals, *just* as individuals, who are the carriers of rights, and rights provide a key concept in modern debates about how to balance individual autonomy with social obligations and state power. The idea that we live under a "social contract" provides modern Westerners with our own potent myth—one that is incompatible with the theory of estates—and reveals how we build our thinking on the individual.[4] Naturally, theories of individualism are themselves disputed and controversial, but I would argue that even totalitarian ideologies that seek to dissolve the individual in some larger collectivity still start by recognizing the priority of the individual. Modern theories may disagree energetically about the proper balance between individual and society or between individual and the state, but the very concepts of "society" and "state" already take for granted that individuals stand in some relation to these larger categories.[5]

To be sure, this modern understanding of the individual has roots far older than the social contract theories that emerged in the works of seventeenth-century authors such as Thomas Hobbes and John Locke. For example, modern individualism has important roots in the radical spiritual egalitarianism of early Christianity. A tension between the collective obligations of estates and the individual salvation that was offered to Christian believers thus characterized European thinking not just among elites, but at every level of society, throughout the premodern period. Nevertheless, ideas like the theory of estates had such a tenacious hold, even in Jenatsch's seventeenth century, that belief in individual salvation did not lead to the conclusion that individuals were the foundation of human society. Individual identity therefore took on a distinctive meaning. Early modern Europeans, when they thought about what we call identity, generally saw it as the visible expression of a person's participation in a group or a community. Such groups, as they saw it, provided the foundations for society—groups understood not in our modern sense as a "collection of individuals," but rather as social institutions that enabled humans to *become* persons, with specific characteristics, virtues, and responsibilities defined by the group.[6] In this cultural environment, the theory of estates remained alive because it provided an explanation for why groups defined people, even if actual groups interacted in far more complex ways than the simple relationship of three estates suggested.

The previous chapter demonstrated how this understanding of identity worked in religious matters, where orthodox faith long remained a precondition for becoming a full person. Only those who professed and practiced true religion could belong fully to their communities and thus enjoy the benefits of membership. Even though salvation belonged in the spiritual sphere as a matter between God and the individual, it was mediated by the institutions that God had appointed, the Church and the orthodox community. Whatever a person believed in private, visible conformity in religion set the standard for inclusion or exclusion, according to this view.[7] After the Reformation divided western European Christians, this perspective increasingly clashed with the direction taken by Protestant theologians, and also with the reality that people could and did begin choosing their faith. Change was slow, however, and even a century after the Reformation, most Europeans refused to treat faith as a choice made by individuals, rather than as an obligation that *created* complete persons. Even when Jenatsch confronted this issue, the old way of looking at things had only just begun to yield to the notion of individual choice in faith.

Similarly, although the theory of estates had long since diverged from the way people in Europe lived their lives, it remained a potent myth in the sixteenth and seventeenth centuries. Jenatsch's life, especially the way his career crossed the traditional boundaries between the three estates, illustrates this with particular clarity. Most of his contemporaries thought about him from the vantage point of the old model, as a pastor and member of the clerical estate, though ultimately a renegade from his given station. His own efforts to gain a noble title reveal both the value he put on ennoblement and the very traditional reasoning he thought justified his efforts. Simultaneously, the fact that he was able to cross the boundaries of estate, and particularly the unstable position he occupied during the decade between his departure from the clergy in 1620 and his rise to real prominence after 1630, reveal how the traditional understanding of the estates was teetering on the brink of collapse. In itself, mobility among the estates was nothing new, yet for centuries this fact had scarcely affected the way people thought about the estates in everyday life.[8] Throughout the Middle Ages, for example, the seemingly clear distinction between "clergy" and "laity" had been blurred by various practices that allowed laypeople to enjoy the "benefit of clergy," from the creation of lay tertiary religious orders to the practice of burying pious laypeople in clerical garb. By the end of the Middle Ages, anxiety about what it meant to be a cleric or a nobleman often became acute. Protestant theology, which insisted on the priesthood of all believers, further destabilized not only the sacral but also the social position of the clergy, while aristocrats across sixteenth- and seventeenth-century Europe engaged in bitter debates about whether their nobility derived from their "virtue" in fighting for the common good, or resulted automatically from their "pedigree."[9]

How, then, did people think about social estate in Graubünden, a state with no lords where two religions were legal? The answer to this question reveals both Graubünden's peculiarities as well as its continuing connection with larger European developments. That is, while the voices we hear from Graubünden often rejected the explicit formulas found in estate theory, local ways of thinking still reflected the theory's underlying assumptions about people and society. Like most Europeans at this time, most Bündner saw individualism *per se* as neither natural nor plausible, even when their actions revealed that they were behaving more and more as individuals. As in religion, then, Jenatsch's life helps identify a cusp between two worlds, one that he highlighted by cutting across old boundaries even as he continued to accept their restrictions.

To begin with, estate in Graubünden lost at an early date the legal and political relevance it still possessed in much of Europe. The century-long transformation after 1400 that had produced a republic of communes had also fatally undermined the formal authority of the region's nobility. Political power itself remained, of course, and those lords who retained enough power also continued to claim lordly privileges over their domains. But even the most powerful of these, the mighty Habsburg family, saw their lordly authority in Graubünden whittled away to mere remnants during the sixteenth century. The Habsburgs were unable to block or even to slow the progress of the Reformation in their Bündner domains, and their appointed officers exercised little control over communal political decisions.[10] Elsewhere, the lesser aristocracy of Graubünden lost all *legal* claims to special status, although their property rights over land, income, and even people in the form of serfs did survive. The distinction is significant, since one of the key elements in the theory of three estates was that the nobility deserved a special political and legal status because of their role as defenders of the community.

In Graubünden, every male citizen fought under his communal banner. The assertion that the nobles ruled because only they fought—a notion that the rapid growth of European armies around 1600 was already starting to change—made little sense under such circumstances. Indeed, the armed commoners in Graubünden were able to invert this deeply-rooted theory in order to demand and obtain the power to vote on policy for their village and for the Three Leagues.[11] Communal votes thus replaced lordly authority in politics, an arrangement still justified by the fact that those who decided—now the members of the citizen militias—were those who fought.[12] The new elite families that rose to power after 1500 in Graubünden, meanwhile, were those with the wealth, education, and ability to persuade their fellow citizens to vote in certain ways. A noble background no longer mattered, though leadership of a commune's militia in times of war remained one of their obligations.[13] Some of the new magnate families had noble roots, but many came out of the peasantry or from merchant families in Chur. Noble status, as we will see in Jenatsch's case, could still confer prestige and influence inside and especially outside Graubünden, but it had lost the ascriptive quality that it had once had.

Similarly, the clerical estate in Graubünden had by 1600 lost the automatic respect that it supposedly deserved. Even before the Protestant Reformation, Bündner villages began treating their clergymen as employees, and not as especially trustworthy employees at that. The commune of Davos provides an example. In 1466, the commune recorded its relationship with its parish priest in a written charter that described the house, land, and income that was due to him and his chaplains, but also imposed certain obligations. For example, the priest had to read and write for the commune without additional payment, and if he wanted to collect on his debts, he was to use only the local court, not the bishop's court.[14] By the early sixteenth century, the commune's claims had expanded considerably, to the point that the priest was described as an employee serving at the pleasure of the communal magistrates:

> First, we have a free parish church that we lease to a priest on an annual basis honorably for God's sake and for no fee. Whatever the priest owes the Bishop of Chur or his vicar, he should pay without putting any burden on the church or the village, and he should not say "the church is mine," since he is only hired for a year. And if any priest tried to introduce any novelties that were harmful to the village, then the village will always have the power to send him away.[15]

After the Reformation began to spread in Graubünden, all the clergy found themselves in a similar position. Under Graubünden's unusual religious settlement, each commune gained the authority to appoint or dismiss either a Catholic priest or a Reformed pastor at will, thus making the clergy dependent on communal approval. Their low status was reflected in their miserable salaries: Reformed pastors in particular often earned barely enough to survive, which became a cause for frequent complaints.[16]

Once the first and second estate had lost their privileges, being in the third estate no longer meant what it had before. A poem called "Prosopopeia Raetica," written by Jenatsch's contemporary, Adam Saluz, captures the transition. One of the poem's central arguments was that Graubünden's travails had come about because "no one wants to remain in his estate."[17] This accusation, surprisingly, was directed not at the peasants and ordinary citizens who carried their communal banners to popular tribunals, but rather at the magnate families who did the bidding of foreign princes. Saluz made his point in part by playing on the multiple meanings of the German word for estate, *Stand*. He reminded the Bündner, "Because you have a common estate, you also have honor or shame in common."[18] Here, estate meant both the shared political organization that communities in the Three Leagues had in common, and also the single legal estate ("commoners") of all people living in Graubünden, since neither clerics nor nobles enjoyed any special legal privileges. In Saluz's description of the idyllic past:

> Our pious fathers enjoyed all this
> in peace, and preserved it,
> After they endured a great deal
> before winning their freedom . . .
> Good and rural, without pride and splendor
> they honored the work of their hands,
> They considered leisure shameful
> nor were there any excesses in the land.[19]

Saluz imagined an ideal society with only one estate, namely those who worked; he compared this ideal to the present, when too many people sought to join the nobility and get rich—as did Jenatsch.[20]

At one level, Saluz thus rejected the traditional doctrine of the three estates by calling for a single unified estate as the foundation of peaceful government. Ironically, however, his vision still assumed that violating the boundaries of the estate system was causing disorder in Graubünden, because the local elite attempted to act like nobles. Incidentally, Saluz remained equally critical of the "base mob" and denied that his ideal one-estate society should practice democratic governance. Instead, he maintained that everyone should still do the work God had given him, whether it was to rule or to farm. Thus, Saluz implied that ruling, too, was an office limited to a few.[21] Such a view resonated with the opinion, strong in Bündner political culture, that magistrates were officers whose authority rested on the will of the commune: they were employees of a kind, just like the Davos clergymen discussed earlier. In short, Jenatsch's contemporary Saluz captured in his poem the transition from a mental world in which personhood followed, in part, from social role, to one in which individuals took on—and could therefore drop or change—different offices during their lives.

The whole meaning of estate and its relation to personhood was in turmoil during Jenatsch's life, especially in Graubünden and similar regions. Not only were the specific roles assigned to "those who pray," "those who fight," and "those who work" becoming less persuasive, so was the deeper assumption that personhood arose out of social roles with specific duties and virtues. For an ambitious and talented young man, it was an exciting time, rich with possibilities but equally shaded by frustration, since the local magnates as well as the world outside Graubünden gave little respect indeed to a defrocked Protestant pastor. Old ideas about status and identity remained an obstacle for Jenatsch, shaping people's expectations even though they rarely conformed to his actual circumstances.

Jenatsch in the Clerical Estate

George Jenatsch was the son of a pastor who became a pastor himself. As a boy in the Engadine, he began preparing for a clerical career by learning Latin, and his entire education in Zurich and Basel revolved around preparation to become a Reformed minister. One could hardly imagine a background better designed to instill the values and outlook of the clerical estate into a young man, had those values been vibrant and widely accepted. The Protestant Reformation had deeply undermined the social prestige belonging to the first estate, however, and the unusual political system in Graubünden only heightened the problem. That Jenatsch followed his father's footsteps as a young man certainly reflected strong traditions of this era, but did not in itself reflect any personal attachment to the system of estates.

Indeed, deep structural ambivalence accompanied Jenatsch's entry into the clergy—in addition to his unsuitable temperament, which many observers noted. At one level, his training and dedication to religion really did provide him with authority and respect, as had always been the case for the first estate in European society. Clergymen were not only educated and literate but also responsible for existentially important rituals such as baptism and communion, putting them, as it seemed to many, closer to God than other mortals. At another level, however, Jenatsch could look forward to little more than employment by a penny-pinching commune that might listen to him during Sunday sermons but would expect his obedience in everyday matters. Through his control of the pulpit, a critical channel for communication as well as a site of spiritual authority, he could be sure that whatever he did and said would be heard and attended to. If, however, he became too insistent in telling his parishioners what to do—especially if his sermons turned to political affairs—he could expect to be brusquely silenced.[22] Ultimately, the contradiction between his ambitions and the limitations that the Graubünden clergy faced made it easier for Jenatsch to give up his clerical robes and become a soldier.

Jenatsch's path into the clergy began with his father, but once he was on it, the sophisticated and focused institutions that trained him, especially in Zurich, shaped his views. Perhaps the experience of watching his father preach before his entire congregation every Sunday also made an impression on the young Jenatsch, though he says nothing about it in his letters. Such early influences lacked the concentrated focus on producing theologically reliable and politically active ministers found at the school for future pastors in Zurich, at the heart of the Swiss Reformed Church.[23] Close cooperation between the city authorities and the teachers at the school ensured that the young men working on their languages, liberal arts, and theology were under constant scrutiny. Leading men in the city also helped place boys like Jenatsch with proper families for lodging and oversight.[24] Jenatsch took his rooms with one of the school's directors. A few years later, he also became the tutor to Giovanni Baptista de Salis's four sons, who had recently begun their studies in Zurich as well.

Zurich's schools and church succeeded in turning Jenatsch into a zealous pastor and a spiritual activist, as described in the last chapter. Arriving back in Graubünden and appointed to serve in the church at Scharans, he threw himself into the political defense of his church and his allies, leading up to the tumultuous court at Thusis. The positions he and his fellow activists took showed how far they had moved beyond any theoretical view of the clergy as a first estate that served the other estates by their prayers. Indeed, the activist pastors in Graubünden energetically insisted that they were citizens, not mere clergy, even as they claimed the authority of God for their declarations. These contradictory arguments opened them up to the criticism that they were no longer fulfilling their proper role. Even though Graubünden in no way conformed to the model of three harmonious social estates, the model still was available for anyone wishing to criticize inconvenient pastors as well as ambitious commoners, as in Saluz's poem.

In contrast to Jenatsch's generation, earlier leaders of the Graubünden Reformed clergy had persistently denied that they had any interest in mere political questions. Even when the ministers did attempt to influence political decision making, they did so by supporting the leaders of the Protestant majority at assemblies of the Three Leagues, rather than by rousing their congregations or by speaking out on their own. During a conflict about the bishop of Chur's rights in 1560, for example, a letter from the pastor of Chur to Heinrich Bullinger, head of the Zurich church, carefully limited the synod's goals: "These articles are all that we want; the rest are political matters and nothing to us, lest anyone think that we were stepping beyond the boundaries of our calling."[25] When Graubünden ministers did get caught up in politics, moreover, the backlash was quick and ferocious. During a major political crisis in 1572, several ministers who tried to intervene found themselves under attack from all sides. Even before the tumult reached its peak, the Three Leagues' highest assembly warned the clergy, "whether they be Reformed pastors or Catholic priests, . . . to encourage no further unrest, but to leave our common lands in peace, prosperity and unity."[26] After the crisis, this warning became a new law, requiring that "ministers and priests from both religions . . . should see only to their offices and not get involved in any secular affairs."[27] In Graubünden, the touchiness of the magistrates about clerical interference was heightened because the leagues were religiously mixed, with partisans on each side closely observing the clergy on the other. As the magnate families made clear, the first estate should stick to its books and pulpits, leaving politics to them.

Yet the pastors could not in fact be ignored politically. Through the pulpit, they possessed unparalleled access to the communal citizens who assembled to hear their words every Sunday. Moreover, the magistrates lacked any institutional way to control clerical voices, Protestant or Catholic. This fact set Graubünden apart from most of Protestant Europe at this time, where princes or city magistrates were firmly in control of their churches, and pastors worked under the watchful eye of growing bureaucracies. Among Graubünden's Alpine valleys, in contrast, pastors gained their employment village by village, and though they certainly faced loose oversight from the synod and pressure from the local big shots, the so-called *grosse Hansen*, they were basically independent agents. One strategy that the most powerful families employed, therefore, was to domesticate individual pastors through various forms of clientage. For example, Jenatsch retained close ties to the Salis family long after he began working for them in Zurich.[28] (These connections and their consequences are discussed in the next chapter.) Nevertheless, disagreement over the clerics' proper role grew in Graubünden from the 1560s to the 1620s, and in this discussion, the language of estate turned up most often in the voices of critics.

In this atmosphere, many of the synod's members turned toward the activist position that Jenatsch represented. Over the years, several Reformed pastors wrote learned tracts insisting that Graubünden was, in fact, a Protestant state.[29] The reality that one of the Three Leagues retained a Catholic majority among its communes, however, meant that such efforts had little impact. After 1600, the synod also energetically supported political reform in the Three Leagues. As in 1572, however, the pastors' every effort to exert political influence simply provoked the magistrates to insist more loudly that clerics should stick to their prayers and sermons. By the time Jenatsch arrived home from Zurich in 1616 to join the firebrands among the Reformed pastors, things were at a boil. Confessional zeal combined with political crisis helped trigger the Thusis Tribunal, which provides us an excellent crystallization point for examining expectations about the clerical estate in early-seventeenth-century Graubünden.

Let us begin by looking again at the letter that the Reformed Synod drafted at their meeting in Bergün early in 1618, before the tumult at Thusis took shape. The letter began by lamenting the cruel persecution that the pastors had faced for trying to advise the people of Graubünden:

> The current miserable condition of our common beloved Fatherland demands of us that we greet you and speak up on such matters, with the confident expectation that you will receive this well. For we do not doubt that you, as people well experienced in God's word, know how much the office that we bear demands of us with great urgency that we condemn all kinds of current misbehavior.[30]

Appealing to their office put the Graubünden pastors firmly in the Protestant mainstream that separated person from function, in contrast to the estate model's tendency to combine the two. The next section of the letter reinforces the conclusion that these pastors, at least, were not thinking of themselves as an estate. Their enemies, the pastors said, abused them in many ways, but the worst was that "they have (to our particular dishonor) forbidden us to speak about public affairs, *something that every goatherd can to do.*"[31] It was quite extraordinary for the pastors to compare themselves to lowly goatherds. But the comparison made a point: even a goatherd could speak out in the communal assemblies of the Three Leagues, the pastors claimed, yet they were supposed to be silent. Having first laid out the obligation that their *office* laid on them to advise their flocks, they now claimed a *citizen's* right to speak as well. Thus, flowing boundaries between different visions of social order are on display within the paragraphs of this single letter. Were the clergy an estate defined by its members' prayers? Did the pastors hold an office that obligated its holders to speak out, or were they individual citizens who had the right to participate in public assemblies like anyone else?

The Thusis overseers used a quite different line of argument when speaking with their brothers within the synod. Let us go back to the passage where the overseers claimed God's mandate to manage not just churches, but also public affairs:

> Clerics should pay attention not only to spiritual affairs and matters of faith, but should also be concerned that things proceed properly in worldly governance.

For when God had chosen the people of Israel as his special people and property, and had given them their church and political laws, he provided them not just with ceremonies and church rituals, but also with laws that demanded good morals and upright discipline, and also told them how to manage judicial affairs.[32]

Their brief continued with examples from the Old Testament that showed how prophets and kings from Moses to Jehoshaphat had combined spiritual and secular power. The letter then continued by claiming that Christ and his apostles had also preached about secular matters, setting an example the overseers felt obliged to follow. The line of argument here clashed directly with the claims of the second estate to manage "worldly governance"; indeed, the letter's arguments echoed far older social theories, such as the divine kingship of the ancient Mediterranean world. At the same time, the overseers' letter to their fellow pastors dropped the "citizenship for goatherds" argument that was so effective when speaking to laymen in Graubünden. While it is tempting to say that the overseers were simply talking out of different sides of their mouth, we may also conclude that around 1620, wildly inconsistent social theories were in circulation that seemed plausible to different audiences.

Looking for ways to defend their role, the Thusis pastors drew on different, even clashing justifications that ranged from biblical commands to their common citizenship. Their enemies, in contrast, concentrated on a single, very conservative point: the clergy had been dishonored and stained by these diabolical pastors who refused to follow the rules of their proper estate. A series of manuscript poems attacking the Thusis court relied on this approach. As one put it,

The estate of pastors
(curse the shame) has not just
become like the Jesuit order:
Hangman's helpers are what they are.

The poem continued with a warning:

You Graubünden lords, what can't you handle,
Do we need to light you a candle?
Are you idiots, and such naked fools,
That the clergy can make you their tools?
Can't you take care of justice and courts?
No, instead to the clergy you resort;
You follow those rebellious pastors,
Hearing lies, songs, and sayings from your masters.
Take off your pants and put on some skirts,
Foolishness and games are your just desserts.[33]

The poem left no doubt at all: the ministers were at the root of Graubünden's unrest because they refused "to learn to stay in their estate, and to leave worldly affairs to those God has ordained to rule them."[34] The term "estate" again had more than one implication here: it meant the clerical first estate, but it was also a jab at the modest family background and low social condition of most pastors, their "common" (*Gemein*) estate. As a line in another poem put it, "before this unfortunate and untimely rebellion started, lots of pastors had to go on foot; now, though, they ride like noblemen, with thugs and servants at their side."[35] In either case, the anonymous authors who attacked Jenatsch and the other Thusis overseers promoted the conservative view that a man's estate was a destiny that should determine his actions.

The views unleashed by the debate about the spiritual overseers at Thusis were thus asymmetrical. The pastors and their supporters reached out in various directions to defend their actions, looking from the politics of ancient Israel to their office to their claims of citizenship. Since these arguments did not hang together well, the activist pastors often found themselves at rhetorical as well as political disadvantage, whereas their opponents could hammer away at how the pastors violated the natural limits of their estate.

Jenatsch the Soldier

The vulnerability of the synod and its pastors eventually drove some of its members to leave the clergy and its limitations behind them. For Jenatsch, the critical moment came when he left Berbenno in the Valtellina in July 1620, saving his own and his young wife's lives by headlong flight over the mountain passes to Graubünden. The chronicler and pastor Bartholomäus Anhorn, who recorded Jenatsch's entire career in his modest chronicle, captured this moment when writing Jenatsch's obituary:

> But when the murder of the Protestants began in the Valtellina on July 9, 1620, he escaped the murderers with his wife and made it to the Engadine. And when at that time the war in the Valtellina began, and the Bündner marched into the Valtellina with help from Zurich and Bern, he took off his toga or pastor's robes and belted on the sword, marching along into war.[36]

Given Jenatsch's later successes, his turn to military action by abandoning his career as a pastor represented a critical moment, as those around him recognized. In fact, he had been acting more politically than pastorally ever since the Thusis court had concluded its actions. By January 1619, even his fellow pastors had begun to complain about this, though it was his best friend and companion Blasius Alexander who attracted the most ire. Alexander, it seems, had been visiting his fellow pastors to "persuade' them to support his faction and the Venetian alliance.

In Ftan in the Lower Engadine, he had appeared with a gang of armed men and forced his way into pastor Andreas Stuppan's house for a conversation. The synod sent a delegation to complain to him, insisting "that he should above all fear to do anything unplanned, since they should consider that our weapons are spiritual, not material."[37] When unhappiness about the Thusis verdicts boiled over later that spring, Jenatsch and Alexander set out for Chur at the head of military companies from the Lower Engadine, together with their military ally Captain Giacomo Ruinelli and the heads of the Salis clan. Their effort to force their way into Chur, where the pro-Catholic communes had gathered, ended when they met their rivals outside the town gates and lost the hand-to-hand fight that took place. As the resulting pro-Spanish court in Chur began canceling the Thusis court's actions and indicting the Thusis leaders, Jenatsch along with his activist colleagues found it wise to leave the area, though they continued to act in support of their cause. Indeed, it seems they formed something like a "pastors' gang" led by Blasius Alexander. At one point, reports came in that they had beaten up a Catholic sexton in the Valtellina, and that Blasius was raging about his superiors among the Engadine clergy. In July 1619, finally, the entire synod suspended Jenatsch as a pastor for six months.[38] Hardly had he returned to service in Berbenno when the massacre in July of 1620 once again left him unemployed. This time, he left the clergy forever.

What status did an ex-pastor have in those troubled times? Jenatsch became extremely active as a military recruiter and agent of the Protestants in Graubünden over the next few years, and in most of the surviving documents, it was his new persona—as a soldier and leader—that was relevant. Although his status was uncertain, he quickly found a place among the shiftless mercenaries and ambitious commanders of the Thirty Years' War that raged around him. His past as a member of the clergy was no obstacle to recruiting soldiers, it seems; indeed, it might even have been helpful when recruiting or negotiating with the fiercely Protestant inhabitants of the Lower Engadine. For Catholic sources, like the pamphlets attacking him after Pompeius von Planta's murder, his prior career as a clergyman was also worth highlighting because it made his brutality even more shocking.[39] Otherwise, his past career left few marks as Jenatsch lived the violent life of an ambitious freelance soldier. During a stint in 1622 as a junior officer in the mercenary army of Ernst von Mansfeld in Germany, he advanced to the rank of captain in the course of several battles against the imperial army of Tilly. Although Jenatsch was there scarcely four months, the chronicler Sprecher reported that Jenatsch had carried out eight murders. Whether these were duels or attacks similar to the murder of Planta is unknown.

The Thirty Years' War was a pivotal moment in the evolution of European military culture. The large armies and endless campaigning opened up many pathways of advancement for young men who were capable and brutal.[40] As in previous wars, it was above all those who were at the edges of the noble estate who found the greatest opportunities. Ernst von Mansfeld, for example, went from being an illegitimate son of the Count of Mansfeld to one of the most effective generals fighting against Austria in the early part of the war. Most famous of all was Count Albrecht of Wallenstein, a nearly exact contemporary of Jenatsch who followed a similar path to military prominence and assassination, though on a much larger scale than Graubünden. Rising from the petty nobility of Bohemia, Wallenstein became the virtual arbiter of Germany, commanding a powerful army as well as ruling extensive territories in Bohemia and Mecklenburg, before he was murdered with the emperor's connivance in 1634.

Very few commoners made it to the highest military ranks as Jenatsch did. Doing so required luck as well as skill, and those who did succeed often sought a noble title to validate their membership in the military and in the social elite that the nobility represented. Tied to noble identity was noble honor, as well. Thus, in addition to the eight shadowy duels that Jenatsch may have fought while with Mansfeld's forces, his adaptation to noble values shows up in one very well-documented duel he fought in 1627. The course of that event, during which he killed his long-time patron and ally Giacomo Ruinelli, reveals both how much Jenatsch had adopted the code of military honor, and also how far he had already moved from the tempestuous violence of his earlier years.

Before looking at the fight of March 6, 1627, we need a broader picture of how dueling changed during the sixteenth and seventeenth centuries. No single formal, static code ever guided and legalized dueling in early modern Europe. Of course, men in Europe, especially powerful and violent ones, had long resorted to hand-to-hand fighting in conflicts involving their honor, and their societies developed ways of limiting such fights to the combatants, though such limits were often ineffective. In that sense, European dueling belongs to the broader phenomenon of ritualized combat. It was most likely in Renaissance Italy that duels began to be treated as special fights regulated by special rules. From the outset, the notion of dueling was closely related to notions of estate: only noblemen, it was usually argued, had the kind of honor that had to be defended in a duel, and being noble, they were also qualified to fight for their honor on their own behalf. Ironically, some evidence suggests that it was wealthy patricians in the towns, who were not necessarily militarily trained and whose noble status was open to question, who seized upon dueling as a way to prove themselves noble after all.[41]

In Graubünden, although family feuds were frequent and often violent, there are few signs of formal dueling before Jenatsch's time.[42] When conflict in Bündner villages turned violent, it generally took the form of large-scale riots rather than following any formal procedures like a duel. In this, the Bündner were like their Romansh-speaking neighbors in the Friuli, who fought their feuds with no holds barred and who often resorted to ritualized violence, such as throwing their enemies' bodies to the dogs or the pigs, to emphasize their power and victory.[43] When Jenatsch and others associated with the Salis faction sought out Pompeius von Planta, for example, they paid no attention to any rules of honor or fair play. The group of nineteen armed men cornered Planta, who was wearing only his pajamas.

When he dropped his sword and begged for mercy, they hacked him to death with axes, ultimately leaving one axe driven through his body into the floor.[44] Certainly, Bündner men valued their physical honor and frequently resorted to violence to defend it, but until the seventeenth century, they did not rely on duels to do so.

When Giacomo Ruinelli, Jenatsch, and a number of other officers rode into Chur on March 6, 1627, they were returning home after a relatively successful campaign in the Valtellina. Supported by French money and French troops, Ruinelli had led several Bündner regiments into the valley at the end of 1624 to drive out the Spanish forces defending the rebels there. At the beginning of the campaign, Ruinelli served as a major in the regiment commanded by Rudolf von Salis, but had eventually earned his own regiment directly under French command. When he did, he appointed George Jenatsch as his major and right-hand man. After long negotiations in 1626, the French commanders ordered the Bündner troops to withdraw, since the newly signed treaty of Monsoño provided that papal troops would now hold the Valtellina.[45] Reluctantly, the Bündner obeyed. The regiments were paid with French money, and none of the officers was willing to challenge their paymasters. After marching over the passes to the north and mustering for one last time just up the Rhine from the city of Chur, the troops were released. Consequently, Jenatsch was no longer under Ruinelli's military command when they rode back to Chur.

As they entered the city, one of the officers, Peter Zeggin from Basel, apparently rode his horse through a group of children, injuring at least one. The men proceeded to the tavern Zum Wilden Mann (The Wild Man), where they began drinking heavily. Somewhat later, a representative of the town came to complain to Zeggin. Soon, strong words were flying about what had happened. One of the other captains, Dietrich Jecklin, asked Jenatsch to take Stefan Thyss, a drunken officer who was getting out of control, to the bar's upstairs room, which Jenatsch did. When he came back down, everyone was standing, and Zeggin looked like he was about to attack the townsman. Jecklin again asked Jenatsch to intervene, but as Jenatsch later explained in his own defense, "I answered him: I didn't want to take it on, since he could see how bad it was to get mixed up in things."[46] The confrontation became more and more heated, with Zeggin egging Ruinelli on until the latter became violently angry. Finally—in Jenatsch's version, at least—Jenatsch spoke up:

> I went up with my hat in hand, and spoke the following formal words: "What the Colonel [Ruinelli] says, no one should dispute, his words are just and good. But you other gentlemen are arguing about something that isn't worth the effort and the noise." . . . Upon this the Colonel smiled, took his sword down from the wall, and told me I should take my sword down too. He spoke: "With this I'll teach you how to talk." I said: "No, Colonel Sir, for God's sake; I said nothing against you." And then he said to Zeggin, "Take your sword too, the two of us will call all of you out, and you Major [Jenatsch] as the first one—man for man, one after another," and then he left the room.[47]

Figure 4.1 Outside Chur's lower gate, the Untertor, where Jenatsch killed Giacomo Ruinelli in a duel in 1626. View from the 1820s, printed in Alexandre de La Motte-Baracé de Senonnes and Edouard Pingret, *Promenade sur le Lac Wallenstadt et dans le Pays des Grisons* (Paris: H. Gaugain and F. Didot, 1827). By permission of the Rätisches Museum, Chur (VII 96).

Even if we do not believe Jenatsch's version of the events, the situation was clear: Ruinelli and Zeggin had challenged him to a duel.

At first, it seemed that Ruinelli might be willing to postpone the duel until the following morning since there were too many people in the street outside the Wild Man tavern. Jenatsch also tried to smooth things over again, saying in Italian, "I ask you, Sir, that you should take things for the best." He also added, tellingly, "But if it can't be otherwise, then I am a soldier, and will present myself where you call for me." Whether Ruinelli saw this as a challenge or whether his drunkenness had overcome his common sense we cannot tell. Regardless, he made a fight inevitable with his subsequent words, spoken in German, the language of the people in Chur who were standing around: "You are a dog's ass if you don't come fight right now."[48] The crowd of men headed to the nearest city gate so that they could go outside and fight, though Jenatsch later claimed that he still hoped someone from the city would intervene before swords were drawn.[49]

The actual duel was nothing like the stereotyped encounters found in romantic novels and Hollywood movies. There were no seconds, no pacing of distances, no formal agreements about anything. Ruinelli and Zeggin stormed out the gate onto the street outside, Jenatsch following with a limp. He was not even wearing both boots but only a slipper on one foot, since he had had some corns cut off his feet that morning. As the crowd swirled, both Zeggin and Ruinelli seem to have started attacking Jenatsch even as several people tried to throw themselves in between. In the confusion, Ruinelli was fatally stabbed, perhaps because an onlooker blocked his sword, giving Jenatsch an opening. One witness claimed to have seen Jenatsch cleaning blood from his dagger in the snow and then on his pants before sheathing it. In any event, Ruinelli's last words were a complaint that the men trying to separate them had not played fair. Jenatsch himself started to return to the city, but his friends persuaded him to leave instead, since fighting after peace had been called for was a serious crime. Between the city officials' outrage over a murder and Ruinelli's angry relatives, it would be too dangerous to stay in Chur. Instead, Jenatsch fled to Grüsch, where he would be safe in the hands of the Salis faction. He stayed for a night with his future rival Ulysses von Salis, who later reported that Jenatsch was downcast and worried by the events in Chur.[50]

We cannot know what Jenatsch felt as his efforts to calm a bad situation led him into a duel, nor do we know if some deeper tension had arisen between Ruinelli and Jenatsch. But we can look at how Jenatsch behaved during the event, and even more at his written defense that he submitted to the court in Chur that adjudicated between the parties. These reveal not his psychological state but rather his public stance, which offers some fascinating clues to Jenatsch's transition from pastor in the first estate to soldier, somewhere between the third and second estates. Indeed, the very uncertainty of his social location at the time contributed to his behavior during the duel with Ruinelli. This becomes particularly clear in his letter to the court, in which he sought to clear himself of murder charges and to preserve his honor and position in Graubünden. We should not treat this letter as a personal statement: it was a piece of legal and social positioning.

Jenatsch's letter repeated the basic facts of how Ruinelli had died, which were not in dispute. His account agreed with most of the witnesses about what happened, though of course he could also speak about his own intentions at the time in a way that the witnesses could not. He thus started by emphasizing the warm friendship he had had with Ruinelli. Anyone could see this friendship through their long relationship, he wrote, and he himself "thought I had no better friend in the world than the late colonel, I counted on that friendship, and I always behaved towards him as a upright, honorable friend and captain should."[51] Then, before narrating the actual events, Jenatsch inserted a paragraph describing how the Ruinelli regiment had been dissolved "in the German manner" before the captains rode to Chur. He went into some detail about a particular point that would reemerge later. The German custom was that when a regiment was disbanded, the officers all spoke before the gathered troops, saying that they were now comrades rather than superiors and that they would answer any complaint "with good will if it is possible, and if not, with the sword at my side."[52] These German customs, Jenatsch insisted, obliged him to respond to Ruinelli and Zeggin's challenge later in the day.

The most interesting passage in Jenatsch's letter, though, came as an aside after he described the original challenge. It deserves to be quoted in full:

> Now every honorable captain and every upright man should put himself in my place. I have spent some seven years now, mostly in foreign princes' service, for the good of my fatherland, as those lords' and princes' testimony shows; and I am still inclined at this hour to seek my fortune at war. In the last war, those who commanded me know my deeds and attitude. I had the honor of leading two companies into the field, and if I had asked for more, my generals would not have refused it. . . . Consequently, my honor is of fiery importance to me. Nothing is more damaging to a captain's honor among the Germans than if he is called out during a [regiment's] release and does not show up. But not just my late Colonel called me out, so did Zeggin along with him. I was therefore obliged to appear, though I thought that there were honorable men there when he called me out who would stand between us, so that no accident would occur. . . .
>
> And if I had held back, then when I met honorable people in foreign lands, I would have to hang my head. For every Imperial city that is in Germany allows one to appear at a duel, even though they forbid challenges. And thus it is a great black mark for a soldier if it is said about him that he had avoided an honest duel, so that it would be better if he showed up on crutches to explain why he couldn't appear.[53]

Jenatsch set up his defense by placing himself in a very specific context, one that revealed how far he had moved from his origins as a Reformed pastor. Curiously enough, he explained a duel in Chur—a violation of local law—by talking about German military customs! The earlier part of the letter established that answering such a challenge was an unavoidable obligation for an officer. Jenatsch then built on that point by extolling his past military service with its contributions to his fatherland as well as confessing his ambition to persevere and rise in military service, as he indeed did in the following years.

Above all, it is striking how Jenatsch consciously chose the context he wanted to belong in—again, not as a psychological, but rather as a legal and social act. Even though he was in his native country, he framed his defense according to the rules of German military honor. Since he intended to be a soldier in the larger world, he wanted to be judged by the standards of that world, not by those of his neighbors and friends. He emphasized this point again later in the letter: "If an eye should count for an eye, then every soldier, and all honorable people who defend themselves, would have to leave their lives: An eye for an eye only counts for dishonorable things."[54] By choosing this defense, rather than falling back on his privileges as a clergyman or appealing for help to his kin and patrons, Jenatsch provides us with a concrete example of how the world was changing. The ideals of estates, clans, or hereditary subjugation had to give way under the corrosive pressure of war, and under the pressure of shifting notions of identity. The court in Chur accepted his defense, although it assessed him a heavy fine for breaking the city's laws against dueling. Specifically, the court publicly preserved his honor, the thing he had fought to protect. Interestingly, they also instructed him to avoid Ruinelli's kin and heirs for a year, and to yield any space to them whenever he might encounter them. The older ties of blood feud still bound people in Graubünden, as the court knew. In fact, Jenatsch was nearly assassinated by a hitman hired by Ruinelli's sister while taking the waters in the summer of 1627.

The Soldier in Search of a Title: Jenatsch as a Nobleman

Jenatsch's career in the following years confirmed the wisdom of his plan to seek his fortune as a soldier. He fought successfully in all of the campaigns in Graubünden and the Valtellina, as well as in Venetian service. That he had risen to the rank of captain in Ruinelli's regiment was already unusual, given his background.[55] When this regiment disbanded in 1627, Jenatsch first traveled to Paris, hoping to recruit a company in direct service to the French crown. When he failed to achieve this end, he persuaded the Venetian government to allow him to recruit troops for service there. By early 1629, he had sent some 1,200 soldiers over the passes into Venetian territory despite angry protests from the Bündner magistrates, who at the time favored a policy more friendly to Austria and Spain. In a letter signed by several other mercenaries working for Venice, Jenatsch wrote:

> I do not think that I offended you my lords and patrons [the magistrates in Chur] in any way, even if I did go to Venice on account of my own personal business matters; . . . so I say reverently to your lordships that I am certain that my actions (which were those of a private captain) were in no way prejudicial to my fatherland.[56]

In the spring of 1629, he finally followed his troops into Venetian territory, hoping to take command of the companies he had raised. He still called himself *Capitano*, the position he had held under Ruinelli, though some Venetian documents already referred to him as *Colonello*, that is, as the head of an entire mercenary regiment.

Disease and desertion soon reduced his men to well under four hundred, even as Jenatsch fell into disagreement with the general commanding the Venetian mercenary regiments. When the Venetian Senate ordered him to consolidate his two companies into one, thus cutting his income and forcing him to demote his own brother, Jenatsch left his post on the Friulian border to protest in the city. He was promptly thrown in jail when he arrived. Only after long months, which he spent reading theological books, was he cleared of the charges of insubordination and spying that had been lodged against him.[57] The precious colonelcy still remained beyond his reach, though, and his hopes of rising higher in Venetian service were stymied.

Jenatsch therefore left Venice early in 1630, but conditions in Graubünden were too dangerous for him to live there, since Austrian troops again occupied all of the main transit routes. Additionally, the plague was raging in Graubünden and the Valtellina, carried in part by the thousands of troops that were using the Bündner passes for transit, meaning that Jenatsch had another good reason to stay away for the moment.[58] He moved instead to the safer territory of the Swiss Thurgau, outside the little town of Bischofszell, and bought a small castle called Katzensteig, well located for recruiting Swiss and south German troops for any nation that wanted their services.[59] That he had not given up his military hopes is shown by another trip he took to Paris "to seek his fortune," once his wife and family were safely settled in Katzensteig.[60] His timing seemed good. Under the newly confirmed guidance of Cardinal Richelieu, French diplomats were hard at work planning a new occupation of Graubünden and seizure of the Valtellina, all part of their grand strategy to neutralize Habsburg power across Europe. Ever since 1620, meanwhile, the Bündner leadership had seen the recovery of the Valtellina as their highest goal, and was willing to work with any power that seemed likely to help them toward that goal. In 1631 and 1632, France appeared to be the best ally. Since Jenatsch had already served with distinction during the first French occupation, his opportunities for advancement and profits looked excellent.

By the end of 1631, the French had authorized three Bündner regiments, and Jenatsch had received a position in one of them as lieutenant colonel to Colonel Andreas von Brugger. Shortly thereafter, the new French general for the troops arrived in Chur. Henri, Duke of Rohan, was a high French nobleman now in exile, since he had been the leader of the Huguenot (Protestant) faction in France that Cardinal Richelieu had finally crushed in 1629. Over the next five years, Jenatsch first became Rohan's confidant and then his nemesis. By late 1632, Jenatsch was captain of his own independent company, which continued to receive French pay even as the other Bündner regiments were disbanded and the soldiers gathered for the reconquest of the Valtellina melted away.[61] Action remained slow as the great powers maneuvered and negotiated. Without war, Jenatsch's chances to rise further remained blocked. Eventually he, along with many other leading Bündner, even began thinking about negotiating with the Spanish and Austrians again.[62] In 1635, though, after France openly entered the Thirty Years' War, Jenatsch finally got his opportunity. Rohan returned to Graubünden with many more troops, and when he was ready, formed three Bündner regiments to accompany his army of Frenchmen into the Valtellina. Jenatsch, who had already been actively defending the Lower Engadine with his company, finally gained the rank of colonel as the head of one of these regiments.[63]

The campaign that the Duke of Rohan led against the Spanish and Austrian troops defending the Valtellina remains a classic example of effective mountain warfare. He relied on both French regulars and on the three Bündner regiments that France was financing. Late in 1635, Rohan's forces successively defeated a major Austrian army that attacked the valley across the passes to the east and a Spanish Italian army that entered the valley from the west. As Jenatsch was one of Rohan's colonels, this campaign also marked Jenatsch's final ascent to the highest military level, a move that promised to bring him both great influence in Graubünden and also ongoing profits from managing his regiment. As was common for men in his situation, he began seeking a noble title to match his accomplishments, something that would vault him and perhaps even his descendants into the noble second estate.

The fact that Graubünden's strategic location made it a political football, with control hotly sought by both the French and Habsburg forces that were dividing continental Europe at this time, must have encouraged Jenatsch in his pursuit. After all, Jenatsch now had the power in his hands to help one side or the other. If his regiment continued to support Rohan, it was unlikely that the Habsburgs would be able to dislodge France's control over the crucial passes. Such loyalty would deserve a rich reward. If he switched sides—something that many influential magnates in Graubünden were contemplating—his regiment would make a French defense of their position nearly impossible. Surely, the powers in Madrid and Vienna would recognize this reality and reward him with the noble title he sought. In fact, each time Rohan won a victory, Jenatsch became more valuable to the defeated Habsburgs. Jenatsch's search for a title thus became much more intense and much more promising at this point.

In 1636, Jenatsch directly requested that the Habsburgs award him the noble fief of Rhäzüns in Graubünden.[64] Rhäzüns was an old lordship possessed by the Habsburgs, although the local commune was simultaneously a member of the Grey League. The Habsburgs routinely awarded their rights to the lordship on a lifetime basis to leading Graubünden men, mostly from the Planta family. Strategically located and possessing a lovely castle that still stands above one branch of the Rhine, Rhäzüns with its lordly title would have been a fine reward indeed for Jenatsch's efforts to swing Graubünden into the Habsburg column. In fact, his request was almost certainly futile, since aside from his commoner status and very recent conversion to Catholicism, the Habsburg court still needed ongoing support from the Planta faction in Graubünden.

Nevertheless, Jenatsch's approach was characteristically bold. He sent a letter to Archduchess Claudia of Habsburg, who administered the Habsburgs' possessions in the region, while he was in the middle of his secret negotiations about a new Austrian-Bündner treaty. In fact, he wrote the letter while in Innsbruck, the Habsburg regional capital. After enumerating the political benefits that would accrue to the Habsburgs if they awarded him Rhäzüns, he also pointed out that "it would give me the chance to leave more boldly the service of other princes, which

I would have to do at great expense because of the large sums of money that are owed to me."[65] After all, if Jenatsch switched sides, he could hardly expect the French to cover all of the back pay for his troops. Without the French money, he as the recruiter and colonel was personally responsible for his soldiers' claims. Jenatsch's letter was thus blunt and realistic about how things stood, though it provoked no response at all from the Austrians. Jenatsch did carry away considerable cash as well as promises of future Spanish gifts from the Christmas negotiations in Innsbruck, but not the noble title he desired.[66]

A year later, in 1637, Jenatsch made another explicit request to be ennobled by the Habsburgs, requesting not only the nearby Austrian lordship of Megdberg bei Hohentwil as his fief to rule but also an explicit improvement of his coat of arms to reflect the lordly status that holding such a fief implied.[67] By now he had delivered the crucial treaty, and the Habsburg alliance was enjoying the benefits of being able to march troops through the Valtellina without interruption. The issue of Jenatsch's ennoblement thus moved forward from the regional Habsburg center in Innsbruck to the imperial capital in Vienna, where the necessary political and bureaucratic wheels turned slowly. Only shortly before his death was the decision made to ennoble him and to approve Jenatsch's new coat of arms; the fief of Megdberg remained on the table but had not yet been awarded when he died. Jenatsch's requests for *mercedes* (rewards) from the Spanish crown were also left pending. As the Milanese viceroy put it in a letter to Madrid on the subject, "the state of that Republic [of the Three Leagues] does not permit any noteworthy partiality."[68] The Spanish could see that Jenatsch's enemies were growing more powerful, and did not hasten to reward him now that they had the Valtellina safely in hand.

The "state of the Republic" clearly referred to Jenatsch's increasing involvement in the affairs of the local patriciate, most notably his intervention in a long-running inheritance dispute among the Planta family.[69] Not only was he attempting to gain the fiefs that would allow him to demonstrate his new noble quality; his growing power also allowed him to become the arbiter of conflicts among the most powerful local families. The most likely planners of the axe murder in 1639 came from the Planta family, who could cite as their motivation not only Jenatsch's murder of Pompeius in 1621, but also his long adherence to the Salis faction and his new ability to threaten their family affairs. In one sense, then, Jenatsch's drive toward ennoblement represented another step in his internal acculturation, one consistent with his shift to Catholicism. He had hitched his star to the nobility and the system of estates that it represented. At the same time, however, the "nobility" in Graubünden constituted a real social group that used all available means to defend its boundaries against interlopers just like Jenatsch. His assassination thus punished him for violating entirely too many boundaries: those between commoner and noble, but also those between factions and between religions.

*   *   *

A characteristic shift took place along the path Jenatsch followed from simple pastor to powerful almost-nobleman, matching one found in his religious career and even in his attachment to place and language. As a young pastor, he and the radicals he consorted with seized on any argument to justify their engagement in Graubünden's political life, whether it fit with the traditional certainties of estate and social place or not. Their flexible adoption of contradictory arguments reveals that the contemporary social order, and the very concept of personhood, were experiencing profound instability. Jenatsch found it possible to cross so many boundaries because those boundaries were far weaker than they had once been. Yet as his power increased, he moved into positions where he began adopting the very values that his mobility had effectively violated. In religion, he was a convert, or as his former colleagues would have put it, an apostate—but he was an apostate to Catholicism, whose very certainty about authority and long tradition made the faith attractive to him. Likewise, despite his fluid movement across the tenacious if weakening boundaries of social estate, the place he was seeking just before he died was among the nobility, the one group that clung to the theory of estates and to the privileges it awarded them long after reality had undermined the theory's foundations. In effect, Jenatsch repeatedly broke the rules set by tradition while moving toward a position that fundamentally supported the authority of tradition. The same pattern emerges, though in a more fragmentary way, when we look at how Jenatsch challenged—but also adapted to and exploited—the boundaries of blood, kin, and gender that shaped the society of seventeenth-century Europe.

Chapter 5

HIDDEN BOUNDARIES?

Behind Conventional Views of Jenatsch

Earlier historians and biographers typically concentrated on certain favored issues when looking at European history before the modern era. One common theme was the creation of the modern nation-state and the emergence of distinct ethnic and national identities, both seen as defining features of the European path to modernity. Researchers have looked for national character in everything from the actions of political leaders to the making of cheese. Similarly, the complex evolution of Latin Christianity and other religions in Europe, along with the eventual spread of secular ideas, have provoked endless research and heated debates that continue today. Finally, the inner organization of European societies and their transition from traditional hierarchies, however imagined, to modern mass societies organized along lines of class and wealth have always been a key interest for historians. Nationality, religion, and social organization thus framed most historical research about the early modern period until at least the 1950s. It is no coincidence that study of Jenatsch's life and its meaning began with these same issues.

As the study of early modern Europe has continued in recent years, however, other aspects of European society have gained fresh attention. For example, larger personal networks—clans, kin-based factions, patron-client networks, and the like—turn out to have been a powerful force shaping European society and politics throughout the early modern period, even where historians thought that bureaucratic states and modern individualism were on the rise. For a long time, professional historians seemed oddly blind to how common such phenomena were, perhaps in part because studies of our contemporary society paid relatively little attention to such extended person-to-person networks.[1] The picture of George Jenatsch's life found in both biography and literature mirrors this blindness, since most authors underplayed the way kin-based factions shaped his career—except, significantly, when explaining his murder.

Speculation about who killed George Jenatsch has gone on almost since he fell to the murderer's axe in 1639. The only people who were not very interested, it seems, were the city authorities who investigated the crime. Other contemporaries discussing his death focused on the Planta family's desire for blood revenge, on the Salis clan's anger at Jenatsch's "treachery" in pushing them aside, or even on the wounded honor of the villagers of Haldenstein owing to incidents earlier during the war. Similar explanations also played a major role in the work of historians and biographers; in this, they followed the historical sources, which make it obvious that most Bündner at the time concluded that revenge, blood, and honor lay behind Jenatsch's death. What is odd, though, is how far the biographers leave these powerful themes in the background *until* Jenatsch's murder, even though they clearly operated throughout his life. This is true not only of the scholarly biographies by Ernst Haffter and Alexander Pfister, but even in Conrad Ferdinand Meyer's novel. Meyer does not ignore kinship and revenge as motives, as we will see, but he balances them against the higher good of nationalism. His character Lucas, the loyal Planta servant who grimly saves the bloody axe for eighteen years, is held in check by the higher intentions of mistress "Lucretia" von Planta, the (semi-fictional) daughter of Pompeius.[2] Meyer's murderer is ultimately Lucretia, but she kills Jenatsch not for the revenge that Lucas demands throughout the novel, but because Jenatsch's personal ambitions are undermining the national survival of the Three Leagues. Even where kinship and faction appear in later stories of Jenatsch, it seems, they do so as primitive remnants of a past society.

A closer look at the sources highlights another issue that has recently been getting much more attention from historians of early modern Europe: how honor provided the key vocabulary for talking about both family and loyalty to one's patrons or clients. Early modern politics involved very real material stakes, of course, including power, wealth, and influence. The actors themselves, though, often explained their deeds in terms of honor and dishonor.[3] We have already seen how the demands of honor crucially defined Jenatsch's duel with Giacomo Ruinelli and its aftermath. Jenatsch's honor as an officer forced him to respond to Ruinelli's challenge and shaped his efforts to explain Ruinelli's death. Indeed, since his first appeareances on the public stage, Jenatsch's honor had been under attack. What is curious, however, is the form some of these attacks took: efforts to smear Jenatsch often included slurs against his sexual behavior, which this chapter will explore.

Both the invention of Lucretia von Planta and the fate of Jenatsch's honor also provide clues about important social boundaries that long remained hidden in plain sight because scholars paid little systematic attention to them. The most obvious of these is gender. The differences between the sexes have interested humans since the beginning of time, of course, but analytical studies of gender and sexuality in history are a relatively recent phenomenon. The best current research on gender reveals how sexual difference and its cultural expression shape fundamental aspects of every society, whether or not those living at the time thought in such terms. Equally, women's history has helped us see how past tellings of history often took for granted that only men were real historical actors, with rare and therefore fascinating exceptions. Recent research, in contrast, has demonstrated how women have always been makers of history at every scale, from the family to trade, religion, and politics.[4]

The story of Jenatsch, both as historical reality and as it has been retold since his death, vividly demonstrates how earlier writers simply overlooked women. On the one hand, previous accounts all portray Jenatsch as a man in a world of men. In the two major biographies as well as in dozens of articles and essays, women scarcely appear at all. (It is worth noting that this form of "not seeing women" was common in Switzerland, where women gained the right to vote everywhere only in 1991.) On the other hand, literary and poetic versions of Jenatsch's life have often inserted an exceptional woman into his life, but by using women who did not in fact exist.[5] Since both the historical record and writings of historians paid so little attention to real women in Graubünden, it seems, novelists and playwrights had to invent them. Drawing from the methods of women's history, however, which can help uncover the reality of women's lives even when relying on historical records that largely ignored women, we can begin to understand the role that gender played in Jenatsch's world, and how the crucial distinction between the sexes created powerful boundaries that shaped his experience. Looking at Jenatsch's career from these angles clarifies his own behavior, and also makes us aware how even the most profound boundaries in human society sometimes become invisible because they are neglected or romanticized (like gender) or because they do not fit our expectations of how society and the state ought to work (like kin networks).

The Ubiquity of Kin, Faction, and Vendetta

When we take a careful look at Jenatsch's early career, from his days in school through his first exile in 1621, an important observation emerges: at every step, he was closely associated with the Salis family. After losing his student's stipend in Zurich for bad behavior, he supported himself by tutoring and supervising the Salis boys, whom he followed to Basel when they began university. As pastor in Scharans in 1616, he joined the activist wing of the Reformed synod that worked hand-in-glove with Hercules von Salis in triggering the Thusis Tribunal. After he left the clergy in 1620, he went to Grüsch, home base of the Salis faction, where he soon joined the band of Salis retainers on the fateful ride to Rietberg to murder Pompeius von Planta. These associations did not mean that his faith and his patriotism were unimportant to him, of course, but they certainly deserve closer examination. Who were the Salis and their great rivals, the Planta? What role did they and other powerful clans play in Graubünden's social order and politics, and how did their power create boundaries and challenges for Jenatsch?

We must remember that social power and kinship in Europe had been connected for centuries before the early modern period. Indeed, the feudal society of the Middle Ages organized itself largely along bloodlines, in fact if not in theory. Aside from the few European families enjoying the special charisma of kingship, most power belonged to the network of families that made up the feudal aristocracy. Although feudal ideology celebrated these men as the noble second estate, "those who fight," the nobility in practice consisted of kin groups that controlled people and property. Through service, marriage, and (when needed) violence against their subjects, lords, and neighbors, each lineage sought to accumulate land and influence to pass on to the next generation. The merchant elites in Europe's great cities behaved little differently, as shown with particular clarity in studies of Renaissance Italy. In between designing buildings and writing poems, the Renaissance polymath Leon Battista Alberti wrote an immensely influential study titled *On the Family* that celebrated loyalty to kin, while few European families enjoyed greater success in maneuvering than the Medici of Florence. The Medici relied on family loyalty, wealth, political savvy, and systematic building of kin-based patronage networks to cement their control over the Republic of Florence, which ultimately became the Medici-ruled Duchy of Florence. In addition, they managed to capture the papacy and marry into the French royal house.[6]

Aristocratic kinship was never the only system of distributing power in Europe, however, and the familial networks of the nobility faced growing challenges after 1400. On the one side, powerful kings and princes began building bureaucratic regimes that undermined the power of the great nobles, often by giving men from modest families greater authority in the central government. The resulting tensions between hereditary nobles and royal servants did not lessen the importance of having relatives in high positions, to be sure, but they did qualify the claim that noble blood was an automatic qualification for power and influence. On the other side, particularly in well-organized cities, communal regimes emerged that demonized the feudal aristocracy for its rapaciousness and corruption. Again, these attacks did not target the principle of family solidarity directly. Still, by criticizing the nobility for putting blood above communal loyalty and by celebrating the ability of free men to choose their own leaders regardless of birth, urban communalism offered an alternative to hereditary noble power. Switzerland in particular became a hotbed of anti-noble rhetoric that celebrated the "hardworking virtuous forefathers" who had thrown off the yoke of noble tyranny.[7]

Graubünden experienced similar changes at about the same time. Up to the 1400s, noble families, lesser and greater, utterly controlled the political life of the region. Regional dynasts like the Werdenberg and the Matsch families built up territorial complexes, competing with the bishops of Chur, themselves mostly from regional noble families, to extract revenue and military manpower from the mountain peasants. The dynastic nobles in turn often relied on local families for their bailiffs and agents, while the bishops built up a following of ministerials, semi-noble families who served as administrators and local judges in episcopal fiefs for generation after generation. Because the position of bishop itself was not hereditary, these ministerial families—most notably the Planta and the Salis—were able to build up independent authority to the point that they began thinking of themselves as born to rule too. The Planta originated in the Upper Engadine, Jenatsch's home commune, while the Salis began their rise from the neighboring Val Bregaglia to the southwest. Eventually, both spread branches all across Graubünden and beyond. Other Bündner families—the Capaul, the Travers, the Demont, and the Castelberg—began taking similar paths in the other leagues, though none achieved the wealth and influence of the two biggest clans.[8]

Before 1500, however, the situation in Graubünden began to change significantly, producing some highly unusual trends compared to most of Europe. Most important, the regional noble dynasties died out. This was not simply a matter of biological bad luck; previously, others had simply replaced noble families who failed to reproduce. Rather, the economic and political environment had undermined the middling nobility to the point that their collected lands and titles dissipated unless an heir stood ready to hold them together. The process had begun in the region with the failure of the Counts of Toggenburg in 1436 and continued with the extinction of the Matsch family and the Counts of Werdenberg-Sargans. Lying in wait for their territories were two contenders: the cities and rural cantons of the Swiss Confederation on the one hand, and the mighty Austrian Habsburg dynasty on the other. Many of the Toggenburg and Matsch lordships in Graubünden fell under Habsburg control in the late 1400s, so that the Habsburgs became lords over eight of the Ten Jurisdictions, for example, while the Swiss purchased several Werdenberg territories right next to Graubünden. When the Protestant Reformation arrived in Graubünden, another set of political players, clerics like the bishop of Chur and the abbots of Disentis and Pfäffers, were effectively knocked out of the political game. As the new Republic of the Three Leagues took shape, therefore, the most powerful non-noble families of Graubünden, led by the Planta and Salis, moved into the vacuum left by the dynasts and the bishop to become leaders of the developing state.

The Three Leagues formed a most unusual state, however, which meant that these families had to defend their prominence in unusual ways. Graubünden was ruled as a confederation in which a majority of communes in each league had to agree on all significant decisions. The individual communes usually followed the leadership of a few powerful local families that lived in them. Ambitious families like the Planta and Salis therefore began spreading to more and more communes in order to improve their chances of controlling the affairs of the Three Leagues as a whole. By 1600, in fact, branches of the Salis family were leading citizens in at least six communes of the Three Leagues, though they trailed the Planta, who settled in at least nine.[9] A side effect of this dispersion was that members of these wide-ranging clans began to find themselves on opposite sides of many issues. Even as Planta and Salis presence became more pervasive in the Three Lleagues as a whole, the clans themselves fell victim to internal divisions. For example, the sly Venetian ambassador reported in 1603 that "these two Messers Salis may come from the same family, but since they are not related closely, their interests and their followers are far apart."[10] Men from the same clan competed not only for the prestige of guiding their fatherland, but also for public pensions (which successful politicians could bring home to their fellow citizens as an early form of "pork") and the private bribes that Spain, France, and Venice were eager to spread among influential men.

Hercules von Salis's decision as a young man to settle in Grüsch in 1588 provides a perfect example of how an ambitious Salis could move into a new commune. The case is especially interesting because Jenatsch later worked closely with Hercules' sons, Rudolf and Ulysses. Hercules was born in the Val Bregaglia, the homeland of the Salis, but found his path to prominence blocked there. Not that the Salis lacked influence in the valley: in fact, they totally controlled its political and economic life. Rather, because there were *too many* Salis in the Bregaglia, Hercules faced countless rivals for office and influence. The situation was even worse because his father and grandfather had made some powerful enemies. Hercules therefore leapt at the chance for a good marriage in Grüsch, a German-speaking commune in the League of the Ten Jurisdictions, and quickly made himself a leading man there with the support of his father-in-law.[11]

Jenatsch's first known contact with the Salis came only after he began his studies in Zurich. The public support he obtained when he first arrived in Zurich suggests he had some kind of patron, but most likely it was the clerical network his father belonged to, not the Salis family, that helped him.[12] However, Jenatsch's temper and his wild behavior eventually got him in trouble with the Zurich authorities in 1613, when he faced first the loss of his stipend and then expulsion from school. This was when Salis patronage became an important factor for Jenatsch personally. Hearing of his son's problems, his father turned to Giovanni Baptista de Salis from Soglio, the powerful and wealthy leader of the Venetian faction in Graubünden, who agreed to employ Jenatsch as tutor and supervisor for his three sons in Zurich, paying Jenatsch fifty gulden per year, a generous salary. However, Jenatsch's income and status as a student now depended on Giovanni Baptista and his sons. Sometime in 1614, Jenatsch wrote his new patron a letter in which he exploited the well-established patron-client system of the era even as he balked at the submission that clientage demanded of him. The letter opened by acknowledging an advance of twenty gulden that Salis had provided. Jenatsch employed the typically humble language of a grateful servitor: "I will beg the Almighty, that he will on my account reward and pay all those who have shown and demonstrated such goodness to me." Having shown his humility, Jenatsch spent the next several paragraphs trying to renegotiate the arrangement that his father had arranged:

> It may be that my father agreed that I should serve your Grace for three years for this salary, but this does not please me; it is true that something like this was mentioned, but it was also included that either party could try things out for half a year. After that, either party would be free to continue, or not, and now that half year is over. Whether your Grace is pleased with my service, I cannot know, since you have not yet made your feelings known. For my part, I will gladly keep instructing your children to the best of my ability, as long as my expenses

continue to be paid; and if not, I have given your Grace notice that I will seek another position in the spring, as others have done, too.[13]

Depending on which part of the letter one reads, one could equally say that Jenatsch was entering a relationship of loyal clientage to the Salis or that he was already a tough-minded negotiator intent on getting the best pay for his services. He did continue with the Salis boys, suggesting that his boldness did not anger Giovanni Baptista.

Early in 1615, two of the Salis boys got into a fight with a local youth, Salomon Bühler. It seems that Jenatsch's pupils started it, but they ended up the losers once the fists started flying. They turned to their tutor for help, and instead of admonishing them as the school authorities expected, he joined the fray. Fighting was a serious offense by itself, of course, but Jenatsch made the situation much worse by announcing that he was going to "give [Salomon] such a reward that no one else will want to harm my disciples."[14] He followed up on this premeditated threat by beating up young Bühler, "so that the whole neighborhood heard him screaming, and afterwards the lumps and bruises were visible."[15] Jenatsch then ignored several invitations to explain himself to the school board; when he finally did appear before them, he refused to apologize and was expelled from the school. Surprisingly, though, the punishment was never carried out. Giovanni Baptista de Salis was not only a powerful man on his own account; he was also an in-law of the city treasurer. Since punishing Jenatsch would have been an insult to Giovanni Baptista, the treasurer intervened to protect Jenatsch.

This incident is revealing in several ways. Jenatsch's father originally appealed to Giovanni Baptista on behalf of his son, making Jenatsch in effect a client of the Salis clan. Jenatsch evidently thought that his father had sold his services too cheaply, but he also took his role seriously, striking out to protect and revenge his charges even at risk to his own situation in Zurich. Punishing Bühler was a matter of honor for the Salis, and most adults around Jenatsch, though not the school officials, ultimately understood the incident this way. Since he had acted on behalf of a powerful clan, moreover, a network of kinship and patronage protected him from any consequences, even though his behavior had been outrageous. After all, Jenatsch was not simply a poor, backcountry student under the school's authority, but also a future pastor. Violent threats and premeditated retaliation hardly matched a vocation to serve the church, it might seem. In the seventeenth century, however, even theology students lived in a world of patronage, kin, and honor that often took precedence over the abstract standards of schoolmasters and clergymen.

What played out as schoolboy fights in Zurich could become bloody and violent in Graubünden itself. Clan and patron-client networks intertwined with both notions of honor and the realities of power. As a result, they could influence actions ranging from routine intimidation in village assemblies to large-scale riots when powerful clans faced each other within a single community.[16] Since most struggles of this kind took place locally in an oral, rather than literate, context, they rarely entered the historical record. Fortunately for historians, though, Jenatsch's later notoriety meant that people kept closer track of what happened to him, thus preserving some evidence about how kin and patronage worked at the time.

As in other aspects of Jenatsch's life, major transitions were underway. The world of coherent if often violent patronage by a few powerful clans who operated through honor and revenge was giving way to more complicated politics, as foreign powers sought to intervene in Graubünden and as the Three Leagues began operating more and more like a state.[17] The transition actually increased the potential for explosive and unpredictable violence. Rivalry for public offices and foreign pensions, disagreements over new laws and their implementation, or religious differences could trigger chains of actions and reactions that depended on blood and kin, and vice versa. As a transitional character himself, Jenatsch participated in both systems, though his biographers have usually looked at him through lenses shaped by the newer rather than older modes of exercising power.

There can be no doubt, in any event, that by 1618, Jenatsch operated as a client and supporter of the Salis clan, specifically of Hercules von Salis from Grüsch, who became the head of the pro-Venetian faction of Bündner magnates after Giovanni Battista died.[18] Having worked under Salis's guidance to trigger the Thusis Tribunal, Jenatsch fled to Grüsch, the center of Salis plotting, after the 1620 Valtellina massacre. From there, he joined the band of Salis retainers who rode by night to Rietberg Castle in order to murder Pompeius von Planta. Indeed, Planta's murder shows vividly how traditional honor revenge and modern politics could form a potent mixture.

Planta became a target for many reasons. First, Planta-Salis rivalry had intensified after 1600 because most of the Salis family firmly supported both a Venetian alliance and the Protestant religion. Although most of the Planta lived in Protestant Engadine communes and remained Protestants in their religion, their clan's political alignment swung increasingly toward Spain, which ruled nearby Milan and eagerly sought to increase its influence in the Three Leagues.[19] One sign of growing polarization was that a number of prominent Planta magnates converted to Catholicism, none more visibly than Pompeius. His brother Rudolf, generally recognized as the leader of the pro-Spanish faction, only converted to Catholicism later in the 1620s. Clan identity, politics, and religion became increasingly aligned and polarized in this period, heightened by the virtual civil war and massive outside intervention that was tearing the Three Leagues apart.[20] Even so, the public murder of one party's leading light shocked contemporaries, both because of its brutality and because of the shameless behavior of the murderers. More was at stake for the killers than just political advantage, it seems. To find out what, we need to trace the lines of vendetta and power in the Lower Engadine and Val Müstair.

The key is the actual men who murdered Planta. Jenatsch may have been at the forefront when the troop of murderers, nineteen in all, found Planta in his

Rietberg castle, but the actual killer was most likely Niklaus Carl von Hohenbalcken, a huge, powerful man who was the head of a well-established Val Müstair family.[21] The Hohenbalcken, who were Catholic, were rivals of the Lower Engadine Planta leaders, including Pompeius and his brother Rudolf, and therefore led the Val Müstair in supporting the Venetian alliance. In the wake of the Valtellina massacre in July 1620, Rudolf von Planta therefore led a troop of Planta retainers and Austrian troops into the Val Müstair. Hohenbalcken, the head magistrate, had to flee into exile while Planta's men burned his house and those of his wife and his brother.[22] In an account that described and defended the attack on Pompeius, an anonymous Salis supporter divided Pompeius's crimes into two categories: general (that is to say, political) and particular. The author relied on Pompeius's particular crimes to justify the participation of the men who carried out the murder, including Blasius Alexander, Jenatsch, and the Hohenbalcken brothers. Alexander's complaint, according to this document, was that Pompeius had banished him from the Three Leagues and put a price on his head, while Jenatsch's was that Pompeius had "threatened to tear him to pieces if he ever caught him."[23]

The sources therefore make it clear that the murder was simultaneously political and personal. Pompeius and his brother had helped organize the Valtellina massacre and Spain's seizure of the Valtellina, yet the Three Leagues had not acted—indeed, in their chaotic state, could not act—to punish him. The Salis raiding party therefore claimed to be acting in legitimate defense of their fatherland by carrying out the judgments of the 1618 Thusis Tribunal. The personal dimension, however, explains the exact identities of the murderers and the brutality of the act:

> First, he was knocked down, and then hit in the head. As he lay on the floor, still breathing through his blood, an axe was driven through his chest and stomach, while another one split his head open. Both remained stuck there in his body.[24]

The very earliest account of the attack—written, it says, by someone who participated—adds the final, gruesome detail: "he was struck down, cut open, and his heart and guts were torn out of his corpse."[25] The author of another account claimed that multiple desecrations of Pompeius's corpse took place because "each one of them wanted to leave a sign on the traitor's body."[26] As historian Edward Muir has shown for the nearby Friuli region, this kind of demonstrative violence was not merely a random expression of rage, but rather sent a message of vengeance and power to the associates of a defeated enemy.[27]

To further taunt the Planta, another anonymous pamphleteer wrote to defend Planta's murderers and celebrate the good effects that the killing had, both political and religious. Spanish partisans had taken a fright, the author claimed, whereas "all goodhearted patriotic people" were filled with joy. The wavering Protestants living near Planta's castle had returned to their faith, and the local

Catholics even agreed to restore the pulpits in the churches for Protestant preaching. When the author turned to the personal, however, he laid on the scorn with a heavy hand:

> [Pompeius's] accomplices are happy about his death, just like some of his relatives, since they no longer have to put up with his pride; thus they seek no revenge, but rather thank God that he left the world honorably in this way, instead of at the hangman's hand. From his brother, captain Rudolf, nothing is heard.[28]

To claim that Pompeius deserved to hang was itself profoundly insulting, since only common criminals died this way. To suggest that the way Pompeius *did* die, pinned to the floor by a murderer's axe, was "honorable" taunted the Planta clan even further with their own weakness. Even if Blasius, Jenatsch, and the Hohenbalcken brothers had political goals, they carried them out through actions rich in symbolism about blood and honor. The similarities with Jenatsch's own murder are striking.

The tables quickly turned in the Three Leagues, despite Pompeius's death. Blasius Alexander was soon in an Austrian prison, where he was eventually executed, while Jenatsch had to flee Graubünden to avoid the same fate. In exile, he continued onward in a spectacular career that lasted another eighteen years until another axe—or was it the same axe?—ended his own life in 1639. During those years, public politics, secret diplomacy, and religion were his apparent concerns. Blood revenge and factional passions seemed to give way to tough-minded military and political pragmatism. He even went through formal reconciliations with both the Ruinelli heirs and the Planta family, whose members he had killed so ruthlessly.[29] When the axe struck down Jenatsch in February 1639, though, the forces of blood and revenge came back into his life.

Who Killed George Jenatsch?

The assault on Jenatsch in January 1639 involved a band of costumed men; the actual murderer was dressed as a bear, and none of the witnesses, as they claimed, could identify him. The local authorities in Chur carried out a lackadaisical investigation that interviewed a number of witnesses but never officially identified a suspect.[30] Meanwhile, the wild circumstances surrounding the murder, as well as the prominence and extraordinary career of the victim, ensured that rumors began swirling immediately. Jenatsch's murder was notably bloody: he was not simply gunned down, but killed in a ritualistic way. The murderers shot him first, but they had also brought along an axe, and this was the weapon actually used to strike him down. Once Jenatsch was on the floor, moreover, another man from the band deliberately crushed his head with a war hammer.

Most Bündner quickly concluded that Rudolf von Planta, son of the murdered Pompeius, had instigated the murder, quite possibly using the same notorious axe

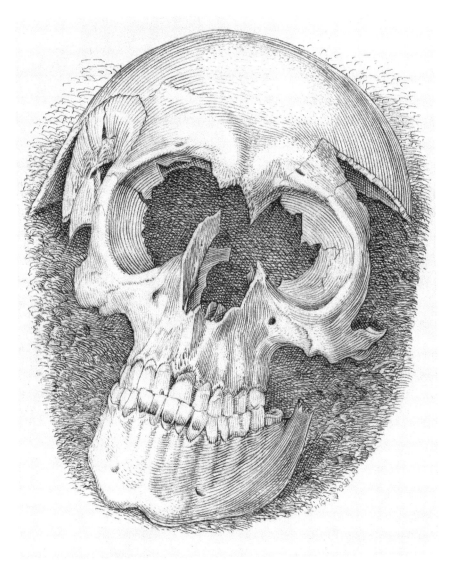

Figure 5.1 Jenatsch's skull as excavated in 1959, with the slice of an axe visible on its left side (to the right in the illustration) and the blunt impact of the hammer on its right side. Original etching by Toni Nigg, 1959. By permission of the Rätisches Museum, Chur (H 1973, 1376).

that had once cleaved his own father's body.[31] At a wedding party not long after the murder, Planta even confessed his part in the murder in a scene that echoes one of Shakespeare's most brilliant moments, the players' scene in *Hamlet*. The younger Planta entertained the wedding guests with his personal company of actors, who performed with great energy, seeking to outdo one another in amusing the assembled notables. As the performance reached its peak, however, Planta and his sidekick Giovanni Baptista Prevost joined the actors in their performance: "But [Planta and Prevost] didn't want to amuse the guests, but rather to make a tragedy out of this wedding comedy," as the chronicler Jacob Wigeli from Chur reported. They seized a gun and aimed it at several men from the Prättigau who had served under Jenatsch. As the panic-stricken guests threw themselves aside, Planta turned to the groom and bride and spoke, pointing to his friend Prevost:

> This is the man who murdered Jenatsch, and I am the true head of the Planta faction, and I will not relent until every one of Jenatsch's followers is executed just as he was, for reasons that you all know.[32]

Motive, opportunity, and confession: the culprit seems clear![33]

One might therefore think that the question "who killed Jenatsch?" would quickly fade away, yet it did not. Although feverish speculation did not last long in Graubünden itself, the question remained irresistible for later biographers and historians, since the myth of Jenatsch always found its high point in his murder. Two things kept interest alive. First, Jenatsch had been murdered not by a single man but by a crowd, which opened the door for conspiracy theories about who else might have taken part. Both contemporaries and later historians were free to wonder about the motives for and impact of the murder, as a 1639 report illustrates:

> As for what was discussed [in Chur] about it, well, there are nearly as many opinions as there are people. Good, honest, patriotic people feel that it was a special necessity for the common fatherland to get that kind of man out of the middle of things, so that better opinions about common affairs could be reached. Others, however, hold it for a foolish deed; one could have gotten rid of him in some other way.[34]

The second reason the issue remained open is that Jenatsch had so many enemies. It therefore remained tempting to connect more of them to his spectacular murder. Giovanni Baptista Prevost and Rudolf von Planta had obvious reasons for blood revenge, but so did the descendants of Colonel Ruinelli and other men Jenatsch had killed. Politics and diplomacy provided another whole range of suspects. The most powerful branch of the Salis family, for example, had supported the French alliance and felt betrayed politically by Jenatsch, as did French partisans in general. But the Spanish party might also have been involved: after all, shortly before his death, Jenatsch had sent out feelers to France again, probably as a way to put pressure on Spain to finalize its treaty with the Three Leagues. Indeed, many candidates emerged right after Jenatsch's death as possible murderers; not surprisingly, all of them were men.

When Jenatsch entered the literary world in the late 1700s, astonishingly, a woman began to replace all other suspects: "Lucretia" von Planta. Aside from the lack of any evidence that a woman had killed Jenatsch, Lucretia suffered from an additional weakness as a suspect: a Lucretia von Planta never existed. Several pieces of evidence did help support the late emergence of Lucretia as a suspect, however. To begin with, people knew that Pompeius von Planta's daughter Katharina had been present at her father's murder in 1621, at least according to several sympathetic accounts.[35] It was appealing to think that the trauma of this event had set her mind on revenge, however long it might take. A second clue appeared in the testimony taken by the Chur city council after the murder. Conrad Matthis was the innkeeper at Die Glocke (The Bell), an elegant inn next to the less reputable Staubiges Hüetli (The Dusty Cap) where Jenatsch died. Among his guests that February night were Colonel Rudolf von Travers and his wife Katharina, the daughter of Pompeius. When Matthis heard the commotion caused by Jenatsch's death, he went downstairs, where several witnesses told him about the crime. He also observed a peculiar exchange, which he described in his testimony. As Matthis listened, Travers's servant came back from the Dusty Cap carrying a pistol, which, he said, was the pistol that had killed Jenatsch (though as we know, it had only injured him). The servant then offered the pistol not to Travers or to Matthis, but to Katharina von Planta. Matthis testified that she examined it and said, "Maybe my departed father's death has been revenged with this."[36] This is the first (and only) piece of evidence suggesting that a woman was involved in some way with the murder. Mathis's testimony played no further part in the official investigation, however, nor did anyone at the time associate Katharina directly with the murder. As the historical events faded into myth, in contrast, more and more versions of the story added a female protagonist. Given the intensely patriarchal nature of Bündner society, such a twist may seem peculiar. Yet gender and sexual boundaries are powerful forces in every human society. Perhaps the return of a woman to stories about Jenatsch—however hidden real women were at the time—is not so surprising after all.

Honor and Gender: Jenatsch the Whoremonger or Misogynist?

As we learned earlier, kinship and even political tensions in the seventeenth century often found expression through the language of honor. If honor was everywhere in public life, helping sharpen the boundaries created in other ways, did it also connect with gender and sexual identity? Since he lived in a deeply patriarchal culture that we study through sources that largely ignored the existence of women, Jenatsch's life is not the place to examine early modern attitudes about women, gender, or sexuality in general. We can do the converse, however: we can look at how the powerful human forces of gender and sexuality found an echo even in a life like his. When we do, not surprisingly, honor and dishonor provide some of the most intriguing clues, though Jenatsch himself also delivered a few insights through his surviving comments about his family. This chapter will therefore conclude by looking at two issues: Jenatsch's own statements about women, and some attacks on Jenatsch's sexual honor after 1618. First we briefly need to summarize the little that is known about his family life.

It is telling, in a way, that we do not know the exact date of Jenatsch's marriage or even whether he married once or twice.[37] From a political and patronage perspective, the important thing for earlier biographers was simply that he had married into the powerful Buol family from Davos in the Ten Jurisdictions. Like Hercules von Salis a generation earlier, Jenatsch soon relied on his father-in-law for local support during critical moments in the politics of the Three Leagues. A few scraps of evidence indicate that his (first?) marriage took place in 1620, and that he took his young wife with him to his parish in Berbenno in the Valtellina. The couple fled together during the Valtellina massacre in July 1620.[38] An entry in the baptismal register in Davos when his (second?) daughter was born in 1627 indicates that his wife's name at that time was Anna.[39] One genealogist has speculated that Jenatsch first married Anna's older sister Katharina in 1620, then Anna around 1625, since most of his children were born after 1627. The only evidence for his (first?) daughter, named Catharina, comes from a much later property deed that mentions her as a (half?) sister of Jenatsch's youngest son, Jörg—though without giving a birth date. This daughter could have been a daughter of the first wife Katharina, who might have died during the plague that struck Graubünden in the early 1620s, or she equally might be a daughter of the (only) wife Anna. We are unlikely ever to know.

The real message from all this indirect evidence is not about the details of Jenatsch's immediate family, though. Rather, what it reveals is how far women were pushed out of the public sphere in Graubünden during this period, both in the minds of contemporaries and in the work of many historians since. From such a perspective, the only important thing about Jenatsch's marriage was his father-in-law, whose political and financial connections helped as he was changing his career from pastor to military entrepreneur. Such a pattern is typical for traditional patriarchal societies: whatever the complex realities of family life and the emotional connections between men and women, the public sphere *represented* marriages as relationships between men carried out by means of women. Only lucky finds of evidence, such as the writings of Hortensia von Salis (1659–1715) in Graubünden, give us glimpses into the more complex realities of women's lives.[40]

Further evidence about Jenatsch's family life is equally scarce. We do know that he stood as a godfather fairly often in Davos. The spiritual kinship established through this ritual provided a good way for an outsider like Jenatsch to create connections in his new commune. Although he began godfathering local children as early as 1621, a major burst of christenings came in 1627, just before he became an official citizen of Davos. Even after he converted to Catholicism, he continued to stand as godfather for local (Protestant) children, though he became a less popular choice. Instead, his wife Anna became a frequent godmother after 1636.[41] The sense of domesticity and local networking conveyed by Jenatsch's godfathering also echoes in his defense of his family in his conversion letters. With some heat, he insisted to his former colleague Stephan Gabriel in 1637 that "I do not want anyone in our Rhaetia to be driven away from liberty of conscience either by force or by law: the proof comes from my wife and children and all my friends."[42] All this is enough to lead one biographer, Alexander Pfister, to conclude that Jenatsch was "a good dutiful father to his family."[43] Without more letters or diaries from him and those around him, however, this remains little more than a wishful guess.

There was a darker side to Jenatsch's attitudes about women, as well, which we can glimpse through some marginal notations he made in his family Bible. Though these comments are undated, they do show that at some point he harbored considerable anger toward women. For example, when reading the Old Testament book of Proverbs, which contains several misogynistic outbursts, he wrote several bitter-sounding comments.[44] Next to chapter 5, which contains the verses,

> For the lips of a strange woman drop as an honeycomb,
> And her mouth is smoother than oil:
> But her end is bitter as wormwood, sharp as a two-edged sword.
> Her feet go down to death; her steps take hold on hell,

Jenatsch wrote, "Pay attention!" A few pages later, next to the word "woman" in chapter 8, he simply wrote, "Satan!"[45] We simply cannot tell whether Jenatsch was echoing conventional patriarchal sentiments here or was revealing some deeper streak of hostility toward women.

In any event, his enemies also saw his relations with women as a vulnerable point, though for quite different reasons. Various sources make it clear that Jenatsch had a reputation as a ladies' man for whom marital chastity was not an important virtue. As he rose to prominence, those who hated him spread the rumor that he was a proper whoremonger whose lustful misdeeds began in his student days and never stopped. Such accusations began as soon as Jenatsch appeared on the public stage as one of the spiritual overseers of the Thusis Tribunal. These attacks emphasized sexual misconduct as well as other crimes, since it was especially dishonorable for a clergyman to fall into fornication. Indeed, from a Catholic perspective, clergy were supposed to be celibate and not even married.

Some of the first accusations against Jenatsch appear in anonymous songs that circulated shortly after the Thusis Tribunal closed. The leading men of the tribunal came under harsh attack, as did the spiritual overseers, including Jenatsch. The tone of the songs is dire:

> You are locusts from hell, who destroy everything down your throats,
> What have you started, you strangers from heaven, devil's children?
> Is this your new faith: causing rebellion, torturing, robbing, rebelling,
> burning, writing, giving verdicts,
> prosecuting, lying, raging, and persecuting?[46]

Jenatsch himself appears in this song only under a pseudonym, "Carnatsch," which echoes the Italian *carnaccio*, meaning fleshly or lustful, though with overtones of the butcher's shop as well.[47] The rant continues at some length, ending with the observation that letting the clergy run things meant that the Bündner authorities might as well "take off your pants and put on some skirts, foolishness and games are your just deserts."[48] Although the Protestant clergy had been marrying for nearly a century, the political insult here carried sexual overtones. If the clergy were in charge, it meant that the real men who were supposed to rule were behaving like women or children.

Even harsher (and more sexually loaded) accusations followed a few years later in an anonymous pamphlet that circulated in the Three Leagues, quite possibly written by Pompeius von Planta himself. The author employed aggressive slurs intended not only to defame, but also to enrage his targets. The poem in this pamphlet described the inhabitants of the Lower Engadine, for example, as "rogues, thieves and murderers" for at least a hundred years, while the troops gathered in Thusis were so bad that "if God wanted to punish a land, he would appoint no other people than these." The leader of the men from the Val Müstair, Niklaus Carl von Hohenbalcken (who was later Planta's killer), was a "bewhored man, who was always comfortable with rebellions." The author used similar violent language to slander one secular leader after another.[49] When the anonymous author turned to the Reformed ministers, especially the ones who had served at Thusis, his tone became even more hysterical. Fools and knaves were bad enough, but the pamphlet accused these men of direct ties with Satan. According to the pamphlet, pastor Johann à Porta was the son of a black magician and had been "wrought in hell." Blasius Alexander, Jenatsch's closest friend and ally, was "a public thief, incestuous, a perverter of children, and a traitor to his country."[50] Jenatsch himself gained attention specifically for his sexual behavior:

> The fifth was Georgie Jenatsch, a godless lad well suited criminally—when he lived on welfare in Zurich, he had more whores than schoolbooks, and he can outfox practiced deceivers when it comes to lying and treachery.[51]

Enraged by the course of events at Thusis, the author used sexually colored slander to attack the men he most hated, the Reformed pastors, including Jenatsch.

Given the era's sensitivity to honor, we can assume that the targets of such abuse harbored their own rage and waited for revenge.

*   *   *

Seventeenth-century Europe in general, and seventeenth-century Switzerland in particular, were profoundly male-centered societies.[52] Of course, men did care about women, positively or negatively, and women could and did play diverse roles in everything from household management to political influence to spirituality. The divide between the sexes, a profound boundary in all human societies, was therefore an omnipresent reality for Jenatsch, even if the silences in the evidence force us to look for it in unexpected places. In fact, Jenatsch's own background as a pastor made gender a particularly loaded part of his identity. Christianity's views about spirituality and sexuality ensured that the clergy remained an estate apart in sexual terms as well as in other ways. Clerics were men of peace rather than violence, marked by special clothing and, at least for Catholics, by sexual celibacy. Jenatsch himself seems to have harbored mixed feelings about women, judging from the sparse evidence we have, but he was also particularly vulnerable to sexual slander because of his past identity as a clergyman.

The sharp distinction between men and women in early modern Europe, as in many societies, correlated with the enormous importance of kinship networks in all aspects of everyday life. The kinship established through women's biological and cultural role in reproduction found parallels in the spiritual kinship of godparenting and in the formation of kin-like patron-client networks. By attaching himself as a client to the widespread Salis patronage network, Jenatsch achieved his first dangerous prominence on the public stage at Thusis and never looked back. Kinship and patronage, in turn, often found expression in the potent language of honor, blood, and revenge. The logic of honor and dishonor helped frame and explain the events of Jenatsch's era, ranging from the subtle negotiations of diplomats to the brutal symbolism of Pompeius von Planta's body split by axes or Jenatsch's skull crumpled by a war hammer.

Even so, both contemporary chroniclers as well as later Jenatsch biographers often left such forces in the background. Sex, kin, patronage, and honor—and the boundaries they generated—played a minor role in their narratives, since the authors chose instead to concentrate on what they regarded as the masculine and rational spheres of political maneuver, national identity, and spiritual authenticity. When poets, novelists, and playwrights living in the very different nineteenth century became fascinated by Jenatsch's life, however, they found that they needed to treat his personal life in order to make his story seem complete. They often did so by creating fictional archetypes, rather than relying on historical evidence.

Chapter 6

JENATSCH AFTER 1639

Storytelling in Biography and Myth

A study of the historical Jenatsch reveals that the novel's beauty . . . must be attributed not to the historical material, but to the author. It is what the author made out of the material that turned Meyer's Jürg Jenatsch into the work of art that we now possess.

—Julius Sahr, *C. Ferd. Meyer: Jürg Jenatsch,* 1904

A figure as complex and ambiguous as George Jenatsch was bound to leave strong impressions on the men and women who knew him. His accomplishments during his period of genuine prominence in the 1630s, moreover, made him highly visible within the narrow confines of the Three Leagues, thus ensuring that he would indeed be remembered, though not always in a positive way. It is to the richness and ambiguity of memories about him, and thus in a sense to Jenatsch's career after his death in 1639, that this chapter turns. The man himself crossed cultural and social boundaries repeatedly while alive; once dead, the memory of him soon challenged the boundary between history and myth, as diversely placed authors sought to bring him back to life in their works.

Two seemingly contradictory conclusions become visible when one looks at the literature about Jenatsch, from the earliest mentions in chronicles written shortly after he died, through a famous nineteenth-century novel and two major scholarly biographies, right up to Daniel Schmid's quirky 1987 movie. The first is that Jenatsch's story kept being retold in different ways. Issues or approaches that seemed compelling to authors in one period gave way to entirely different viewpoints, which routinely required major reworking of both people and events, for later writers of both fiction and history. Secondly, however, certain motifs showed enormous durability, already appearing in Graubünden memoirs from authors like Fortunat Sprecher and Ulysses von Salis and retaining their fascination for later authors as well. The flow of telling and retelling falls roughly into four major movements.

The first two can be treated quickly: an initial wave of records written within a lifetime of Jenatsch's death, then a long and largely invisible period when stories about his life found their way into local folklore without gaining much echo in printed form. The third period, beginning around 1800, represented a total reversal from the sporadic notices of the second period. Historians, novelists, and poets in the nineteenth century found Jenatsch absolutely fascinating, which led to a flood of histories, plays, poems, and, most notably, Conrad Ferdinand Meyer's 1874 novel. Meyer's work had such an impact that it set a permanent benchmark for all later representations. The texts from this third period often echoed the old themes, including the fateful axe, but added an entirely new and anachronistic admiration for Jenatsch as the "savior of his nation." Moreover, unlike their seventeenth-century predecessors, nineteenth-century authors found it impossible to tell Jenatsch's story without making room for important women who influenced or even controlled his fate. The double concern for national heroism and personal character found in this literature reached a perverse high point in the 1930s, when authors sympathetic to the fascist cause wrote about Jenatsch as a model patriot who had pushed aside the Three Leagues' inconvenient democratic institutions in order to save his people. The collapse of Romanticism (not to mention fascism) in the ashes of World Wars I and II put an end to stories that glorified Jenatsch's heroism, leading to the fourth and final phase. After 1945, Jenatsch's character lost much of its fascination and retellings of his story split in two directions. On the one hand, serious literature that spoke of his life began taking a skeptical or even ironic tone toward his accomplishments, while on the other, popular reception of Jenatsch moved mostly into the commercial sphere, where his historic identity could help attract tourists and sell products.

Through all these dizzying changes, a few aspects of Jenatsch's wild career retained their appeal. Prime among them was the idea that Jenatsch had died with his skull split by the same axe that had killed Pompeius von Planta. Rumors that this was the case began circulating within weeks of Jenatsch's death, and travelers who visited Planta's castle at Rietberg over the next two centuries claimed that they had seen the fateful weapon carefully preserved there, still crusted with blood.[1] When the Romantic dramatists of the nineteenth century took up this story, they soon linked the identity of the axe with the supposed identity of the murderer. More and more versions assumed that the killer behind the bear mask had been none other than Lucretia von Planta, daughter of the murdered Pompeius and (in some versions) tragic lover of the demonic ex-pastor. Even before Meyer built his novel around the tortured love between Lucretia and Jenatsch, Lucretia and her axe had become essential icons in his biography.

The tragic juxtaposition of characters so dear to Romantic authors also points to a second motif that dominates every version of Jenatsch's life: a profound ambivalence. From the outset, authors wrestled with the relationship between his good qualities and his bad deeds. Even the obituary that the Protestant pastor Bartholomäus Anhorn wrote in 1639 gave praise to Jenatsch's "ingenious spirit," though it deplored his conversion to Catholicism and his diplomatic efforts to bring about a Spanish alliance for Graubünden.[2] Later authors, mostly from the Protestant camp, continued in Anhorn's footsteps. Even Ernst Haffter, whose sober 1894 biography followed the rigorous rules of Germanic scholarship, ended up contrasting Jenatsch's patriotic motives with his violent methods and apparently limitless egoism. Alexander Pfister, the most recent comprehensive biographer, consistently described Jenatsch as a man "who, in the style of his violent nature, was too easily ready to put the demands of necessity before his human and Christian duty."[3] Indeed, the lasting ambivalence that has characterized depictions of Jenatsch may reflect the fact that, for all their differences, most authors who wrote about him found it unsettling how often and easily he crossed social boundaries and transformed who he was. What was new in the nineteenth century, though, was a tendency to search for the roots of such ambivalence in Jenatsch's "character" rather than in his situation.

Tellingly, from the most scholarly pedants to the most passionate romantics, authors writing about Jenatsch all found it irresistible to juxtapose a deeply flawed Jenatsch with the "good duke," Henri de Rohan.[4] The close association between the two men during the spectacular mountain campaigns in the early 1630s made such a link attractive and set the stage for their tragic entanglement. Jenatsch's role in betraying Rohan, and the latter's relatively graceful retreat from Graubünden in 1636 represented the high point of their drama. Through these events, Jenatsch's vices seemed, perversely, to cooperate with Rohan's virtues in restoring independence to the Republic of the Three Leagues. If Jenatsch had been less treacherous, or Rohan more so, the critical moment in 1637 when the French retreated peacefully might have gone much more badly for Graubünden. Moreover, both men died dramatically in 1639, Jenatsch under the murderer's axe, Rohan by throwing himself into battle in Germany after having been repudiated by Cardinal Richelieu and the French court. The temptation to play these two men off against each other, or in some cases to create a trio with the crafty Richelieu as the third player, colored most late versions of Jenatsch's life. The requirements of storytelling—that every character needs his icon, and that every agonist calls for an antagonist—thus built on the genuinely dramatic historical material to produce shifting versions of a hero's story.

The Initial Deposit: Jenatsch Immediately after His Death

The early 1600s, when Jenatsch lived and died, also produced an unusually dense cluster of chronicles from authors active in Graubünden. These men, including Bartholomäus Anhorn, Fortunat Sprecher, Ulysses von Salis, and Fortunat von Juvalta, recorded in great detail the dramatic events that shook the Three Leagues during the Thirty Years' War. Only Sprecher's works were published before the modern period, but manuscripts of all these authors' work circulated among

educated readers in Graubünden for generations. When interest in the region's
history began growing late in the 1700s, these texts were among the first to be edited and published for a broader readership.[5] Their prominence and popularity
therefore ensured that later pictures of Jenatsch drew primarily on their contents.
Only in 1894 did Haffter publish his biography, based not on these chronicles but
on manuscript records from the archives of Graubünden, Zurich, Paris, Milan,
and Venice. By this time, Jenatsch's image was already firmly fixed in the region's
popular and learned imagination.[6] The chroniclers' works thus played a decisive
role in shaping stories about Jenatsch. It is notable that every one of these chroniclers was a Protestant.

Bartholomäus Anhorn was a Reformed pastor who knew Jenatsch personally
as a fellow member of the Rhaetian Synod until Jenatsch left it in 1620. The troubles of the war years also drove Anhorn into permanent exile in the Swiss region
of St. Gallen. His major work was his *War in Graubünden*, a rambling assemblage of
copied documents, commentary, and miscellaneous material that concentrated on
the period until 1629. He and his son continued the collection into the 1630s,
however, so the high points of Jenatsch's career were included, including Anhorn's obituary of Jenatsch in 1639.[7] Fortunat Sprecher was a Humanist lawyer
and magistrate from Davos who filled high political offices and compiled many
historical works about the Three Leagues. His *Pallas Raetica* became a standard
reference work across Europe for people interested in Graubünden, and he also
compiled a two-volume history of the wars from 1621 to 1636. The first volume
covering the period through 1629 appeared in print, but his second volume remained in manuscript form at his death in 1645.[8] Among the chroniclers, Ulysses
von Salis probably knew Jenatsch most closely, since the two men fought together
through the 1620s and 1630s in French service. Ulysses was the son of Hercules
von Salis in Grüsch, the patron and faction head whom Jenatsch had served so violently after 1618. Ulysses remained loyal to his French patrons and his Protestant
religion when Jenatsch and the *Kettenbund* engineered the Three Leagues' shift of
alliance in 1636; not surprisingly, therefore, his memoirs bitterly criticize Jenatsch
as a traitor and turncoat to his faith.[9] Finally, the last of our major chroniclers,
Fortunat von Juvalta, had reason to despise Jenatsch as well. A magistrate and local leader from the Domleschg Valley, which included Jenatsch's first pastorate in
Scharans, Juvalta generally leaned toward closer ties with Spanish Milan in the
1610s and 1620s. This earned him the hatred of the Venetian faction, even
though Juvalta was a moderate Protestant and a respected leader locally. Accused
of being a Spanish sympathizer, Juvalta faced charges and rough questioning during the notorious court of Thusis in 1618. His memoirs express his rage at the un-
fair treatment he received. Since he wrote long after the actual events, though,
one wonders how much his knowledge about Jenatsch's later prominence colored
his depiction of the young pastor he first encountered in 1618.[10]

No surprise, then, that none of these pivotal authors looked kindly on Jenatsch. All condemned his conversion as a crucial betrayal, and all but Anhorn

looked down on him as a social climber who threatened to upset the social order they themselves sat on top of. Jenatsch's violent behavior also offended Anhorn, Sprecher, and Juvalta, all learned men who frequently deplored the "wildness" of the Bündner people. Salis, in contrast, was himself a soldier who shared complicity in Pompeius von Planta's murder through his membership in the activist Salis faction in Grüsch. For him, it was not Jenatsch's violence but his betrayal of France (and, more personally, the way he pushed leaders like Salis out of the limelight) that shaped his account. The critical perspective contained in these chroniclers' works lay ready, once interest increased, to influence later accounts of Jenatsch's life, since their narratives provided the most compact and accessible body of information available. At the same time, Jenatsch has a surprisingly small role in their chronicles: these four authors all sought to encompass a much broader view, within which Jenatsch appeared and disappeared relatively swiftly.[11]

Information about Jenatsch also found its way to posterity through a second channel: popular songs and sayings that circulated while he was alive or after his death (and in some cases much longer). A first wave of such material dated from the Thusis court of 1618, though the songs and slanders from the early years do not appear to have reached a wide audience and are found today only in rare manuscript copies. Jenatsch then largely disappeared from contemporary rhetoric until his conversion to Catholicism in 1635. This event triggered a series of attacks from local Protestant clergy, including one in Latin that criticized him as an ass, a flighty bird, an epicurean atheist, and a pagan apostate—all through clever anagrams of his name.[12] We should not underestimate the impact of such poems, which circulated by letter among the region's clergymen. Even if their parishioners could not read the Latin originals, the pastors' network of correspondence provided material that shaped their weekly sermons and their conversations with local inhabitants. In a world in which information was scarce, well-informed clergymen could exert considerable influence on public opinion.

It was probably another pastor who celebrated Jenatsch's murder in short, easily remembered verses in 1639:

> Here lies a man,
> I can't say his name
> here in the land
> because of his shame.[13]

Verse after verse excoriated Jenatsch with particular emphasis on his hostility toward God and true religion—though his lying, cheating, stealing, and murdering received considerable attention as well. The poem ended in a satisfied tone:

> You've now received your wage,
> The devil's honored guest,

Who lets your sins all weigh,
And leaves you no more rest.

Suffer the glowing coals,
For the innocents you've slain,
God's set it as his goal,
To make you feel some pain.[14]

Romansh rhyming chronicles took up Jenatsch's fate as well, suggesting that many Protestant Bündner celebrated his death by singing songs about him.

The first phase of reception ended when written versions of such songs became scarce and interest in Jenatsch faded, as the people of the Three Leagues moved on to different problems. Scattered evidence from the long, quiet second phase suggests that the story of the apostate who murdered Pompeius von Planta and rose to great power during the crisis of the Three Leagues, only to be murdered by Planta's heirs with the same axe, continued to circulate.[15] By the early eighteenth century, though, Jenatsch's deeds had largely vanished from the consciousness of people in Graubünden and Switzerland. The first publication of the manuscript chronicles after 1750 did make available some information about his role during the Thirty Years' War, but only as one man among a welter of other facts and personalities. Similarly, the first systematic surveys of the Three Leagues' history included him as described in Sprecher's and Juvalta's chronicles, but without giving him a particularly prominent role.[16]

The Glory Days: Jenatsch as National Hero in the 1800s

It took another existential crisis for the Three Leagues to reawaken interest in an earlier national hero, though now in the very different world of Europe's consolidating national states. During the era of the French Revolution and its aftermath, Graubünden again suffered invasion from French armies, the loss of the Valtellina (this time permanently), and eventual restoration of its independence. The men who lived through these crises faced repeated struggles over the nature and future of their unusual federal states. For them, the figure of Jenatsch offered a powerful way to express their understandings of Graubünden's or even Switzerland's political essence and its relation to the larger world.

When Louis Vulliemin published the first systematic history of seventeenth-century Switzerland in 1845, he gave the Three Leagues considerable attention since they were the only part of Switzerland drawn directly into the Thirty Years' War. Jenatsch appeared primarily as an actor during the diplomatic maneuvering of the 1630s, but Vulliemin included as fact the entire folkloric story of Jenatsch's death, including the bloody axe of Pompeius von Planta and the presence of Lucretia von Planta, who Vulliemin thought had instigated the murder.[17] The first biographical study to concentrate exclusively on Jenatsch appeared only in 1852, in a local Graubünden magazine. The author, Alfons Flugi, had given a talk to the local historical society that was so well received that he decided to expand and publish it for other local readers.[18] Another biography by Balthasar Reber in Basel appeared in 1860, aimed at Swiss readers more broadly.

The very fact that Graubünden had its own historical society by this point was no coincidence, nor was the timing of the interest in "Graubünden's pastor and hero," as Reber called him. Events across Europe in the mid-1800s drove growing public interest in—and anxiety about—the nature of the nation-state. Particularly in German-speaking Europe, the political crisis that began during the French Revolution and the Napoleonic invasions, which had temporarily subjected all of Germany to the French, triggered a powerful nationalist backlash. Across Germany, statesmen, poets, and activist students argued about the German nation's place in Europe, and about its proper shape. This debate also touched Switzerland. Although Napoleon had restored the traditional federal organization of the Swiss Confederation in 1807 after a brief fling with French-imposed central government, deep divisions of language, confession, and historical identity continued to trouble the loosely united cantons. Anxiety in Graubünden was even greater, since official participation in a Swiss nation—which happened as a consequence of Napoleon's meddling—was a novelty for the Bündner. Since the 1640s, the Three Leagues had largely gone their own ways, connected in sympathy and in European perception with the Swiss, but effectively part of a different trans-European coalition most of the time. The Three Leagues also operated as an independent state, possessing a legal charter, political customs, and claims to control an identifiable territory.[19] After 1815, however, Graubünden (shorn of its former subjects in the Valtellina) became an official part of Switzerland, one canton among others, and joined in the generation-long debate about what kind of a nation Switzerland ought to be.[20]

One can thus understand why historically minded laypeople in Graubünden during this period searched the past for parallel situations when their identity and autonomy had been at stake. The period from 1618 to 1639, when the Three Leagues had confronted internal paralysis combined with intense foreign pressure, seemed to fit the bill, and was thus (in their minds) ideally suited for drawing lessons relevant to the troubled 1840s and 1850s. George Jenatsch had been a key figure in both managing foreign pressure and in restoring relative domestic autonomy and stability after 1636. To many in the mid-1800s, therefore, he clearly seemed to offer a model for their times, since the Bündner once again had to balance political change against local tradition.

From our modern perspective, in contrast, the 1840s and 1850s seem profoundly different from the world Jenatsch inhabited in the 1630s. The most important new element, which plays a major role in every nineteenth-century literary or historical version of Jenatsch, was precisely the problematic nation-state. The more extreme nationalists in Europe after 1800 were fond of claiming that Switzerland, as a nation with three official languages, made no sense. Some German nationalists even suggested that this conundrum should be resolved by allowing the German-Swiss to rejoin their cultural and linguistic cousins in the new Germany. Given that the Swiss and Bündner had enjoyed three centuries of political separation from the Holy Roman Empire, such proposals met with little enthusiasm. Instead, Swiss centralizers tried to create a national government that could participate in an international Concert of Europe, though they faced determined opposition from devotees of local particularism—what the Swiss still call the *Kantönligeist*—in struggles that often amplified existing divisions over religion, language, and political ideology. The tensions finally unloaded in a brief civil war in 1847, during which the centralizers associated with the liberal and Protestant cantons won a clear victory over the conservative Catholic particularists.[21] A new national constitution followed in 1848, though its firm insistence on national, not local, sovereignty meant that Graubünden did not officially accept it and give up communal sovereignty until 1854.[22]

This reluctance in Graubünden had deep roots. The historical Three Leagues had certainly *not* conformed to the nineteenth-century ideal of a nation-state— that is, a sovereign people united by government, language, and culture, and sharing a coherent political identity. Rather, the leagues' territories had accumulated on the basis of complex feudal and post-feudal privileges, including substantial domains where other sovereigns claimed significant rights, and the Bündner remained divided by religious confession, language, and legal systems. As we have seen, Jenatsch operated within this complex terrain by showing diverse loyalties to his local culture ("Engadino-Rhetus"), to his church, to various outside powers (Venice, the Holy Roman Empire), and to Graubünden's home-grown political authorities. He was ambitious, and even a patriot, but nothing he did during his lifetime suggested that he considered himself a "national hero."

For many in Switzerland and Graubünden in the 1850s, however, national heroes were what they needed. Thus, Jenatsch's first appearance as a character in a drama took place in 1848, exactly as the Swiss and Bündner were wrestling with the problem of creating a new constitution and new national state. Peter Conradin von Planta, a liberal Protestant Bündner, wrote a play that year that juxtaposed his own kinsman Rudolf von Planta with a fiery Protestant hero, Jenatsch. In the drama, Planta seeks absolute power in Graubünden in alliance with the sinister Catholic powers of Austria and Spain, while Jenatsch pursues him in the name of "God and Fatherland."[23] After Jenatsch kills Rudolf (not Pompeius, and not with an axe), the play ends with a hearty celebration:

> It is done! The entry point of evil has been removed, and our Fatherland's freedom and Reformation have been freed from the shattered prison of their shame. O God of Zabaoth, praise and honor to you for the happily completed deed.[24]

It did not take a particularly subtle eye to equate Rudolf in the play with the conservative Catholic Swiss who in 1847 had sought an alliance with reactionary Austria. The author thus presented a Jenatsch who was above all a suitable hero for liberal Protestant nationalists—a curious fate indeed for an authoritarian convert to Catholicism.

Protestant historians also celebrated Jenatsch as a patriot and liberator, most conspicuously Balthasar Reber in his 1860 biography, which served as a foundation for most literary versions for the next thirty-five years, including Conrad Ferdinand Meyer's. Reber drew his evidence almost exclusively from seventeenth-century chroniclers like Sprecher and Juvalta, but the man he described was quite different from the ambitious apostate we have seen in the original sources. Reber, like the chroniclers, wrote from a clearly Protestant perspective and did not hesitate to repeat anti-Catholic stereotypes. Unlike the chroniclers, however, Jenatsch's conversion seemed a minor issue to him. Reber's explanation was that Jenatsch's seeming switch to Catholicism was merely a maneuver, justifiable because he did it for the sake of his fatherland. As was typical for these nineteenth-century authors, Jenatsch's importance for Reber was primarily national.

Reber also concentrated on a second dimension of Jenatsch's life that appeared frequently in this period: personal character. Nineteenth-century writers showed a strong tendency to look for individual qualities that could explain political actions and outcomes. They therefore pored through the historical evidence searching for clues about notable individuals' personal lives and attitudes. Finding the true character of a fluid and complex character like Jenatsch represented a challenge. Reber, for example, found himself trapped in ambivalence:

> Let us show all respect for the first half of Jenatsch's life, but no respect for his dark side, which powerfully overshadowed the light. He had a dark side because he was not only a patriot, but also a much bigger egoist than he was a patriot: an egoist in public affairs as in his private life. Jenatsch was an extraordinarily beneficial man for his Fatherland as a whole, but he was essentially a bad man.[25]

This same contradiction—a bad man who was good for his fatherland—recurred constantly in other works. Meyer captured the dilemma in his novel as well. In a speech Jenatsch makes to Lucretia von Planta, whom he loves and whom he is recruiting to help carry out his bold plan to liberate Graubünden from the French, he asks her:

> Don't you see, Lucretia, how all of us who are born amidst these civil wars are a disobedient, guilty tribe?—and a wretched one! There a brother has struck down his brother, and here a corpse divides two who love and belong to each other. Let us not be lesser than our fate! I stand at the helm with hands already covered in blood, and will navigate our little boat, Graubünden, through the cliffs.[26]

For the novelist as for the biographer writing in the mid-1800s, only patriotic virtue could explain—and perhaps even justify—the violence inherent in Jenatsch's deeply flawed character.

A similar juxtaposition of approval and ambivalence appeared in a wide variety of works, dominating characterizations of Jenatsch at every turn. As Heinrich Zschokke explained as early as 1798:

> Posterity has placed him among the greatest Bündner, because we look more at what he did for his Fatherland than at the dark stains in his behavior. Brutality, sensuality and ambition distorted his character, but his public actions formed a chain in which each act gave witness to his patriotism, his overpowering spirit, his courage, and his cleverness. This man therefore stands like an Alcibiades of his people, who leaves us uncertain whether we should react more with wonder or more with disgust.[27]

Meyer echoed this judgment in his novel in a way perhaps more subtle than the historians. As Jenatsch's power waxed in his version, Meyer staged a discussion among several leading men in Chur, including the novel's narrator and Jenatsch's old friend, Heinrich Waser from Zurich. After the other men complain of Jenatsch's greed and his religious conversion, Waser seeks to defend him:

> In one respect, George Jenatsch stands above our greatest contemporaries: in his overpowering love of his Fatherland. . . . That is the only key to his many-sided character. . . . And is it not a good fortune for us, honorable statesmen as we are, if deeds that are needful for the salvation of our Fatherland—deeds that cannot be carried out with clean hands—can be done by such lawless men of power . . . ?[28]

Few authors could express the commonly recognized tension between Jenatsch's virtues and his vices so vividly.

Later assessments only heightened the impression that Jenatsch was a man who did everything for his fatherland. Indeed, as European nationalism intensified, reaching a tragic high point during the era of the World Wars, Jenatsch's supposed national identity made him useful to a wide variety of ideological agendas. Whereas liberals in the nineteenth century found in Jenatsch a man who bravely put national interest ahead of his religious confession and even his personal interest, twentieth-century antiliberals built on the same elements to describe a Jenatsch who (correctly, they thought) seized power from a weak, directionless democracy in the name of the authentic destiny of his *Volk*, his people. Both approaches, however, shared the fact that they were responding to contemporary crises by projecting them onto a complex historical figure from the past. In one depiction from the 1930s, Rudolf Joho portrayed Jenatsch as a democrat who finds that his people are unready for the task of leadership. Having freed

Graubünden from foreign powers and killed Pompeius von Planta, Joho's Jenatsch first tries to restore power to the communes and the people so that they can build "an Alpine Empire in which every citizen, no matter his estate, his country of origin, or his religion, stands alike in law and duty."[29] When his fellow citizens fall into hopeless strife, however, Jenatsch realizes that only a true leader, a Führer, can bring about peace. Declaring himself the "national magistrate" (*Landamman*) of the Three Leagues, Joho's Jenatsch takes charge, accompanied by the joyful assent of the masses.[30] When his true love Lucretia commits suicide, he loses his will to action and allows her brother Rudolf to exact his revenge:

> Let my Reich collapse after me. The time is not yet ripe, and I was born too early. In a century, perhaps two—who knows!—one man will achieve the unity of all peoples, and bring peace, perhaps.[31]

Clearly, Jenatsch's astonishing career, along with his accumulation of power before his death, gave his story mobilizing potential for antiliberal as well as liberal causes. Both the patriotic pathos of most literary versions and the passionate authoritarianism of a few lost their potency, however, when nationalism itself came into question.

Telling the Story Differently: Character, and Some New Characters

Literary versions of Jenatsch's life deserve a little more attention, because they help illustrate not only the slippery distinction between history and myth, but also how notions about telling historical stories have been changing since the seventeenth century—as well as how they have remained the same. We can start by noting that Jenatsch's story as it appeared both in the surviving manuscript sources and in the historical chronicles of his own era was almost exclusively a *political* story. Jenatsch's importance to his contemporaries rested on his actions in the political sphere as both a soldier and a diplomat. He first drew attention at the political tribunal in Thusis, rose to prominence in and outside Graubünden as a soldier and military recruiter, and drew hatred or praise for his role in the tense political negotiations that pitted Spain against France as the desired ally of the Three Leagues. Even when contemporaries criticized Jenatsch's personal behavior, they did so for partisan reasons. In short, the historical record tells us almost exclusively about the public man.

This public man was not enough for nineteenth-century authors, though, who wanted to connect public action to private character. Their desire to understand the "true Jenatsch" thus put his inner thoughts at the focus of their attention, even though the available sources had almost nothing to say on this subject. We lack a diary or intimate correspondence that might give us insight into the inner workings of our subject's mind. Some authors responded to this vacuum of information by stressing the ambivalent character of Jenatsch and left it at that, but others, especially poets and dramatists, filled in the void differently. Going beyond the mere recognition of ambivalence, they sought to portray Jenatsch as a man torn between his real self and something else. Even more important, they sought to illuminate the darkness they saw in him by introducing new characters into the drama. Strikingly, almost every character they invented (or inflated from sketchy information) was a woman. This represents a major change from the original sources from Graubünden, in which women remained virtually invisible, as we have seen.

The most important invented woman in Jenatsch's mythical life was doubtless "Lucretia" von Planta—a character based on a real woman but massively changed by different authors to fit the needs of their stories. That real woman was the daughter of Pompeius von Planta, Katharina von Planta, who married Rudolf von Travers, another Bündner military captain. The first puzzle here is where the name Lucretia came from. It was hardly an insignificant choice, since the original Lucretia in Rome was a heroine of the republican tradition whose suicide motivated her husband and father to overthrow the foreign kings ruling in Rome.[32] Swiss authors had long proposed that there were strong parallels between Lucretia and the founders of the Swiss republic. As Heinrich Bullinger, pastor and dramatist from Zurich in the early sixteenth century had put it—perhaps oddly, from our perspective—her situation "matches the drama of William Tell very well."[33] The name change from Katharina to Lucretia seems to have taken place sometime in the 1700s, though some later authors familiar with the historical sources tried to split the difference, as Haffter did by naming her "Lukrezia Katharina Planta."[34] The early appearance of the name Lucretia was already connected with the idea that she had murdered Jenatsch. The sources for this invention are quite obscure, but it seems quite possible that it represents a theme coming out of popular mythology and memory. As we have seen, it was already reported as fact in Vulliemin's history of seventeenth-century Switzerland, published in German in 1844.

Wherever the story came from, it proved impossible to shake off. Thus, the historian Reber points to Lucretia's cousin Rudolf as the murderer—an entirely plausible perpetrator, as we have seen—but then hedges his historical tale by adding that "Lucretia, daughter of Pompeius, is said to have been among the masked murderers, and the axe was the one that killed her father, which she had preserved for twenty years for her revenge."[35] Theodore de Saussure wrote an early dramatic version of Jenatsch's life in 1868. He set the climactic murder of Jenatsch at a ball, held to celebrate Jenatsch's entirely fictional marriage to Clothilde von Travers—yet another invented woman in his life.[36] Lucretia enters the ballroom with masked men and announces Jenatsch's doom:

The time is over for vain threats.
From the tomb you are called with grave words,
By Pompeius Planta, speaking through my mouth.[37]

In Saussure's version, the hired men use swords, not an axe, to bring Jenatsch down, with Lucretia as the avenging angel who led them on.

By far the most influential version of the Lucretia myth appeared in Conrad Ferdinand Meyer's novel. He was the first to combine the motif of revenge with that of love. Indeed, the relationship between Lucretia and Jenatsch forms the core of his novel, beginning with the very first scene. There, the young Lucretia, still just a girl, sends a message to her childhood hero Jenatsch: "Guardati, Giorgio" (Watch out, George), she writes, because she knows that her father is planning the murder of Protestants in the Valtellina where Jenatsch is serving as a pastor. Meyer even rendered his fictional Jenatsch several years younger than the real man in order to make a childhood friendship between the two plausible, and he transplanted Jenatsch as a boy from Samedan in the Engadine to Scharans, close to the Planta castle of Rietberg.[38] We learn later in the novel that the teenage Jenatsch protected Lucretia when she was a child from her reckless cousin Rudolf, and that they had exchanged gifts while he was a student in Zurich. This strong childhood tie forms the foundation for what comes later in Meyer's story. At the beginning of the novel, Jenatsch is already married to another (fictional) woman, Lucia, who was his only convert as he preached in the hostile Valtellina village of Berbenno. She, the most beautiful and faithful of wives, dies violently during the Valtellina massacre, which Jenatsch flees with her lifeless body in his arms. Before Jenatsch can act on his love for Lucretia, though, politics intervenes: after helping murder Pompeius von Planta, he leads the resistance against the Austrian and Spanish invasions. As a result, he must then flee Graubünden and enter Venetian service until the day of liberation.

In book 2 of Meyer's novel, titled simply "Lucretia," the profoundly torn relationship between the two lovers develops further. When they meet at the Duke of Rohan's palazzo in Venice, Jenatsch offers Lucretia his life:

> You shall have your right, Lucretia. The man who murdered Planta owes you his life. Here he presents himself, and awaits your decision. He is yours, twice yours, since the boy would have offered himself already. Since I laid hand on your father, you must hate my existence, unless I can put it into service in place of thousands of our people. . . . Think, Lucretia von Planta. You must make the decision, who has the greatest right to my blood: Graubünden, or you?[39]

Here, and in a second pivotal scene set at the summit of the San Bernardino Pass, Jenatsch acknowledges Lucretia's power over him. Meyer thus turns their love into a kind of fateful bargain: as long as he serves their fatherland faithfully, she will not claim the revenge that is hers. Rather, they will work together, though rarely seeing each other, to ensure that Graubünden regains its honor and independence. In Meyer's imagination, Jenatsch's success thus leads directly to his death sentence as well. At the end of the novel, he has reached his goal and restored the Three Leagues. His boundless ambition and egoistical drive remain untamed, however,

Figure 6.1 The murder of Jenatsch, after Meyer. Jenatsch, center, defends himself with
a candlestick against masked men and a bear. Lucretia stands before him with her axe.
Xylographic print based on an original painting by E. Sturtevant. By permission of
the Rätisches Museum, Chur (H 1972, 1748).

and he is well on his way to making himself absolute ruler over Graubünden. In-
timidated and overawed, the magistrates of Chur prepare a festival to celebrate the
new Spanish treaty, but the party ends when the news of Henri de Rohan's death
arrives.[40] Most of the guests abandon the ballroom, but Jenatsch refuses to postpone his moment of glory and ignores Lucretia's warning, once again, to watch
out. He is thus isolated and vulnerable when Rudolf von Planta and his men arrive
to murder him. At the crucial moment, though, when Jenatsch is already bleeding
from countless wounds, Lucretia seizes and swings the fatal axe: she must be the
one to kill him, because Jenatsch is *hers*!

   At the heart of Meyer's novel, and of many other literary versions of Jenatsch's
life, we thus find an attempt to bring unity to his complex identity and frequent
boundary crossings by personalizing his motivations and connecting them to influential women in his life. Although the exact configuration that each writer used
was different, they shared two crucial convictions: that human beings have a coherent core identity that can explain all of their actions, if only understood correctly, and that both good and bad politics rest fundamentally on the personal
character and emotional attachments of political heroes. For the novelist Meyer as
for the historian Reber, Jenatsch could save Graubünden, despite his bad character,

because of his love for his nation. For the novelist, moreover, his love for a woman, Lucretia, shaped and enhanced his national love. Only she could tame the demonic side of her lover, and only her forbearance, holding back from the revenge that was hers, freed him to unfold his patriotic love. When the demons of ambition and lust finally won out in Meyer's Jenatsch, Lucretia was the only one entitled to claim his life.

Such concern for personal identity and its coherence in these authors leads to a curious concern that crops up in several versions of Jenatsch's life: that Jenatsch is in danger of "losing his self." For writers convinced that they could uncover Jenatsch's true identity, it made sense that the conflicting forces in his soul put him at risk of losing his true self. In the view of a patriotic writer like Reber, "Graubünden's pastor and hero" faced a conflict between his better self, defined by love of fatherland, and his demonic self, defined by love of himself.[41] Despite the deeds he accomplished for Graubünden, Jenatsch's failure was to let his egoism win out in both his public and his private life, and it was that failure that justified, even required, that he be murdered at the end of his saga. In Meyer's version, too, love of the fatherland—passionate, but also domesticated because it lay under the power of a woman, Lucretia—faced a self-love so consuming that Jenatsch lost all sense of reality by the end of the novel. In the climactic scene that culminates in Lucretia's killing of Jenatsch, he displays a wildness that violates discipline and propriety. Refusing to give up the feast in his honor after hearing the news of Rohan's death, Meyer's Jenatsch greets Lucretia's arrival ecstatically:

> Welcome, Lucretia . . . you bring me joy! The world has become flat, gifts and honors nauseate me! Give me my young, fresh soul again! I lost my soul long ago, but it stayed with you.[42]

As wild dancing fills the room, he seeks to sweep her out of her world into his, until the murderers' arrival interrupts him.

Theodore de Saussure makes the danger that Jenatsch will lose his self even more explicit, if less romantic. Saussure's play opens with a scene between Jenatsch and his mother—another figure invented by the playwright, since we know almost nothing about the real woman. In the drama, the two are about to hold their evening prayer in the Valtellina parish of Berbenno, but Jenatsch is distracted: during his sermon the day before, he saw a beautiful woman in the congregation, and now he knows no rest. His mother recognizes the threat at once: "Enough! You speak in a fever! You no longer have control over yourself. Conquer yourself!" After all, her son's identity as pastor and champion of his faith should be clear. Alas, her worst fears are fulfilled. Driven by his yearning for the woman, Clothilde von Travers, Jenatsch abandons his vocation as pastor and takes up the sword. He hopes to love a noble lady and to revenge his mother's death at the hand of the brutal Catholic mob. Saussure's firmly Protestant point of view did not stop him from adopting the typical covert admiration of Jenatsch's forcefulness. Even so, for Saussure, Jenatsch's choice to lay down his spiritual weapons required him to lose his true self once again.

Variations on the Bloody Axe

Despite all of the mutations that Jenatsch's story experienced at the hands of dramatists, poets, and novelists, many held fast to one crucial element whose roots lay in popular mythology: the identity of the fatal axe. From anonymous tales in the eighteenth century to Daniel Schmid's motion picture, the axe kept on coming back. A few authors, to be sure, chose other weapons both for Pompeius von Planta and for Jenatsch himself. In Richard Voss's much-maligned stage version from 1893, for example, Jenatsch kills Pompeius in a duel with swords, though Pompeius's ghost does choose an axe for his revenge at the end of the play.[43] Saussure, too, gives no details about Planta's murder, and the revenge at his version's climax takes place with daggers.[44] In Hans von Mühlestein's *Death and the Dictator* from 1933, Lucretia shoots Jenatsch, though the bloody deed does take place in the historically documented tavern.[45]

Most authors, though, followed both historical evidence and narrative impulses as they worked out their versions of the "same axe." After all, both Planta and Jenatsch *had* in fact been killed with axes, according to the best contemporary documents. Moreover, the brutal violence that such a weapon vividly conveyed also suited many narrative agendas, from moral revulsion to shocked fascination. In this respect, then, Meyer's version may have been the most influential, but it was not particularly original. Indeed, the most creative version I have found came from Peter Conradin von Planta. After his 1848 drama discussed earlier, he wrote three more versions of Jenatsch's story, and one of them has the best "axe story" of all. In 1885—that is, after Meyer's novel had become a best-seller—and still a convinced Protestant and liberal, Planta wrote his *Jenatsch und Lucretia*.[46] The story begins with Pompeius von Planta, who feels threatened by Jenatsch's passionate preaching from the pulpit in Scharans. To end this threat, Planta takes an axe to the pulpit, though he follows up this hostile act with an offer to Jenatsch to become a captain in a foreign regiment. Jenatsch wavers, but the image of the shattered pulpit enters his mind, and he resists the temptation to lose himself:

> Am I still Jörg Jenatsch? And can I now,
> turn my back on those ruins like a coward,
> and quietly let my country's freedom be strangled,
> though I just called the people to defend it?

Instead, Jenatsch goes to Thusis, where he helps have Pompeius declared guilty of treason. To carry out the bloody verdict, Jenatsch uses the very same axe that

Planta used to destroy his pulpit. Lucretia—no lover in this version—urges her husband, Travers, to take revenge. Naturally, the same busy axe once again ends Jenatsch's life. This version is thus unique in putting the axe to use not twice, but three times. The bloody axe obviously made for a powerful and romantic story. Still, the lack of success that Planta's three-ring version encountered suggests that even the best motif can be pushed too far.

Demystifying the Hero: Jenatsch after the World Wars

Jenatsch's story inspired many authors—indeed, many more than are discussed here. What ensured his renewed entry into historical memory, even beyond Graubünden, was the success of a single book: Conrad Ferdinand Meyer's novel, *Jürg Jenatsch*. After appearing as a magazine serial in 1874, the book officially came out in 1876. Sales were slow at first, but they steadily increased. Ever since the author issued his definitive revision of the novel in 1885, it has been nearly constantly in print. As a recent Internet review at a German bookseller's site suggests, "The book is not just for people about to go to Graubünden on vacation, but also for people who would like to read about a Swiss hero, for once."[47] More important, the book became a standard assignment in Graubünden's secondary schools, ensuring that for most of the local population, Meyer's Jenatsch is the one they know best—or, for most people, simply the only Jenatsch they know.

This does not mean that serious scholars, along with the many literary scholars who continue to study Meyer's novel, stopped writing about the historical Jenatsch. One key figure was Ernst Haffter, who wrote a full-scale biography of Jenatsch in 1894 that was based on extensive research in multiple archives. Like most earlier historians, Haffter came from a Protestant milieu oriented toward the liberal state, and his assessment of Jenatsch emphasizes patriotism as Jenatsch's decisive virtue. Haffter's narrative certainly made use of the chroniclers, but he was able to avoid many misinterpretations by comparing what Sprecher, Juvalta, and Salis said to actual documents and letters from the period. In 1936, a second definitive biography appeared. Its author, Alexander Pfister, was a Catholic from Graubünden who gave the question of Jenatsch's religious conversion special attention from a more sympathetic eye. Pfister expanded on Haffter's research by drawing on further archives outside Switzerland, and he also collected and edited all of Jenatsch's surviving letters for publication. Beyond these major works, various specific issues—above all, the question of who murdered Jenatsch—have led to a number of essays and articles that are available to the interested reader.

Jenatsch's real success in the later twentieth century, however, was not in the scholarly realm. Our hero owes his modern public prominence to the fact that his story—or rather, Meyer's version of his story—is so well known. The wide variety of readers acquainted with Meyer's Jenatsch, from schoolchildren to tourists to fans of historical novels, resulted in an audience primed for new uses of the myth.

To close our analysis, we will focus on two areas in particular: newer dramatizations of Jenatsch's life in novels and film, and the public deployment of "Jenatschiana" for marketing and tourism. Prime examples on the literary side include Hans Mohler's 1960 novel, Reto Hänni's 1988 literary commentary, and Daniel Schmid's 1987 film; a brief look at Hotel Jenatsch, the Jenatsch Alpine shelter, and a new public sculpture in Chur, *Lucretia's Tears*, will follow.

Looking at the post-1945 literature on Jenatsch, one striking difference from earlier versions becomes immediately visible. Jenatsch may still be fascinating, but he has lost his aura of heroism. Accompanying this shift is a second, subtler change: although various artists continue to draw on the key motifs we have already seen, including the fatal axe, they no longer take these stories at face value. Earlier authors seemed attracted to moments of high drama because they made the story itself exciting; modern authors, in contrast, seem to approach the same moments with skepticism or irony. One clear example appears in the way Hans Mohler sets up the story of the axe in his novel, *The Battle with the Dragon: A Jenatsch Novel*. Mohler himself is a prolific author of historical novels as well as a published local historian. In his novel about Jenatsch, he makes careful use of the historical sources, though of course he also adds a great deal of detail and personal conversation from his imagination. Drawing on his profound knowledge of local culture and history, he seeks to capture the excitement and danger of the 1620s and 1630s without diverging from the evidence as Meyer did. Even so, the way Mohler frames Jenatsch's death reveals much about the cultural changes of the postwar era.

The outline of Jenatsch's fate in Mohler's novel follows the real events, but the motivations that Mohler provides the various characters are quite different. In Mohler's novel, as in reality, Jenatsch quickly accumulates enemies after the expulsion of the French in 1637. His political ambitions alienate the magistrates and public officials, while his social ambition to join the nobility infuriates the existing local noble families. His fellow officers resent Jenatsch's influence with the Spanish and Austrians and his control over the flow of money that follows it, while older enemies lurk, hoping to revenge Pompeius von Planta, Giacomo Ruinelli, and even Zambra Prevost, who had died in Thusis. Mohler follows Mathis Berger's theory that the prime conspirators were Johan Guler, a young (and hotheaded) officer, and Heinrich Otto von Schauenstein, a local magnate supposedly offended by events that had taken place in his private feudal domain of Haldenstein, across the Rhine from Chur.[48] Mohler adds his own twist to the story in a conversation he depicts between Guler and Schauenstein. Guler speaks first:

> "Do you know who's in Chur? The castellan Rudolf von Planta and Captain Prevost. That puts a new face on things. Everyone will assume that the son of Pompeius and the son of old Zambra have taken the step to blood revenge . . ."
> "Blood revenge after nearly 20 years?" Schauenstein laughed. "Not even the thickest Bündner is that stupid. If those two brave boys had wanted to avenge their fathers, they would already have found a hundred chances."

"Who adds up the number in such a case? Besides, we could reinforce the idea of blood vengeance a little. Every one knows that Pompeius was struck down with an axe. We should absolutely use an axe, too. Then, all someone has to do is claim that it is the *same* axe, and that Pompeius' blood was still clinging to it. The people suck up that kind of story like honey!"[49]

In Mohler's version, the story of the same axe becomes an intentional rumor spread to divert attention from the real murderers. Though "the people" may love the myth, sophisticated men like Mohler (and his readers) know that such a story is *too* perfect to have happened outside of a novel. After all, Mohler must have known when he wrote the novel that the old version of the story would not be enough to titillate his audience, since most of them would already be familiar with Meyer's version. As a novelist, he therefore sought to surprise his readers and engage them by interpreting the events in a new way. Making the "same axe" a ploy rather than the climax of Jenatsch's life adds another layer of sophistication. Mohler's distancing tactic turns his own ending into a comment on the fact that Meyer's novel took the old myth too literally. Such ironic emphasis on the machinery of storytelling characterizes much post-1945 literature. Even though it relies more closely on the historical sources, therefore, Mohler's book adopts a sensibility that undermines both the nineteenth century's willingness to accept dramatic narrative principles like patriotism or personal character, as well as the seventeenth-century reality of Jenatsch's struggles over power, wealth, and faith.

Daniel Schmid's film version of *Jenatsch* confirms that Mohler's turn was no fluke, since Schmid builds his whole movie around the way history becomes entangled in myth. The movie's protagonist, Christoph Sprecher, is a journalist from Zurich assigned to interview a decrepit archaeologist named Tobler. After reviewing an old newsreel reporting Tobler's excavation of George Jenatsch's tomb in the 1950s, Sprecher visits the old man, who leads him through a step-by-step reenactment of Jenatsch's murder in 1639.[50] Tobler describes Lucretia standing across the room and hypnotically driving the murderer on with her commanding gaze as the axe falls on Jenatsch's head. Sprecher leaves, entranced by the tale, with a souvenir he steals: a metal bell that Tobler claimed was found in Jenatsch's skeletal hand in his grave. Although Sprecher's editor wants him to work on a tourist story about the Glacier-Express railway, Sprecher becomes absorbed instead by the bloody tale of Jenatsch. He finds his way to the isolated castle of Rietberg (which the director places high in the mountains, rather than in the fertile Domleschg Valley, where it is really located). The proprietress, a Lady von Planta, shows him the chimney where Pompeius von Planta tried to hide from his murderers, and the axe that laid Planta low, still preserved in the castle's tower. Sprecher asks whether it is really the same axe, and Lady von Planta answers that only time separates the axe from the one that killed Jenatsch: "His legend *is* his truth," she insists, "and what we call history is entirely fiction." As Sprecher fidgets with the mysterious bell, she dismisses him with the odd words: "We will meet again. But for now, avoid people; the Black Death is coming to Chur!"[51]

Indeed, the bell seems to operate as a kind of time machine. As he leaves the castle, Sprecher finds that his taxi has vanished. A peasant with a horse-drawn cart picks him up instead and deposits him in a hamlet where he sees a procession carrying shrouded corpses by hand. He has landed briefly in the seventeenth century! For the remainder of the film, each time the bell rings—even on tape—Sprecher is transported to another scene from Jenatsch's life. His wife, Nina, tries to hold him back, but to no avail. When he returns to Rietberg with Nina, for example, the bell falls from the table, and suddenly it is Sprecher himself who gives away Pompeius von Planta's hiding place to Jenatsch and his band of killers—and he does so in Romansh, a language he does not even speak. At the climax of the film, it is Carnival time in Chur—first in the twentieth century, but then in the seventeenth century. Sprecher finds Lucretia von Planta guiding him to the Staubiges Hüetli pub, where her commanding gaze drives him to take up the axe and strike down Jenatsch. As Jenatsch dies, he clutches Sprecher's carnival costume, pulling off a bell that will be buried with him, and eventually come to the mysterious archaeologist Tobler. Schmid's film thus intertwines past and present in complex ways. As another sinister historian explains to Sprecher, such experiences are like windows on a past life.

Schmid further emphasizes the confusion between experience, history, and myth with frequent postmodern comments on his own narrative. For example, he includes repeated shots taken through the windows of passing trains, during which Sprecher keeps glimpsing characters from his own story and from Jenatsch's. Other parts of the story are seen from multiple perspectives. Pompeius von Planta's murder is filmed through a mirror, while the mysterious Lady von Planta in the modern Rietberg reappears as an innkeeper in one of the flashbacks. How could Tobler, the mysterious archaeologist who had robbed the grave not only of the magical bell, but also of Jenatsch's real skull, know such precise details about Jenatsch's murder—and why did the events he reconstructed draw on the novels and plays, not the historical record? By telling the story, Schmid suggests, Tobler in some sense made it true: "His legend *is* his truth." If the viewer has any doubts about the ironic subtext, Schmid (who was himself a Bündner) uses a comment from Sprecher's editor to drive the point home: "Those poor people in Graubünden: First a Zurich novelist [that is, Meyer] imposed Jenatsch on them as a national hero, now another man from Zurich [the archaeologist, Tobler] has stolen him back again!"

A few years later, another Bündner had the chance to respond to the multiple Jenatsches that populated the region's imagination in the late twentieth century. Noted author Reto Hänny confronts the shards and echoes of history, novel, and film in his essay "Giorgio, Guardati," an afterword to the 1988 edition of Meyer's *Jürg Jenatsch*. Hänny opens by noting that he became acquainted with the historical figure and the novel when he encountered a copy—of the 246th printing!—in his grandfather's bookstore as a boy. "Every Bündner person has been burned by Jenatsch, more or less," he confesses. He and his friends imagined their childhood rivalries "as though we fought the hated Planta clan with halberds and nail-spiked staffs"; riding his bicycle to visit his teenage girlfriend, he felt like Jenatsch searching for Lucretia's lighted window as he made his way down the Domleschg Valley.[52] Romantic versions of Jenatsch's life circulated long before Meyer's novel and continue to circulate today. Hänny repeatedly sets the historical record against the multiple stories and diverse personalities attributed to Jenatsch—from seventeenth-century libels to depictions by Meyer, Mohler, and Schmid—both by quoting or evoking other versions, and by using a fragmented parenthetic style that constantly suspends completion of any sentence about Jenatsch. Hänny concludes by repeating a claim that Hans Mohler had already made: "Jürg Jenatsch lies buried not in the cathedral in Chur, but between the two covers of a book."[53]

The Popular Jenatsch

As twentieth-century literature lost itself in considering the fragmentations that the constant mirroring of history and fiction had produced in the case of Jenatsch, more practical Bündner—"burned by Jenatsch," to be sure, but less concerned about the slippery identity of a man they knew primarily through Meyer's novel—put him and his story to use. One key turning point was the 1959 excavation of Jenatsch's grave in the cathedral in Chur. The local newspapers and even the Swiss national media carried the story, and Jenatsch's remains, especially his clothing, were put on display for audiences ranging from schoolchildren to tour groups. Graubünden has been a tourist destination almost since Jenatsch died, as illustrated by the captivating watercolors of the Dutch artist Jan Haeckert, which showed off the dramatic terrain and ended up in the imperial collections in Vienna.[54] As tourism grew to be Graubünden's preeminent industry, anchored by the great ski complexes in Davos and St. Moritz, a little historical color belonged to good marketing. The Hotel Chesa Guardalej in St. Moritz, "charmingly built in the typical Engadine style," for example, offers its Jenatsch restaurant with "international cuisine and excellent fish specialties."[55] The well-fed mountain climber can then set out for the Chammana Jenatsch, a mountaineering hut located at an altitude of 8,700 feet on the slopes of the Piz Bernina above the Engadine. In addition to running water in both summer and winter, the hut offers local meals accompanied, appropriately, with wine from the Valtellina. Of course, evocation of a vaguely remembered hero is more suitable for advertising than details about Jenatsch's less attractive identities as murderer, traitor, or apostate. None of the tourist enterprises offer much detail about Jenatsch's life on their Web sites, though the hotels no doubt keep a copy of Meyer's novel handy for the curious visitor.

Even more recently, the current restoration project in the Chur cathedral included Jenatsch and his life in its recent newsletter: "One of the best-known names found, together with his coat-of-arms and an inscription, on a cathedral gravestone is that of the Bündner freedom fighter Jörg Jenatsch."[56] The newsletter is historically careful, using the name Jörg, for example—historically defensible, yet close enough to the form that most people recognize, Jürg. Yet history and myth can no longer be separated, as the text makes clear: "His name became famous above all because of Conrad Ferdinand Meyer's novel *Jürg Jenatsch*, which stylized him as a heroic figure and allegory of Graubünden's striving for liberty and independence."[57] The same search for balance is apparent in the new public sculpture and fountain sponsored by the cantonal bank of Graubünden in 2006. Located at the site of the original Staubiges Hüetli bar where Jenatsch died, the fountain is called *Tears of Lucretia*. On a nearby wall, two official plaques tell first the historical story, then the mythical version according to Meyer.[58] Like Daniel Schmid in his film and Reto Hänny in his essays, even the sober authors of a diocesan newsletter and careful bank employees demonstrate through their approach that the historical Jenatsch and the character from fiction have become irrevocably entangled at the beginning of the twenty-first century.

Epilogue

THE PAST, THE PRESENT, AND MAGIC BELLS

George Jenatsch's remains are buried again—probably. After 1959, the contents of his grave in the Chur cathedral floor, including the damaged skull that archaeologist Erik Hug removed, received careful study for several years. The Swiss National Historical Museum restored the luxurious clothing Jenatsch died in and identified the various objects in his grave. In 1972, the clothing and objects (but not his bones) went on display in a glass case as part of the treasures of the Chur cathedral.[1] Some scientific examination of the bones took place between 1959 and 1961, including a dental examination, before Hug apparently took them to his private residence in Zurich. After that, however, their fate becomes uncertain. According to the cantonal archaeological service of Graubünden, "regarding the bones we must consider it very likely that in 1961 they found their way back into the grave, including the skull."[2] Hug definitely kept several pieces of trim from Jenatsch's clothing, and a former colleague later suggested that he kept some small pieces of bone for further research, though this cannot be confirmed.[3] If so, they are probably lost, as are all of Hug's notes from the excavation. In fact, even the exact location in the cathedral where Jenatsch's body was found, and perhaps returned, is once again unknown, according to the archaeological service.[4] Meanwhile, stories about his bones' fate circulate among historians interested in Jenatsch, including one that Jenatsch's bones only returned to Chur after the canton sent a uniformed policeman to retrieve them from Hug, who never had permission to remove them in the first place.[5]

As these final notes about his story illustrate, Jenatsch still resists packaging, no matter how tempting it is to wrap him up neatly. His clothes may now be in a museum case and his bones might be mostly back in his grave, but the historian writing about Jenatsch in the twenty-first century encounters the same challenge as those in the seventeenth, eighteenth, nineteenth, or twentieth centuries did: where does truth end and myth begin? As is the case for all historical figures, close study of Jenatsch and his career reveals that he was more complex than the stories we are able to tell about him: he eludes even the most determined efforts to pin him down definitively. Yet this complexity also offers a real opportunity to understand not just the man, but also the culture that shaped him and his identity, in ways that give us genuine insight.

We see this, for example, in Jenatsch's shifting relationship to the spaces he lived in—the Engadine, the Three Leagues, the Holy Roman Empire, and western Europe as a whole. His attachment to the narrower space of Graubünden became manifest through his repeated returns to it throughout his career. He spent years outside Graubünden, especially during the terrible 1620s, but even then, each swing of events in his party's favor drew him quickly back. The dramatists and historians of the 1800s therefore correctly saw Jenatsch's behavior as revealing his strong connection to his native territory and the people there—his patriotism, in short. Yet closer examination of what he said and did during those years also shows him willing to shift his territorial and political loyalties. At the local scale, we can see this in his marriage and settlement in Davos, in a different league and with a different language from his native Engadine. When he died, moreover, he was angling for a lordship entirely outside Graubünden, which would establish his noble status and reward him for his role in bringing the Three Leagues into the Habsburg orbit. Perhaps he would have continued to live in Chur, serving the Austrian and Spanish cause by rebuilding the Three Leagues as their ally—but it is equally easy to imagine that his ambition would have drawn him to more promising places once they became open to him, such as Vienna, the seat of Habsburg power, or Germany, where marauding armies still provided their mercenary colonels with both power and wealth. How should we assess his local loyalties, then? Even though we can never know whether Jenatsch would have left Graubünden behind, his life clearly does reveal how seventeenth-century patriotism was layered, with parallel and sometimes conflicting attachments to a locality, its people, and ways, on the one hand, and to the trans-European institutions and movements that generated such violence in the period, on the other.

Similarly, Jenatsch's changing statements and actions when religion was at stake may give us only a clouded understanding of his own faith, but they do highlight the shifting relationship between spiritual and political engagement at a pivotal point in European culture and its history. The zeal that drove the young Reformed pastor to participate in the torture of Nicolò Rusca changed after Jenatsch experienced not just the Valtellina massacre of 1620, but the painful years of forced proselytizing and violence that Graubünden suffered afterward. By the time Jenatsch converted to Catholicism, his commitment was different, as shown in his actions. Some saw his willingness to tolerate Protestantism—even in his wife and children—as proof that his conversion was merely a political sham, but this view cannot explain all of his behavior. Lacking a mirror on his soul, any firmer conclusions rest on mere speculation. We should therefore leave Jenatsch's personal religious identity uncertain in our own minds, recognizing that his behavior did not fit any simple pattern. Nevertheless, his life certainly does illustrate how the connection between religious and political loyalties was changing by the 1630s, despite the torrents of pious rhetoric on all sides.

Another, quite different challenge to understanding Jenatsch is that his life—and especially his most unusual murder—began generating myths immediately after he died. Who could resist connecting the axe that killed him to his own part in the murder of Pompeius von Planta, after all? Generation after generation interpreted Jenatsch through their particular expectations about motivation, character, and destiny, and those interpretations have inescapably become part of our own access to his slippery identity. Nowhere is this clearer than among the chroniclers who knew him personally. Their concerns (and their various reasons for hating him) shaped later images of Jenatsch in lasting ways, since their material was the most readily available when writers after 1800 regained interest in Jenatsch. In particular, the first serious biography, by Balthasar Reber, and the most influential literary version, by Conrad Ferdinand Meyer, relied almost entirely on the chronicles from Jenatsch's lifetime in shaping new representations of Jenatsch. Even though these two authors molded Jenatsch's image to reflect their own nineteenth-century anxieties—the peculiarity of Swiss nationalism or the tension between personal virtue and political necessity—they nevertheless relied on the old chronicles not just for raw material, but for judgments about what had really mattered in the seventeenth century. Only later, in 1894 and 1936, did biographers like Ernst Haffter and Alexander Pfister delve into the mounds of routine documents in various European archives, a process that is still going on—and when they did, other dimensions of Jenatsch's experience began to emerge. Haffter's careful examination of Jenatsch's Venetian service, like Pfister's recovery of Jenatsch's letters after his conversion, revealed that the early chroniclers had left out a great deal. More recent research has opened up further areas to our view, such as Jenatsch's entanglement in the Bündner networks of kinship and blood feud.[6]

Meyer's great novel, in turn, shaped the imagination not only of later novelists and playwrights, but also of later historians. Even those aware that Meyer's story strayed from the evidence, for example, had to find creative ways to retell Jenatsch's story to an audience who "knew" that Lucretia von Planta had murdered him. For the historians, this usually meant contrasting the authority of documentary evidence with popular memory as a way to attract interest. For artists, the challenge was to reimagine their narratives by playing off the elements that most readers expected—like Hans Mohler's recasting of the "same axe" as a ruse rather than reality. Meanwhile, advertisers catering to the public simply echoed Meyer's story, while more "serious" institutions, like the Catholic Church when remodeling its cathedral or the cantonal bank when sponsoring a memorial to Jenatsch's murder, awkwardly juxtaposed the historical and the literary Jenatsch in their productions.

Today as much as ever, then, Jenatsch allows us to see how historical and artistic representations of humans in the past remain entangled. One last anecdote I heard as I was finishing my research on Jenatsch illustrates this particularly well. Daniel Schmid's film *Jenatsch*, discussed earlier, intentionally confuses the historical experience of Jenatsch and the seventeenth century with the personalities of journalists, archaeologists, and common Bündner in the twentieth century. Near the beginning of the film, the journalist Sprecher interviews the mysterious archaeologist, called Tobler in the film, who excavated Jenatsch from the Chur cathedral floor. The old man reenacts Jenatsch's murder for Sprecher, foreshadowing a later scene in which Sprecher, transported through time by the magical bell, finds himself swinging the axe that kills Jenatsch.

In September 2007, while I was having dinner with several Swiss colleagues, the well-known Bündner historian Jon Mathieu told me how the filmmaker had gotten the idea for this unusual scene.[7] While still a young scholar, Mathieu received a commission to write an essay on recent Jenatsch research for a new edition of Alexander Pfister's biography, which had not been updated since 1951. As part of his work for this project, Mathieu interviewed Erik Hug, the archaeologist who conducted the 1959 excavations.[8] As Mathieu told me in 2007, Hug had in fact reenacted Jenatsch's murder for him, almost exactly as it occurs in the film. Moreover, when Daniel Schmid, a Bündner who had long enjoyed Meyer's novel, was planning a movie version, he consulted with Mathieu: Switzerland is a small country, and Mathieu had just finished an article about Jenatsch, after all. Mathieu not only relayed the anecdote about the eccentric archaeologist to the filmmaker, but did his best to persuade Schmid to go beyond Meyer's novel in conceiving his script. What seems a fanciful invention in a film by a postmodernist auteur thus rests on actual events.

Shortly after this conversation, I inspected Jenatsch's clothing, which is temporarily in the custody of the cantonal museum in Chur while the cathedral is renovated. The display case with Jenatsch's tunic, undergarments, and other items from his grave has been moved to the museum's storage area in a bombproof underground bunker outside Chur.[9] A friendly museum staffer guided me to a glass case, whose contents are still arranged as they have been since 1976. Two mannequins hold Jenatsch's outer clothing, while the objects that were buried with him, such as the scapular, the rosary, and several small medals, are laid out on the floor of the case. Detailed labels carefully explain the significance of each piece of clothing, the scapular, the rosary and the medals. Only one object in the case, mysteriously, has no label at all: a small metal bell.

Notes

Abbreviations

Anhorn, *Krieg*	Bartholomäus Anhorn. *Graw-Pünter-Krieg, beschrieben von Barthol. Anhorn 1603–1629. Nach dem Manuscript zum ersten Mal herausgegeben.* Ed. Conradin von Moor. Chur: Verlag der Antiquariatsbuchhandlung, 1873.
BK	Traugott Schiess, ed., *Bullingers Korrespondenz mit den Graubündnern.* Quellen zur Schweizer Geschichte, o.s., vols. 23–25 (Basel: Verlag der Basler Buch- und Antiquariatshandlung, 1904–1906; Nieuwkoop: B. de Graaf, 1968).
Briefe	Alexander Pfister, ed., *Jörg Jenatsch: Briefe, 1614–1639* (Chur: Terra Grischuna Buchverlag, 1983).
Gartmann	Balzer Gartmann, *Georg Jenatsch in der Literatur* (Disentis: Buchdruckerei Conradau, 1946).
Haffter	Ernst Haffter, *Georg Jenatsch: Ein Beitrag zur Geschichte der Bündner Wirren* (Davos: Hugo Richter, 1894).
JM	Fritz Jecklin, ed., *Materialien zur Standes- und Landesgeschichte Gem. III Bünde (Graubünden), 1464–1803*, 2 vols. (Basel: Basler Buch- und Antiquariatshandlung, 1907–1909).
Juvalta	Fortunat von Juvalta, *Denkwürdigkeiten des Fortunat von Juvalta, 1567–1649*, ed. Conradin von Moor (Chur: O. Hitz, 1848).
Meyer	Conrad Ferdinand Meyer, *Jürg Jenatsch: Eine Bündnergeschichte* (Munich: Wilhelm Goldmann Verlag, 1984 [based on the 1885 Leipzig edition]).
Pfister	Alexander Pfister, *Georg Jenatsch: Sein Leben und seine Zeit*, 5th ed. (Chur: Verlag Bündner Monatsblatt, 1991).
Sprecher	Fortunat von Sprecher, *Geschichte der bündnerischen Kriegen und Unruhen*, ed. and trans. Conradin von Mohr, 2 vols. (Chur: Leonhard Hitz, 1856).
StAGR	Staatsarchiv Graubünden, Chur, Switzerland.
StAZH	Staatsarchiv Zürich, Zurich, Switzerland.
Urkundenbuch	Ernst Haffter, ed., *Georg Jenatsch: Urkundenbuch, enthaltend Exkurse und Beilagen* (Chur: n.p., 1895). (Also published as part of Haffter's biography of Jenatsch.)
VAD	Vadianische Sammlung, St. Gallische Kantonsbibliothek, St. Gallen, Switzerland.

Zinsli   Philip Zinsli, ed., "Politische Gedichte aus der Zeit der Bündner
                                Wirren 1603–1639. Texte," *Jahresbericht der Historisch-antiquitarische*
                                Gesellschaft Graubündens 40 (1911): 107–239; and 41 (1911): 23–120.
                                (Citations follow internal pagination.)

Prologue

1. What Jenatsch was called—Georg? Jörg? Jürg?—is one of the issues this book will discuss. I have chosen to name him not by one of his contemporary names, but by the modern English equivalent, George. Using the English makes no presuppositions about his linguistic identity, in contrast to using any of the names he used during his life.

2. "Das Grab des Jürg Jenatsch," *Neue Bündner Zeitung*, August 11, 1959.

3. "Das Grab des Jürg Jenatsch: Ergebnisse der wissenschaftlichen Untersuchung des Fundes," *Der Freie Rätier*, December 24, 1959.

4. "Das Grab," *Neue Bündner Zeitung*, August 11, 1959. The slicing wounds to the skull figured prominently in the press coverage (e.g., "Zu den Ausgrabungen in der Kathedrale in Chur," *Der Freie Rätier*, August 12, 1959.)

5. The leader of the excavation team, Dr. Erik Hug, never published a full report on his dig, which he financed himself after getting permission from the bishop to search for Jenatsch's grave. For a discussion of the results, see Jon Mathieu, "33 Jahre nach Pfisters Jenatsch-Biographie: Neue Forschungsergebnisse und -perspektiven," in Pfister, 491–508, here esp. 492–93.

6. "Das Grab," *Der Freie Rätier*, December 24, 1959.

7. Of course, the English "George" is a name he never used. The actual names that Jenatsch used during his life are analyzed in Norbert Furrer, "Paroles de mercenaire: Aspects sociolinguistiques du service étranger," in *Gente ferocissima: Mercenariat et société en Suisse (XVe–XIXe siècle)*, ed. Lucienne Hubler et al. (Lausanne and Zurich: Editions D'en Bas and Chronos Verlag, 1997), 289–315, esp. 312–13.

8. See the investigational report in *Urkundenbuch*, 156.

9. "Das Grab," *Der Freie Rätier*, December 24, 1959.

10. *Urkundenbuch*, 158. The version in Bartholomäus Anhorn's necrology contains the even bloodier line, "dz das hirn an die wend sprützt" ("so that his brain sprayed against the wall"), ibid., 172.

11. "Jürg Jenatsch—ein großer Sohn Bündens," *Neue Bündner Zeitung*, August 15, 1959.

Introduction

1. Pfister; the German subtitle is *Sein Leben und seine Zeit*. The other standard biography, published in 1894 by Ernst Haffter, carries the title (in German): *Georg Jenatsch: A Contribution to the History of the Troubles in Graubünden*, thus throwing the emphasis onto the "times," not the man. Nevertheless, Haffter's work follows the same chronological narrative structure, focused on Jenatsch's life course, as Pfister's.

Chapter 1

1. A vivid description of economic and agrarian life in premodern Graubünden is in Jon Mathieu, *Bauern und Bären: Eine Geschichte des Unterengadins von 1650 bis 1800* (Chur: Octopus, 1987). Here and in his later work, Mathieu argues that balanced agriculture, including successful cereal crops as well as the lucrative cattle products for export, provided the economic foundation for the region's population.

2. This is illustrated vividly by the complicated and ambiguous border between France and Spain in the 1600s and 1700s, analyzed in Peter Sahlins, *Boundaries: The Making of France and Spain in the Pyrenees* (Berkeley: University of California Press, 1989).

3. For a detailed analysis in English of the political history of Graubünden, see Randolph Head, *Early Modern Democracy in the Grisons* (Cambridge: Cambridge University Press, 1995). The standard reference work for all aspects of Graubünden's history is Jürg Simonett, ed., *Handbuch der Bündner Geschichte*, 4 vols. (Chur: Verlag Bündner Monatsblatt, 2000). See esp. vol. 2, *Frühe Neuzeit*.

4. In its earliest years, this league included eleven members and was sometimes called the Eleven Jurisdictions (*einliff Gerichten*).

5. The Three Leagues' domain in Italy, which Benjamin Barber describes as an "empirette," consisted of three lordships: the Valtellina proper, and the two counties of Chiavenna and Bormio. Barber, *The Death of Communal Liberty: A History of Freedom in a Swiss Mountain Canton* (Princeton, NJ: Princeton University Press, 1974).

6. To an early modern mind, there was no contradiction at all in having a "free republic" with relatively democratic government rule over other men and women who were politically disenfranchised feudal subjects or even serfs. This was the relationship between the Three Leagues and the Valtellina, but also between many other early modern republics and the various lordships that they had bought or conquered.

7. For an overview see Guglielmo Scaramellini, "Die Beziehungen zwischen den Drei Bünden und dem Veltlin, Chiavenna und Bormio," in *Handbuch* vol. 2, 141–60.

8. Still useful is the classic essay by Horatio Brown, "The Valtelline," in *Cambridge Modern History*, ed. A. W. Ward et al., vol. 4, *The Thirty Years' War* (Cambridge: Cambridge University Press, 1906), 35–63. See also Andreas Wendland, *Der Nutzen der Pässe und die Gefährdung der Seelen: Spanien, Mailand und der Kampf ums Veltlin 1620–1641* (Zurich: Chronos, 1995).

9. For an introduction to the complexities of Swiss constitutional history, consult Hans Conrad Peyer, *Verfassungsgeschichte der alten Schweiz* (Zurich: Schulthess, 1978).

10. At least, most members of the Swiss Confederation claimed imperial liberty. Eventually, the Treaty of Basel in 1499 confirmed their liberated status, while the Peace of Westphalia in 1648 removed Switzerland (but not Graubünden) from the Holy Roman Empire entirely.

11. Famously in Samuel Pufendorf, *Severini de Monzambano Veronensis De statu Imperii Germanici ad Lælium fratrem, dominum Trezolani* (Geneva [i.e. Den Haag]: Petrus Columesius [i.e. Adrian Vlacq], 1667) (and many later editions), Chapter VI, §9.

12. I have analyzed the interactions of multiple identities in Graubünden in general in Randolph Head, "Comunità di identità e comunità d'azione nei Grigione in età moderna: le istituzioni politiche, confessionali e linguistiche di una repubblica alpina, 1470–1620," *Archivio Storico Ticinese*, no. 132 (2002): 167–82.

13. Two Swiss dissertations provide a superlative analysis of the leading families in the region during our period: Paul Grimm, *Die Anfänge der Bündner Aristokratie im 15. und 16. Jahrhundert* (Zurich: Juris, 1981); and Silvio Färber, *Der bündnerische Herrenstand im 17. Jahrhundert: Politische, soziale, und wirtschaftliche Aspekte seiner Vorherrschaft* (Zurich: Zentralstelle der Studentenschaft, 1983). More generally on the way powerful families coexisted with nominally "democratic" politics in Switzerland, a condition Hans Conrad Peyer terms "aristodemocracy," see Peyer, "Die Anfänge der schweizerischen Aristokratien," in *Könige, Stadt und Kapital: Aufsätze zur Wirtschafts- und Sozialgeschichte des Mittelalters*, eds. Ludwig Schmugge, Roger Sablonier, and Konrad Wanner (Zurich: Verlag Neue Zürcher Zeitung, 1982), 195–218.

14. The way that the Turkish threat helped hold together an Empire increasingly divided by religion is analyzed masterfully in Winfried Schulze, *Reich und Türkengefahr im späten 16. Jahrhundert* (Munich: C. H. Beck, 1978).

15. Of the many fine recent surveys, I still find Euan Cameron, *The European Reformation* (Oxford: Clarendon, 1991) the most illuminating.

16. See Simonett, ed., *Handbuch*; and Head, "Comunità di identità," for a more detailed discussion.

17. The republication of C. V. Wedgewood, *The Thirty Years War* (1938; repr., New York: New York Review of Books, 2005) provides an extremely readable narrative history of the war. For the place of Graubünden in a larger strategic context, see above all Geoffrey Parker, *The Army of Flanders and the Spanish Road, 1567–1659: The Logistics of Spanish Victory and Defeat in the Low Countries' Wars*, 2nd ed. (Cambridge: Cambridge University Press, 2004).

18. Christian Pfister, *Das Klima der Schweiz von 1525–1860 und seine Bedeutung in der Geschichte von Bevölkerung und Landwirtschaft* (Bern: Paul Haupt, 1984).

19. Haffter, 26n11.

20. Pfister, 24–25.

21. The structure of wealth and poverty in nearby Zuoz is analyzed in detail in Paolo Boringhieri, "Pussaunza, richezza e poverted a Zuoz 1521–1801," *Annalas de la Società Retorumantscha* 102 (1988): 79–201.

22. StAZH E II 101, ff. 334^v, article 9, from November 26, 1606.

23. StAZH E II 101, ff. 333^v, article 7. Article 8 condemned fashionable clothing among the students but was aimed primarily at those from good Zurich families, not at outside students like Jenatsch.

24. Haffter, 33–34.

25. Pfister, 35, citing a letter of August 1, 1616. I rely on Pfister's transcription and translation into German.

26. Pfister, 54, and Haffter, 415–16nn86–87, which discusses the problem of Jenatsch's exact appointment date in detail. His predecessor in Scharans was in office until at least April of 1617, when he received a Venetian cash payment of forty-three gulden—a sizeable sum. Pfister comments only that the predecessor was not reelected by the village because of his lifestyle (*Lebenswandel*).

27. Randolph Head, "'Cetera sunt politica et ad nos nihil': Social Power, Legitimacy and Struggles over the Clerical Voice in Post-Reformation Graubünden," in *Debatten über die Legitimation von Herrschaft: Politische Sprachen in der Frühen Neuzeit*, eds. Luise Schorn-Schutte and Sven Tode (Berlin: Akademie Verlag, 2006), 67–85.

28. Padavino was not only a skilled deal maker, but also an astute observer of Graubünden and Swiss politics, whose reports to his superiors in Venice are one of the best

sources of information about the affairs of this period. See his *Del Governo e Stato dei Signori Svizzeri Relazione*, ed. Victor Ceresole (Venice: Tipografia Antonelli, 1874).

29. These uprisings are analyzed at length in Head, *Early Modern Democracy*; see also Michael Valèr, *Die Bestrafung von Staatsvergehen in der Republik der III Bünde: Ein Beitrag zur mittelalterlichen Rügegerichtsbarkeit und zur Geschichte der Demokratie in Graubünden* (Chur: Schuler, 1904).

30. Pfister, 52.

31. StAGR A II Landesakten 1, August 3, 1618.

32. For a detailed, if confessional, celebration of Rusca with valuable documents, see Giovanni da Prada, *L'Arciprete Nicolò Rusca e i cattolici del suo tempo* (Tirano: Tipografia Poletti, 1994). Prada cites at length from contemporary Catholic reports of Rusca's death, which mention Jenatsch by name only in connection with Rusca's capture in the Valtellina. However, Jenatsch was clearly present during Rusca's torture. Most interesting is a comment in Augustin Stöcklin's report from the 1640s about the details of Rusca's death, noting, "Colonel Jenatsch clearly confessed this, who was formerly a pastor and present at Rusca's death" (Prada, 234).

33. Haffter, 67.

34. Haffter, 68.

35. Haffter reports that Jenatsch received several grants of one hundred gulden—a substantial sum—during 1619, and over three hundred gulden in 1620. Haffter, 70, 80.

36. Pfister, 93. Jenatsch was in Davos in May 1620, toward the end of yet another tribunal, since he wrote a letter from there. Haffter, 433n57. Jon Mathieu, "33 Jahre nach Pfisters Jenatsch-Biographie: Neue Forschungsergebnisse und -perspektiven," in Pfister, 495 note c, notes that the identity of this first wife is not entirely clear, since it could conceivably have been Anna's sister, Katherine. Mathieu's comment, and his careful investigation of the issue, highlights the absence of information about women related to Jenatsch in the historical record.

37. In the Valtellina, the policy was a direct consequence of the Protestant majority among the communes in the Three Leagues, which felt entitled—indeed, obligated—to force their Catholic subjects to make room for the "true religion." Further analysis in Randolph Head, "At the Frontiers of Theory: Confession Formation, Anti-Confessionalization and Religious Change in the Valtellina, 1520–1620," in *Konfessionalisierung und Konfessionskonflikt in Graubünden, 16.–18. Jahrhundert*, eds. Georg Jäger and Ulrich Pfister (Zurich: Chronos, 2006), 163–79.

38. The best analysis of the political shifts in the Valtellina during this period is Wendland, *Der Nutzen*.

39. Haffter, 102.

40. Haffter, 107, citing an anonymous description of Planta's murder. The description was sent to Zurich by the city's commander in Graubünden, Colonel Johann Jakob Steiner, and describes from a participant's perspective how the murder was carried out.

41. The pamphlet carries the ironic title "Bloody Meekness of the Calvinist Pastors." *Blutige Sanfftmuet Der Caluinischen Predicanten: Wahrhaffte Relation auß einer Glaubwürdigen Person Sendschreiben* (n.p., 1621), 4. Microfilm in Flugschriftensammlung Gustav Freytag, #5139. Munich and New York: K. V. Sauer Verlag, 1980–1981.

42. Cited in Haffter, 113; my translation from the Italian.

43. This is our only example of Jenatsch as a poet, assuming he is really the author. The clunky rhymes and forced rhythm do not provide evidence of any particular literary

gifts, at least not in German. The poem is reproduced, with the attribution to Jenatsch, in Pfister, 117–18.

44. Haffter, 122–26.

45. Ernst Haffter already used the term "terroristic" to describe the methods of the "goodhearted" faction in his 1894(!) study of Jenatsch (see, e.g., 105), and he provides a thoughtful analysis of how contemporaries reacted to the rising fear and extremism that characterized both parties (see, e.g., 108–10). Jenatsch and Alexander continued using fear as they tried to build an army: for example, when some communes in the Grey League were slow to provide troops, a band headed by Jenatsch and Alexander stormed into Flims, murdered the local magnate Joseph Capaul, and plundered his house. Haffter, 134.

46. In addition, Austria obtained the right to garrison Chur and Maienfeld for twelve years, ensuring complete control over both the passes and the politics of the region. Haffter, 141.

47. Pfister, 165.

48. A formal proceeding against Jenatsch had been moving ahead slowly, but was wrapped up quickly when his services became useful again: the court voted to acquit him of the charges of insubordination and plotting against the Venetian republic by a vote of 9–5. Pfister, 207.

49. Pfister, 268–69.

50. See esp. Wendland, *Der Nutzen.*

51. See below, chapter 3.

52. The local government that had controlled the Valtellina since the massacre of 1620 was a fourth, less influential player, consistently seeking to disrupt plans that would bring the valley back under the Three Leagues' lordship.

53. Demonstrating this, especially with the use of records from the Milanese and Austrian archives, is a major accomplishment of Pfister's biography.

Chapter 2

1. The expression "imagined communities" is Benedict Anderson's, who connects the rise of national feeling both to the role of the press in spreading such convictions, and to the rise of institutions that confirmed and reproduced the nation's supposedly natural identity, such as national censuses, maps, and museums. Benedict Anderson, *Imagined Communities: Reflections on the Origin and Spread of Nationalism,* rev. ed. (New York: Verso, 1991). Two other seminal authors on this question, which has recently produced a great deal of debate, are Ernest Gellner, *Nations and Nationalism* (Oxford: Blackwell, 1983), and subsequent works; and John Breuilly, *Nationalism and the State* (Manchester: Manchester University Press, 1982), and subsequent works. For Switzerland's odd position in this process, see Olivier Zimmer, *A Contested Nation: History, Memory and Nationalism in Switzerland, 1761–1891* (Cambridge: Cambridge University Press, 2002).

2. *Natio* is formed from the Latin verb *nasci,* "to be born." For a lucid essay tracing European "nations" from the erratic ethnogenesis of the early Middle Ages up to the present, see Patrick Geary, *The Myth of Nations: The Medieval Origins of Europe* (Princeton, NJ: Princeton University Press, 2002).

3. An early, if not entirely satisfactory, effort to frame the questions in relation to early modern Europe is in John Armstrong, *Nations before Nationalism* (Chapel Hill: University of North Carolina Press, 1982).

4. The actual phrase, "*rex imperator in regno suo est*," goes back at least to the thirteenth-century jurist Azo. See Gaines Post, "Medieval and Renaissance Ideas of Nation," *Dictionary of the History of Ideas*, vol. 3: 318–24, online at http://etext.virginia.edu/cgi-local/DHI/dhi.cgi?id=dv3–41 (accessed May 4, 2007). For a revisionist update, see Kenneth Pennington, "Learned Law, Droit Savante, Gelehrtes Recht: The Tyranny of a Concept," *Syracuse International Journal of Law and Commerce* 20 (1994): 205–15.

5. Hans Baron's classic study, *The Crisis of the Early Italian Renaissance: Civic Humanism in an Age of Classicism and Tyranny* (Princeton, NJ: Princeton University Press, 1966), explored this connection in detail.

6. For a broad overview of Alpine history, written by an Engadiner, see Jon Mathieu, *Geschichte der Alpen 1500–1900: Umwelt, Entwicklung, Gesellschaft* (Vienna: Böhlau, 1998).

7. Jon Mathieu's careful analysis of the Lower Engadine, lower in altitude but with less land than the Upper Engadine, indicates that local grain crops were important, but not sufficient to feed the population. Mathieu, *Eine Agrargeschichte der Inneren Alpen* (Zurich: Juris, 1992), 43–116.

8. Based on the data in Mathieu, *Agrargeschichte*, tables 2 and 3, pp. 91–100, with my interpretation of his numbers. By his estimate, the Upper Engadine and Lower Engadine each had about five thousand to six thousand inhabitants.

9. The process is described in detail in Richard Weiss, *Das Alpwesen Graubündens: Wirtschaft, Sachkultur, Recht, Älplerarbeit und Älplerleben* (Zurich: E. Rentsch, 1942); see also Jon Mathieu, *Bauern und Bären: Eine Geschichte des Unterengadins von 1650 bis 1800* (Chur: Octopus, 1987).

10. This expression, in Latin, Romansh, or German, appeared at the beginning of every document issued by the commune.

11. Networks of faction and kin, along with family, will be discussed in chapter 5.

12. Erich Wenneker, "Lemnius, Simon," in *Biographisches-Bibliographisches Kirchenlexicon*, http://www.bautz.de/bbkl/l/Lemnius.shtml (accessed May 4, 2007). A slightly longer introduction can be found in Placidus Plattner, "Einführung," introduction to *Die Rateis: Schweizerisch-Deutscher Krieg von 1499. Epos in IX Gesängen* (Chur: Sprecher und Plattner, 1874), i–xxxviii.

13. G. Meyer von Knonau, "Das Album in Schola Tigurina," *Zürcher Taschenbuch*, n.F. 5 (1893): 147–57, discusses Bündner students in Zurich, who numbered about thirty in 1598.

14. For an analysis of wealth distribution in nearby Zuoz during this period, see Paolo Boringhieri, "Pussaunza, richezza e poverted a Zuoz 1521–1801," *Annalas de la Società Retorumantscha* 102 (1988): 79–201." The most sophisticated analysis of the region's society, though for a slightly later period, is Mathieu, *Bauern und Bären*.

15. A well-known example is the Dutch celebration of the Batavians; a lively account of their invention is found in Simon Schama, *The Embarrassment of Riches: An Interpretation of Dutch Culture in the Golden Age* (Berkeley: University of California Press, 1988). A catalog of such cases, from Switzerland to Denmark, can be found in Frank Borchardt, *German Antiquity in Renaissance Myth* (Baltimore, MD: Johns Hopkins University Press, 1971).

16. Aegidius Tschudi, *Die uralt warhafftig Alpisch Rhetia / sampt dem Tract der anderen Alpgebirgen / nach Plinii / Ptolomei / Strabonis / auch anderen Welt und gschichtschribern warer anzeygung . . .* (Basel: M. Isingren & J. Bebel, 1538).

17. Analyzed in detail in Giatgen Fontana, *Rechtshistorische Begriffsanalyse und das Paradigma der Freien: Ein methodischer und rechtssemantischer Begriffsbildungsversuch der mittelalterlicher Freiheit unter besonderer Bezugnahme auf die Historiographie Graubündens* (Zurich: Schulthess, 1987).

18. Johannes Guler von Wyneck, *Raetia: das ist Ausführliche und wahrhaffte Beschreibung der dreyen Loblichen Grawen Bündten uñ anderer Retischen völcker: Darinnen erklärt werden Dero aller begriff, härkommen, thaaten* (Zurich: Joh. Rodolff Wolffen, 1616).

19. Translated (loosely) from Sprecher, "Ein schön neu Lied zu Ehren der drei Bünde," reprinted in Zinsli, 5. The limping translation here matches the clunky German original.

20. Since Jenatsch's letters were written mostly in Italian and Latin, the word he used for "fatherland" was almost always *patria*, which appears in many of his letters. He also used the term "Rhaetian" from time to time.

21. *Briefe*, 59.

22. Ibid.

23. In doing so, he fit into trends emerging across the Holy Roman Empire. See the discussion by Robert von Friedeburg, "Why Did Seventeenth Century Estates Address the Jurisdictions of Their Princes as Fatherlands? War, Territorial Absolutism and the Duties to the Fatherland in German Seventeenth-Century Political Discourse," in *Orthodoxies and Heterodoxies: Order and Creativity in Early Modern German Culture*, eds. Randolph C. Head and Daniel Christensen (Leiden: Brill, 2007); and the volume edited by von Friedeburg: *"Patria" und "Patrioten" vor dem Patriotismus: Pflichten, Rechte, Glauben und die Rekonfigurierung europäischer Gemeinwesen im 17. Jahrhundert* (Wiesbaden: Harassowitz, 2005).

24. *Briefe*, 156.

25. On the complex relationship between politics and religion in Graubünden, and the possible relevance of democratic forms of governing, see Randolph Head, "Rhaetian Ministers, from Shepherds to Citizens: Calvinism and Democracy in the Republic of the Three Leagues, 1550–1620," in *Later Calvinism: International Perspectives*, ed. W. Fred Graham (Kirksville, MO: Sixteenth Century Journal Publishers, 1994), 55–69.

26. The phrase "souveraineté Rhetica" appears in *Briefe*, 111; the connection between "libertà" and "patria" appears in many of Jenatsch's letters.

27. *Briefe*, 76–77.

28. Ibid., 101. For context, see Pfister, 192–94.

29. Ibid., 111. The letter is preserved only in StAGR, and no private copies from the period are known. However, since Jenatsch was writing to the entire assembly of communes in Chur, he could be confident that his message would reach many ears.

30. This last claim was of course completely untrue; he had raised the troops in Graubünden, and maintained them in Venetian service for several years. Pfister, 196–97.

31. *Briefe*, 111.

32. Ibid., 145: "Si Patriae causam assereres, inquis, hoc nunquam dixissem. Num fieri potest, te adeo sinistro affect erga me imbutum, ut credas me Rebellium et non Patriae causam asserere? Jesu bone, quo deveni? Moriar nisi verum sit, Rebelles cane peius et angue me odisse." Pfister notes that "cane peius et angue" is a classical phrase for bitter hatred, one which translates well.

33. The modern French-speaking and Italian-speaking cantons were not yet part of the Swiss Confederation. Some, like Geneva and Neuchâtel, were allies; others, like the Vaud and the Ticino, were subjects. Only in the officially bilingual canton of Fribourg did French take a place next to German—but only in internal affairs. Fribourg's communications with its Swiss allies were conducted in German.

34. To add to the complexity, Alemannic dialects in Graubünden fall into two major groups: the ones that developed locally over a thousand years as the local population switched over from Romansh, and the dialect of the upper Valais, carried into Graubünden in the thirteenth and fourteenth centuries by the Walser migrants from farther west.

35. Linguists and the people of Graubünden generally recognize five major dialects of Rhaeto-Romance or Romansh within Graubünden. From west to east, they are Surselvan, Sutselvan, Surmeiran, and two variants of Ladin, Vallader and Puter. Although there are significant differences—enough that the Bible was translated separately into Surselvan and Ladin—speakers of one can generally understand speakers of another. For a discussion in English, see Robert H. Billigmeier, *A Crisis in Swiss Pluralism: The Romansh and Their Relations with the German- and Italian-Swiss in the Perspective of a Millennium* (The Hague: Mouton, 1979).

36. The translator of the 1560 New Testament, *L'g Nuof Sainc Testamaint da Nos Signer Jesu Christi* ([Basel?], 1560), was himself a notary and polyglot who wrote his notarial documents in both Latin and Romansh. Jachiam Tütschett Bifrun died in 1572 and thus knew Jenatsch's grandfather, the pastor Andreas Jenatsch. Pfister, 21–22. On Romansh printing in Graubünden, see Remo Bornatico, *L'arte tipografica nelle Tre Leghe (1547–1803) e nei Grigioni (1803–1975)*, 2nd ed. (Chur: author, 1976).

37. Analyzed in Randolph Head, "A Plurilingual Family in the Sixteenth Century: Language Use and Linguistic Consciousness in the Salis Correspondence, 1580–1610," *Sixteenth Century Journal* 26, no. 3 (1995): 577–93.

38. For example, by Charles Pascal, a French ambassador to Graubünden in the early seventeenth century, in his published memoirs: "Verum si ea lingua [scl. Romansh] origine Latina est, quo longius a suis initiis provecta est, eo plus Gallicae et Hispanicae peregrinitatis assumpsit." Pascal, *Caroli Paschalii Regis in Sacro Consistorio Consilarii Legatio Rhaetica* (Paris: P. Chevalier, 1620), ff.148ᵛ–149ʳ.

39. *Briefe*, 121–25.

40. His employer, Giovanni Baptista de Salis-Soglio, was not the father, Johannes Baptista von Salis-Samedan, discussed in the section above about multilingual correspondence.

41. *Briefe*, 53–58.

42. Praise of his early schoolboy accomplishments is noted in Pfister, 29–30. Bartholomäus Anhorn described him after his death as "von sonderbarer und gleichsam miraculoser eloquentz" ("of unusual and nearly miraculous eloquence"). *Urkundenbuch*, 154.

43. Based on *Briefe*, which contains the text of all ninety-five letters that are known to survive. The bibliographical apparatus of *Briefe* does not make it clear exactly which letters are autographs and which are not.

44. Code-switching is a shift to a different language in a sentence or paragraph, whether for individual words, phrases, or entire sentences. See Head, "Plurilingual Family."

45. Head, "Plurilingual Family," 586–89.

46. StAGR D II a3a, July 27, 1586.

47. Interestingly, the few such insertions of Romansh phrases in Jenatsch's letters are found primarily in his Latin letters to Stephan Gabriel, another Romansh speaker and (former) fellow pastor. See *Briefe*, 225, 232 (preserved only in copies).

48. Norbert Furrer, "Paroles de mercenaire: Aspects sociolinguistiques du service étranger," in *Gente ferocissima: Mercenariat et société en Suisse (XVe-XIXe siècle)*, eds. Lucienne Hubler et al. (Lausanne and Zurich: Editions D'en Bas and Chronos Verlag, 1997), 312.

49. Reto Hänny, "Guardati, Giorgio," afterword to *Jürg Jenatsch: Eine Bündnergeschichte, Mit einem Nachwort von Reto Hänny*, by Conrad Ferdinand Meyer (Berlin: Suhrkamp/Insel Verlag, 1988), 321–54.

50. Pfister, 5: "Der Buchtitel 'Georg Jenatsch' wurde in Anlehnung an denjenigen der Briefausgabe und unter Berücksichtigung der Verwurzlung der Namensform 'Jörg' im Volksbewusstsein in 'Jörg Jenatsch' abgeändert." The name Jörg has a distinctly Swiss flavor in modern Germany, compared to the North German Jürg or Jürgen. The current director of the cantonal museum in Chur reports that his teachers chided him in school because his parents had named him Jürg, after Meyer's novel, rather than the more native Jörg (Dr. Jürg Simonett, personal communication).

Chapter 3

1. *Briefe*, 185.

2. The classic definition of this understanding came from St. Augustine, as described in his *Confessions*, the Christian world's most influential spiritual autobiography. Conversion took on its modern meaning somewhat earlier for Europe's Jews, some of whom (willingly, or more often under coercion) accepted baptism, though the term "conversion" was not at first applied to this either. See Elisheva Karlebach, *Divided Souls: Converts from Judaism in Germany, 1500–1750* (New Haven, CT: Yale University Press, 2001). Conversion between Catholic and Protestant Christianity is currently the subject of a great deal of research. For Switzerland see esp. Frauke Volkland, *Konfession und Selbstverständnis: Reformierte Rituale in der gemischtkonfessionellen Kleinstadt Bischofszell im 17. Jahrhundert* (Göttingen: Vandenhoek & Ruprecht, 2005); and Daniela Hacke, "Zwischen Konflikt und Konsens: Zur politisch-konfessionellen Kultur in der Alten Eidgenossenschaft des 16. und 17. Jahrhunderts," *Zeitschrift für Historische Forschung* 4 (2005): 575–604.

3. The European encounter with non-Europeans, especially in the Americas, also challenged existing ideas about personhood in social and spiritual terms. My analysis is inspired in part by Anthony Pagden, *The Fall of Natural Man: The American Indian and the Origins of Comparative Ethnology* (Cambridge: Cambridge University Press, 1982).

4. *Briefe*, 59.

5. Ibid., 253.

6. For a critical but powerful analysis, see R. I. Moore, *The Formation of a Persecuting Society: Power and Deviance in Western Europe, 950–1250* (Oxford: Basil Blackwell, 1987).

7. Historians in Germany originally developed the term "confessionalization," and much of what has been written about the process is in German. In defining confessionalization, historians such as Heinz Schilling seek to connect the emergence of separate religious confessions with the modernization of the European state. See Schilling, "Confessional Europe," in *Handbook of European History 1400–1600*, eds. Thomas A. Brady, Heiko A. Oberman, and James D. Tracy (Leiden: Brill, 1995), 2: 640–70. On the (limited) applicability of confessionalization theory to Graubünden, see Randolph Head, "Catholics and Protestants in Graubünden: Confessional Discipline and Confessional Identities without an Early Modern State?" *German History* 17, no. 3 (1999): 321–45.

8. The term "secularization" and the debate about whether such a thing ever took place are older, and in some ways much vaguer, than recent discussions of confessionaliza-

tion. In certain respects, the debate over secular as opposed to spiritual views of the world has been going on since the early Enlightenment—a long historical trend captured in Max Weber's phrase "the disenchantment of the world." For the sixteenth and seventeenth centuries in particular, useful starting points for understanding the relationship between the "spiritual" and the "secular" include: Keith Thomas, *Religion and the Decline of Magic: Studies in Popular Beliefs in Sixteenth- and Seventeenth-Century England* (London: Weidenfeld and Nicholson, 1971); John Bossy, *Christianity in the West, 1400–1700* (Oxford: Oxford University Press, 1985); and for a robust argument about later developments, Jonathan Israel, *Radical Enlightenment: Philosophy and the Making of Modernity 1650–1750* (Oxford: Oxford University Press, 2002).

9. Although de facto coexistence between Christian denominations, and even reluctant toleration of "heretical" private worship next to the official church, existed in various parts of Europe, equal public treatment of Catholics and Protestants (not to mention other groups) was rare in western Europe before the 1800s. In eastern Europe, in contrast, a long tradition with roots before the Reformation made official recognition of more than one church possible in a number of regions, including Poland-Lithuania (before it was re-catholicized), Bohemia (to 1621), and Hungary and Transylvania. See Maria Crăciun, Ovidiu Ghitta, and Graeme Murdock, eds., *Confessional Identity in East-Central Europe* (Aldershot: Ashgate, 2002).

10. A valuable review on the question of successful penetration is Geoffrey Parker, "Success and Failure during the First Century of the Reformation," *Past & Present*, no. 136 (1992): 43–82. For an introduction to forms of coexistence, see Ole Peter Grell and Bob Scribner, eds., *Tolerance and Intolerance in the European Reformation* (Cambridge: Cambridge University Press, 1996).

11. Ronnie Po-Chia Hsia has analyzed this dimension of the post-Reformation period in two very accessible books: *Social Discipline in the Reformation: Central Europe, 1550–1750* (London: Routledge, 1989); and *The World of Catholic Renewal, 1540–1770* (Cambridge: Cambridge University Press, 1998).

12. See esp. Head, "Catholics and Protestants"; and Randolph C. Head, " 'Nit alß zwo Gemeinden, oder Partheyen, sonder ein Gmeind': Kommunalismus zwischen den Konfessionen in Graubünden, 1530–1620," in *Landgemeinde und Kirche im Zeitalter der Konfessionen*, eds. Beat Kümin and Peter Blickle (Zurich: Chronos, 2004); and Immacolata Saulle Hippenmeyer, *Nachbarschaft, Pfarrei und Gemeinde in Graubünden 1400–1600* (Chur: Kommissionsverlag Bündner Monatsblatt/Desertina, 1997).

13. The text of the treaty appears in *Amtliche Sammlung der älteren Eidgenössischen Abschiede* (Various publishers, 1856–1886), IV:2:2: 1590–93 (emphasis added).

14. Abundant recent research, however, shows that far from all Protestant (or Catholic) magistrates accepted the clergy's single-minded insistence on uniform orthodoxy. Without challenging the basic view that religious unity and truth were of great importance, magistrates found ways not only to act much more pragmatically, but also to justify their pragmatism in spiritual terms. See esp. Grell and Scribner, *Tolerance.*

15. See Karin Maag, *Seminary or University?: The Genevan Academy and Reformed Higher Education, 1560–1620* (Aldershot: Ashgate, 1995).

16. Cited in Haffter, 33–34. Such regulations were issued regularly; see, for example, StAZH E II 100–101, ff. 317^r–330^v (1606): "Fürtrag, betreffend die unordnung, so der studierenden Knaben halben eingereissen."

17. For more details, see Pfister, 31.

18. Confessionalism—that is, the reorganization of churches and states in the face of an evidently permanent division among western Europe's Christian majority—is a well-recognized feature of this era, often seen as the result of the "confessionalizing" process discussed above. See Schilling, "Confessional Europe."

19. Mark Juergensmeyer's pathbreaking study, *Terror and the Mind of God: The Global Rise of Religious Violence* (Berkeley: University of California Press, 2000), emphasizes that the distinction between peaceful religious movements and those few that turn to violence, in particular to terrorism, rests on such polarization and silencing of internal dissent. Recall that Ernst Haffter described some of Jenatsch's actions as "terroristic" in 1894. Haffter, 105.

20. Haffter, 42.

21. On pastors in Graubünden, see Head, "'nit alß zwo Gmeinden.'"

22. See Randolph Head, "Rhaetian Ministers, from Shepherds to Citizens: Calvinism and Democracy in the Republic of the Three Leagues, 1550–1620," in *Later Calvinism: International Perspectives*, ed. W. Fred Graham (Kirksville, MO: Sixteenth Century Journal Publishers, 1994), 55–69; and Head, "'Cetera sunt politica et ad nos nihil': Social Power, Legitimacy and Struggles over the Clerical Voice in Post-Reformation Graubünden," in *Debatten über die Legitimation von Herrschaft: Politische Sprachen in der Frühen Neuzeit*, eds. Luise Schorn-Schutte and Sven Tode (Berlin: Akademie Verlag, 2006), 67–85.

23. Pfister concentrates on this aspect of Bündner politics in his biography of Jenatsch; see also his "Partidas e combats ella Ligia Grischa, 1494–1794," *Annalas de la Società Retorumantscha* 40 (1926): 71–208.

24. Haffter, 46, relying on a letter that Alexius and Alexander sent to Zurich after the meeting.

25. Letter of the Synod of Bergün, April 20, 1618 (o.s.), from the copy in VAD, Msc. 233. This is the chronicler Bartholomäus Anhorn's copy.

26. Letter of the Synod of Bergün.

27. Again, the parallel to Juergensmeyer's analysis of modern religious terrorism is striking.

28. The key source of this information is the protocol of the court, StAGR AB 5/13, though it is incomplete and quite chaotic.

29. Though it was driven in part by the religious agenda of the synod and its activists, it is important to note that the 1618 uprising also reflected clan and factional politics internal to the Three Leagues. One of the sharpest observers of the time, chronicler Fortunat von Juvalta, ascribed the outbreak of the 1618 tumult in the Lower Engadine entirely to factional disputes, though his account provides no explanation why one of the first acts was to seize Nicolò Rusca, the Catholic archpriest of Sondrio, in the Valtellina. Juvalta, 47.

30. StAGR A II Landesakten I, August 3, 1618. Fortunat von Juvalta reports, however, that when the assembly sent this measure to the individual communes for ratification, as was necessary for all acts of the Three Leagues, it was roundly rejected. Juvalta, 47–48. See also Sprecher, 76.

31. Anhorn, *Krieg*, 30–32.

32. The surviving records, notably StAGR AB 5/13, as well as the eighteenth-century copy of further documents in StAGR B1592, rarely record individual overseers' opinions or actions; in what follows, I assume that Jenatsch was among peers and colleagues whose views he accepted.

33. Anhorn, *Krieg*, 36.

34. Juvalta, 49. Juvalta also hints that Jenatsch lost his appointment in Scharans at the end of 1617, a claim not confirmed by any other source, though the details of Jenatsch's employment between 1618 and the end of his clerical career in 1620 are unclear.

35. Juvalta, 48.

36. Sprecher, 76–77.

37. The charges are detailed in Anhorn, *Krieg*, 35; Sprecher, 82–83; and in an Italian contemporary copy of the charges published in Giovanni da Prada, *L'Arciprete Nicolò Rusca e i cattolici del suo tempo* (Tirano: Tipografia Poletti, 1994), 225–27.

38. Anhorn, *Krieg*, 32–33.

39. Ibid., paraphrasing the overseers' reply to the synod. Anhorn frequently included excerpts from original documents in his chronicle, although he was not especially careful about exact transliteration.

40. See also Head, " 'Cetera sunt.' "

41. *Grawpündtnerische Handlungen des MDCXVIII Jahrs, Darinnen klärlich unnd wahrhafftig angezeigt werden die rechtmeßigen unnd notzwingenden ursachen der zusammen kunfft deß gemeinen Landvolcks . . .* (n.p., 1618). This pamphlet is analyzed at length in Head, *Early Modern Democracy*, 223–30, with further bibliographical information.

42. *Briefe*, 59.

43. Jenatsch's claim reported in Pfister, 73. Juvalta, 49, makes the following claim about Jenatsch's position in Scharans: "He used to say that his sermons to us bore no fruit, so that he could no longer serve in our church. Nevertheless, after the end of his first year he still sought to remain in his office, but we declined to benefit further from his labors." Since Juvalta was the regional magistrate over Scharans, this comment deserves more attention than the biographers give it.

44. Jenatsch later claimed that he chose to serve in Berbenno because "the churches in the Valtellina are not well provided with clergymen" (Pfister, 73), but Juvalta's comments suggest that he was fired. The little that is known about his stay in Berbenno is summarized in Haffter's notes, 434–35.

45. Haffter, 79–80.

46. Anhorn, obituary published in *Urkundenbuch*, 170; cited in Haffter, 94–95.

47. In 1621, the official matriculation book of the synod recorded his departure with a laconic reference to 2 Timothy 4:10: "For Demas hath forsaken me, having loved this present world." Haffter, 126.

48. Anhorn, *Krieg*, 169.

49. Ibid.

50. *Blutige Sanfftmuet Der Calvinischen Predicanten* (n.p., 1621).

51. Analyzed with important Capuchin material by Andreas Wendland, "Ai confini dell'eresia. Le frontiere religiose ed ecclesiastiche in Valtellina (1550–1640)," in *La Valtellina Crocevia dell'Europa: Politica e Religione nell'Età della Guerra dei Trent'Anni*, ed. Agostino Borromeo (Milan: Monadori, 1998), 163–97.

52. The Lower Engadine in the 1620s is worth a new investigation; the best material relating to its history is found in Felici Maissen, *Die Drei Bünde in der zweiten Hälfte des 17. Jahrhundert in politischer, kirchengeschichtlicher, und volkskundlicher Schau*, vol. 1, *1647–1657* (Aarau: Sauerländer, 1966). My summary here is based on Pfister, 187ff.

53. Pfister, 182–83.

54. For the perspective of the Capuchins, see Andreas Wendland, "Il missionario come politico–Il politico come missionario: Missionari cappucini e politica della controriforma

in Valtellina e nel territorio delle Tre Leghe nel XVII secolo. Il programma di riconquista cattolica di Ignazio da Casnigo," *Archivio Storico Ticinese* 33 (1996), 199–218.

55. *Briefe*, 115.

56. Ibid., 93.

57. Ibid., 122, using Pfister's translation from the original Romansh: "haves bain crett vus havesses gratifichio Sia Excellentzchia in aquaist poick sainza l'g daier ad el et eir ad oters disturbo et fadia da quella vard, siand chia nun s'tscherchia das tegniar our d'baselgia, ma sulettamaing da yr aint dawo ils patres, chia in ogni möd nun s'predgia d'inviern avaunt las desch."

58. *Briefe*, 116.

59. Ibid., 120. A few months later, he once again had to complain, this time about the Capuchins' demands in Tschlins: "In Tschlins, the Fathers want the whole church just for the Catholics, but I didn't help them, because it is not reasonable, since the other church [in the village] is in no condition to be used" (126).

60. Haffter, 235–36.

61. Jon Mathieu, "33 Jahre nach Pfisters Jenatsch-Biographie: Neue Forschungsergebnisse und -perspektiven," in Pfister, 499–500; cf. Andreas Wendland, *Der Nutzen der Pässe und die Gefährdung der Seelen: Spanien, Mailand und der Kampf ums Veltlin 1620–1641* (Zurich: Chronos, 1995), 191–92.

62. On approaches to this (false) dilemma, see Hans Medick and David Sabean, eds., *Interest and Emotion: Essays on the Study of Family and Kinship* (Cambridge and Paris: Cambridge University Press and Éditions de la Maison des sciences de l'homme, 1984), especially the editors' introduction.

63. The letters' current location is given in *Briefe*, 290–91.

64. For example, letter 39, in *Briefe*, 145–47.

65. *Briefe*, 137.

66. See esp. *Briefe*, 151–57, undated but probably about May 1636. In this letter, which is the most theological of the entire series, Jenatsch begins with the issue of real presence, but uses it to address the importance of tradition.

67. *Briefe*, 152–53.

68. Ibid., 157. See also Jenatsch's direct attack on popular power as the source of disorder in the Three Leagues, *Briefe*, 224–26.

69. Ibid., 170.

70. Ibid., 253, from June 22, 1638. This interesting letter also argues from both prudence and justice that the authorities in Innsbruck should not try to exclude a Reformed pastor from preaching to the Protestant minority in Samnaun. He points out that the Catholic minority in the rest of the Lower Engadine was even smaller, so that exclusion of the pastor from a commune that enjoyed freedom of conscience ("*libertà del conscienza*") would justify the Engadiners' exclusion of the Capuchins elsewhere. This provides the context for his claim that the best position was to preserve Catholic preaching in the Lower Engadine by "living and letting live."

71. *Briefe*, 225–26; Pfister, 281–82; see Mathieu, "33 Jahre," 498, noting that one major change that took place in Davos after Jenatsch's conversion was that rather than asking Jenatsch to stand as godfather, the Protestant Davosers asked for his wife as godmother. See also chapter 5.

72. *Briefe*, 225.

73. Ibid., 224–25.

Chapter 4

1. The classic exposition of this model at the beginning of the High Middle Ages is found in Georges Duby, *The Three Orders: Feudal Society Imagined* (Chicago: University of Chicago Press, 1980). The most important scholar researching the three estates in late medieval Germany has been Otto Gerhard Oexle. See, for example, Oexle's "Die funktionale Dreiteilung als Deutungsschema der sozialen Wirklichkeit in der ständischen Gesellschaft des Mittelalters," in *Ständische Gesellschaft und soziale Mobilität*, ed. Winfried Schulze (Munich: R. Oldenbourg, 1988), 19–51.

2. An influential critic of older models of feudalism or "feudal society" is Susan Reynolds; see her *Fiefs and Vassals: The Medieval Evidence Reinterpreted* (Oxford: Oxford University Press, 1994).

3. Like the English term "estate," the German equivalent, *Stand*, had multiple and overlapping meanings, though not quite the same as those in English. *Stand* carries the general meaning of "condition, status," but whereas additional meanings in English tend to relate to property—either land or a person's possessions—the German word's additional connotations are more political. A *Stand* can be a political unit as well as a social category. Thus, not only was the German Imperial Diet, the *Reichstag*, made of three estates (*Stände*)—the electors, the high aristocracy (including high clerics), and the imperial cities—but each individual territory entitled to a seat at the *Reichstag* was called a *Stand*. In Switzerland, each of the thirteen cantons entitled to participate fully in the Swiss Diet was called an *Eidgenössischer Stand*. Such multiple meanings made the terms useful but slippery in political argument, as can be seen in the poem by Adam Saluz discussed in the text that follows.

4. The theory of the three estates does include a contractual dimension in its explanation of the relationship between the first, second, and third estates—but only at the level of estates as a whole. It thus has genealogical connections with later theories of the social contract, but its functional and organic metaphors are entirely different from the voluntarism and emphasis on individuals choosing to make contracts that characterize the most important social contract thinkers. Naturally, as in all social and political theory, multiple positions recombined these and other ideas throughout the Middle Ages and early modern period.

5. The history of individualism, or of the "modern self," has occupied historians and philosophers alike. See Charles Taylor, *Sources of the Self: The Making of the Modern Identity* (Cambridge, MA: Harvard University Press, 1989), from the philosophical direction; and in regard to early modern Germany in particular, see David Sabean, "Production of the Self in the Age of Confessionalism," *Central European History* 29, no. 1 (1996): 1–18.

6. The literature and debate on this theme are endless. Useful starting points are found in the collection by M. Carrithers et al., eds., *The Category of the Person: Anthropology, Philosophy, History* (Cambridge: Cambridge University Press, 1985).

7. The seeming contradiction between individual salvation and collective identities was explained by St. Augustine's separation of the earthly from the heavenly cities. This position found a strong echo in Martin Luther's early thought, which sharply separated the spiritual travails of the individual soul from the collective and social obligations of the Christian in the world. In Luther's famous phrase, "A Christian man is the most free lord of all, and subject to none; a Christian man is the most dutiful servant of all, and subject to

everyone." The phrase comes from Luther's essay "On the Freedom of a Christian," in Jaroslav Pelikan and Helmut T. Lehmann, eds., *Luther's Works*, 55 vols, (Saint Louis and Philadelphia: Concordia Press, 1955–1976), 31: 327–78.

8. A classic and entertaining demonstration is Jack Hexter, "The Myth of the Middle Class," in *Reappraisals in History*, 2nd ed. (Chicago: University of Chicago Press, 1979), 71–115.

9. Ellery Schalk's simple binary description of the conundrum of nobility, in *From Valor to Pedigree: Ideas of Nobility in France in the Sixteenth and Seventeenth Centuries* (Princeton, NJ: Princeton University Press, 1986), has been enriched by the work of George Huppert, Jonathan Dewald, and Kristin Neuschel. For the tensions over virtue, power, and status in Italy, J.G.A. Pocock's analysis in *The Machiavellian Moment: Florentine Political Thought and the Atlantic Republican Tradition* (Princeton, NJ: Princeton University Press, 1975), remains essential.

10. Indeed, the domains where the Habsburgs had hereditary claims—the League of Ten Jurisdictions and the Lower Engadine—were among the most aggressive in introducing the Reformation. Although it is risky to infer a direct causal connection, the outcome is striking.

11. Bündner commoners turned the system on its head against their neighbors, too, claiming to be noble because they bore arms and exercised political authority. Jon Mathieu describes an incident from the eighteenth century in which an Austrian nobleman was pushed off a mountain path by a Graubünden peasant with the comment, "We Bündner rule ourselves, and that makes me as much a prince as you." Jon Mathieu, "Eine Region am Rand: Das Unterengadin 1650–1800" (PhD diss., University of Bern, 1983), 401.

12. Indeed, T. N. Bisson argues that the same logic underlies most modern theories of representation. See Bisson, "The Military Origins of Medieval Representation," *American Historical Review* 71 (1966): 353–73.

13. This point is argued most strenuously in Christian Padrutt, *Staat und Krieg im Alten Bünden: Studien zur Beziehung zwischen Obrigkeit und Kriegertum in den Drei Bünden vornehmlich im 15. und 16. Jahrhundert* (Zurich: Fretz und Wasmuth, 1965).

14. The document was pasted into a new church register created after a fire in 1562 and is printed in F. Jecklin, ed., "Das Davoser Spendbuch vom Jahre 1562," *Jahresbericht der historisch-antiquarischen Gesellschaft von Graubünden* 54 (1924): 197–210, column 1 (also published by Hans Sprecher, ed., "Die gerächtigkeit, so ain gemaind uff Tavas zu ainem pfarrer hat," *Bündnerisches Monatsblatt*, n.s., 6, no. 12 (1901): 253–58). My thanks to Immacolata Saulle Hippenmeyer for drawing my attention to these sources.

15. My translation from the *Kirchenordnung* of ca. 1500, printed in Jecklin, "Das Davoser Spendbuch," 197–98, column 2.

16. The synod complained loudly about inadequate salaries—sometimes as little as forty gulden a year—in its letters to fellow clerics in Zurich. See, for example, *BK* I: 277, 285, 288. Cf. Head, " 'nit alß zwo Gemeinden, oder Partheyen, sonder ein Gmeind': Kommunalismus zwischen den Konfessionen in Graubünden, 1530–1620," in *Landgemeinde und Kirche im Zeitalter der Konfessionen*, eds. Beat Kümin and Peter Blickle (Zurich: Chronos, 2004), 21–57.

17. Saluz, "Prosopopeia Raetica," in Zinsli, 50, line 366.

18. Ibid., 57, lines 678–79.

19. Ibid., 49–50, lines 349–58.

20. Ibid., lines 359–69. Saluz's vision of a society consisting only of one laboring estate echoes the ideas of Michael Gaismair and other publicists of the Peasants' War of 1525.

See Frank Ganseuer, *Der Staat des "gemeinen Mannes": Gattungstypologie und Programmatik des politischen Schrifttums von Reformation und Bauernkrieg* (Frankfurt a.M.: Peter Lang, 1985).

21. In this, his views echoed Lutheran and Reformed ways of defining the clergy: all Christians might be priests, according to Luther, but only some were called to the office of leading congregations.

22. Jon Mathieu describes an eighteenth-century Graubünden pastor who got into hot water because he chided his parishioners for sleeping during church services: "In der Kirche schlafen. Eine sozialgeschichtliche Lektüre von Conradin Riolas 'Geistlicher Trompete' (Strada im Engadin, 1709)," *Schweizerisches Archiv für Volkskunde* 87, no. 3/4 (1991): 121–45.

23. Briefly described in Haffter, 28–29.

24. Pfister, 30.

25. *BK* 2: 205, no. 265 (August 26, 1560), in a marginal note by Johannes Fabricius to Bullinger.

26. *JM* II, no. 410, (January 3, 1572), 414–15.

27. StAGR AB IV 1/3, 178.

28. Haffter, 34.

29. Especially the synod head and author Durisch Chiampell, who wrote a manuscript titled "Concerning the Office of Pious Magistrates over Their Subjects" (De Officio Magistratus erga subiectos suos charissimos, in Religionis causa in ipsorem salutem). A copy of the tract was inserted into the protocol of the Rhaetian Synod during its meeting in 1577 (Archiv der Evangelischen Rhätischen Synode, Msc. B 3, 27–35) and copied meticulously by P.D.R. à Porta in the eighteenth century (StAGR B 721, which preserves the pagination of the synod's copy).

30. Synodal letter, VAD 233.

31. Ibid. (emphasis added).

32. Anhorn, *Krieg*, 32–33.

33. Cited from a group of manuscript poems from 1618, printed in Zinsli, 147–51. This one is labeled only "Aliud." The critical reference to the Jesuits suggests a Protestant author, here, since Calvinists in this period often accused the Jesuits of being a dangerous anti-Christian cult. My translation of both passages is loose to keep the flavor of the original, which is truly bad poetry in German.

34. Zinsli, "Postscripta I," 147–48, lines 27–30.

35. Zinsli, "Aliud II," 149–51. Juvalta, 50, makes exactly the same accusation against Jenatsch.

36. Anhorn's obituary for Jenatsch is contained in his sparse additions to his main chronicle, found in a manuscript now in St. Gallen, and published in *Urkundenbuch*, 168–73, here 169.

37. Cited from the synodal records in Haffter, 63.

38. The synodal records are lost for this period, but the suspension is reported by the generally reliable Sprecher; see Haffter, 69n21.

39. The pamphlet *Blutige Sanfftmuet Der Calvinischen Predicanten* (n.p., 1621) emphasized the point.

40. A detailed study of men much like Jenatsch is found in Fritz Redlich, *The German Military Enterpriser and His Work Force: A Study in European Economic and Social History* (Wiesbaden: F. Steiner, 1964).

41. A succinct review of the recent literature can be found in Marco Bellabarba, "Rituali, Leggi, e Disciplina del Duello: Italia e Germania fra Cinque e Settecento," in *Duelli,*

Faide e Rappacificazioni: Elaborazioni concettuali, esperienze storiche, ed. Marco Cavina (Milan: A. Giuffrè, 2001), 83–118. Duels over honor were quickly distinguished by legal thinkers and by the clergy from trial by combat, a much older form of ritualized fighting, and from the German and feudal notion of noble feuding. The purpose of a trial by combat was to find the truth; a noble feud was conducted in the name of justice. In contrast, a duel specifically involved an individual nobleman's desire to defend his honor.

42. On the relatively minor role dueling played in Switzerland, see Lynn Blattmann, "Duell," *Historisches Lexicon der Schweiz*, http://www.hls-dhs-dss.ch/textes/d/D16330.php (accessed May 4, 2007).

43. As described in Edward Muir's sophisticated and entertaining study, *Mad Blood Stirring: Vendetta and Factions in Friuli during the Renaissance* (Baltimore, MD: Johns Hopkins University Press, 1993).

44. Sprecher, 226–27.

45. The diplomatic situation is described effectively in Horatio Brown, "Valtelline," in *Cambridge Modern History*, eds. A. W. Ward et al., vol. 4, *The Thirty Years' War* (Cambridge: Cambridge University Press, 1906), 35–63.

46. Jenatsch's letter of defense to the court in Chur was copied into the court record and is published in C. Jecklin, "Das Duell G. Jenatschs mit Oberst J. von Ruinelli. 6/16 März 1627," *Jahresbericht der Historisch-antiquarischen Gesellschaft Graubündens* 17 (1887): 55–72, here citing 68.

47. Jecklin, "Das Duell," 68

48. Ibid., 62, testimony of Pellizari, who specifically noted the change in language from Italian for Jenatsch's statement to German for Ruinelli's reply.

49. In most towns and cities, dueling was forbidden and heavily punished, though Jenatsch later claimed that German cities allowed those who were challenged to accept.

50. B[althasar] Reber, "Georg Jenatsch, Graubündtens Pfarrer und Held während des dreißigjährigen Kriegs," *Beiträge zur vaterländischen Geschichte herausgegeben von der historischen Gesellschaft in Basel* 7 (1860): 236.

51. Jecklin, "Das Duell," 67.

52. Ibid.

53. *Briefe*, 96–97.

54. Jecklin, "Das Duell," 71.

55. Ruinelli's regiment was funded primarily by France but consisted of men from Graubünden. Thus, Jenatsch rose to his position of captain among his countrymen. Haffter, 224.

56. *Urkundenbuch*, 93.

57. Pfister, 203–8, is more plausible and complete than Haffter.

58. Brown, "Valtelline," 59–60.

59. Jon Mathieu, "33 Jahre nach Pfisters Jenatsch-Biographie: Neue Forschungsergebnisse und -perspektiven," in Pfister, 499.

60. Haffter, 243. The description is the Venetian consul's, whom Jenatsch met in Zurich on his way to Paris.

61. Haffter, 247, calls it a "Freicompagnie."

62. Pfister, 244–46. That Rohan already had suspicions about Jenatsch, 249.

63. Pfister, 291.

64. Since Graubünden lay in the Holy Roman Empire, the Austrian Habsburgs, as Holy Roman Emperors, were best placed to award Jenatsch a noble title. Rhäzüns was a

lordship possessed by the Habsburgs that was also a member of one of the Three Leagues. It was routinely awarded as a nonhereditary fief to leading Graubünden families, mostly the Planta. Discussed in Pfister, 326–27. There is no record that Jenatsch sought a title from France, though he did seek and receive considerable sums of money.

65. *Briefe*, 99. Strictly speaking, becoming the administrator of Rhäzüns would not have made Jenatsch noble. Still, the previous administrators from the Planta family had all been from ennobled branches of the family or personally noble, and Jenatsch's position would certainly have raised his status in the Three Leagues.

66. Haffter, 294.

67. Pfister, 369–70; Andreas Wendland, *Der Nutzen der Pässe und die Gefährdung der Seelen: Spanien, Mailand und der Kampf ums Veltlin 1620–1641* (Zurich: Chronos, 1995), 249.

68. Wendland, *Nutzen*, 248.

69. Pfister, 379–81.

Chapter 5

1. For an example of how uncomfortable the Western mainstream remains in talking about kin networks, note the response to a recent provocative book by Adam Bellow titled *In Praise of Nepotism: A Natural History* (New York: Doubleday, 2003), which drew not a little criticism.

2. The way that Pompeius von Planta's daughter, Katharina von Planta, became "Lucretia" is complex and more than a little obscure. According to two masters of Graubünden history, she appears in the sources only as Katharina, though she had both a granddaughter and a mother-in-law named Lucretia. Until 1789, there is no reference to her as Lucretia. In the nineteenth-century versions of the Jenatsch story, however, including a family chronicle, Katharina became Katharina Lucretia, a name also used by the historian Haffter in 1894, but disavowed by him in an 1898 article. In Meyer's fictional work, she becomes simply Lucretia. See Fritz Jecklin and Michael Valèr, eds., "Die Ermordung Georg Jenatschs nach dem Churer Verhörprotokoll," *Zeitschrift für Schweizerische Geschichte* 4 (1924): 405n1.

3. Vividly argued for the French nobility in Kristin Neuschel, *Word of Honor: Interpreting Noble Culture in Sixteenth-Century France* (Ithaca, NY: Cornell University Press, 1989).

4. The best introduction to women's history in early modern Europe is Merry Wiesner, *Women and Gender in Early Modern Europe*, 3rd ed. (Cambridge: Cambridge University Press, 2008).

5. See chapter 6.

6. The research of Dale V. Kent has been instrumental in making kinship and faction visible in Florence. See Kent's *The Rise of the Medici: Faction in Florence, 1426–1434* (Oxford: Oxford University Press, 1978) and later works.

7. See Guy Marchal, "Die Antwort der Bauern: Elemente und Schichtungen des eidgenössischen Geschichtsbewußtseins am Ausgang des Mittelalters" in *Geschichtsschreibung und Geschichtsbewusstsein im Späten Mittelalter*, ed. Hans Patze (Sigmaringen: Jan Thorbecke, 1987), 757–90; Randolph Head, "William Tell and His Comrades: Association and Fraternity in the Propaganda of Fifteenth and Sixteenth Century Switzerland," *Journal of Modern History* 67, no. 3 (1995): 527–57; and more sociologically, Ulrich Vonrufs, *Die politische*

Führungsgruppe Zürichs zur Zeit von Hans Waldmann (1450–1489): Struktur, politische Networks und die sozialen Beziehungstypen Verwandschaft, Freundschaft und Patron-Klient-Beziehung (Bern: Peter Lang, 2002).

8. A detailed study can be found in Paul Grimm, *Die Anfänge der Bündner Aristokratie im 15. und 16. Jahrhundert* (Zurich: Juris, 1981); specifically on the late medieval Planta, see Peter Conradin von Planta, *Die Planta im Spätmittelalter* (Chur: Historische Gesellschaft von Graubünden, 1996).

9. Randolph Head, *Early Modern Democracy in the Grisons* (Cambridge: Cambridge University Press, 1995), 141–43. The Salis had major landholdings and branches in the Valtellina and Valchiavenna subject territories as well.

10. Cited in Silvio Färber, *Der bündnerische Herrenstand im 17. Jahrhundert: Politische, soziale, und wirtschaftliche Aspekte seiner Vorherrschaft* (Zurich: Zentralstelle der Studentenschaft, 1983), 249; the phrase I have translated as "not related closely" is *senza alcuna parentela* in the original.

11. Our main source of information is Ulysses von Salis's memoirs. See Ulisse de Salis, *Memorie del Maresciallo di campo Ulisse de Salis-Marschlins*, ed. Conrad Jecklin (Chur: F. Schuler, 1931), 1–4.

12. Both Haffter and Pfister discuss the position of the Jenatsch family in the Upper Engadine, which was richly endowed with Planta and Salis family branches, but neither goes into possible patronage alliances in the generations before George Jenatsch's birth. The Jenatsch family was not powerful enough to gain attention in Färber's detailed analysis in *Der bündnerische Herrenstand*.

13. *Briefe*, 53. The letter (shown in facsimile in *Briefe*, p. 55) is written in German with minor errors as well as several clear dialect constructions, using an Italic hand rather than the conventional Gothic script used for German at the time.

14. Cited in Haffter, 35.

15. Ibid.

16. Jon Mathieu gives a series of examples from the Lower Engadine between 1670 and 1770, where local rivalries led to nighttime murders, violent fights at electoral assemblies, and once to a pitched battle outside one of the villages. See Mathieu's *Bauern und Bären: Eine Geschichte des Unterengadins von 1650 bis 1800* (Chur: Octopus, 1987), 271–72. For a better-documented clan war during the sixteenth century in the neighboring and culturally similar Friuli, see Edward Muir's *Mad Blood Stirring: Vendetta and Factions in Friuli during the Renaissance* (Baltimore, MD: Johns Hopkins University Press, 1993), which provides additional literature.

17. Head, *Early Modern Democracy*, provides the case for state-like developments in Graubünden, though they are distinctive because of the Three Leagues' federal structure.

18. For an analysis of the extensive Salis connections with Venice through the lines of Salis-Soglio, Salis-Samedan, and Salis-Grüsch, see Martin Bundi, *Frühe Beziehungen zwischen Graubünden und Venedig* (Chur: Gasser, 1988), esp. 257–60.

19. It is important to remember, though, that both the Salis and Planta clans had multiple branches: there were Catholic and pro-Spanish Salis, and Protestant and pro-Venetian Planta throughout this period. For a detailed analysis, see Pfister, "Partidas e combats ella Ligia Grischa, 1494–1794," *Annalas de la Società Retorumantscha* 40 (1926), and Färber, *Der bündnerische Herrenstand*.

20. The leading members in each faction are outlined in Färber, *Der bündnerische Herrenstand*.

21. I reach this conclusion on the basis of the earliest reports, though some contemporaries also named Gallus Rieder, ensign from the village of Splügen and another hot-

headed Salis client, as the killer. The earliest accounts are published in *Urkundenbuch*, 58–71, and Anhorn, *Krieg*, 167–68.

22. On the Carl von Hohenbalcken family, see Färber, *Der bündnerische Herrenstand*, 179n522. Pfister, 108–9, summarizes the evidence; see also the contemporary discussion in *Urkundenbuch*, 66.

23. *Urkundenbuch*, 66–67.

24. Ibid., 63–64.

25. Ibid., 60.

26. Haffter, 107.

27. Muir, *Mad Blood Stirring*.

28. *Urkundenbuch*, 67.

29. Jecklin and Valèr, "Die Ermordung," 409.

30. The official depositions of eighteen witnesses are published in Jecklin and Valèr, "Die Ermordung."

31. Rudolf von Planta is reported as the key figure by the chroniclers Sprecher and Anhorn. Their views are summarized (though then ignored) in Jecklin and Valèr, "Die Ermordung"; see also the sober evaluation in *Urkundenbuch*, 33. No one has ever commented on the fact that Pompeius von Planta, at least according to one account, had been killed by two axes. See *Urkundenbuch*, 63.

32. The incident was recorded by the Chur chronicler and gossip Jacob Wigeli; I rely here on the paraphrase in Pfister, 411–12. Prevost, known like his father as "Zambra," had his own reasons to hate Jenatsch, since his father had been seized and executed by the 1618 tribunal in Thusis.

33. Ironically, Rudolf himself was murdered in 1640 by a gang of masked men, as a result of a factional blood feud *within* the Planta clan. Rudolf had murdered his cousin (also a Rudolf) over the same disputed inheritance that Jenatsch had tried to help resolve.

34. From one of the nearly identical reports sent to Zurich and Bern, cited in Haffter, 394.

35. For example, *Blutige Sanfftmuet Der Caluinischen Predicanten: Wahrhaffte Relation auß einer Glaubwürdigen Person Sendschreiben* (n.p., 1621), 2.

36. Jecklin and Valèr, "Ermordung," 402. Katharina's husband immediately told her not to say such things.

37. Jon Mathieu, "33 Jahre nach Pfisters Jenatsch-Biographie: Neue Forschungsergebnisse und -perspektiven," in Pfister, 493.

38. Pfister, 95–96. Pfister assumes that the wife's name is Anna, although no document before 1627 contains this name.

39. Details in Mathieu, "33 Jahre," table on p. 495. A letter written in Davos (*Briefe*, 62) in May 1620 mentions a father-in-law.

40. Hortensia von Salis, *Glaubens-Rechenschaft; Conversations-Gespräche; Gebät*, ed. Maya Widmer (Bern: Haupt, 2003).

41. Data from Mathieu, "33 Jahre," 498.

42. *Briefe*, 225.

43. Pfister, 281.

44. Esther Fuchs, "Woman and the Discourse of Patriarchal Wisdom: A Study of Proverbs 1–9," in *Women in the Hebrew Bible: A Reader*, ed. Alice Bach (New York: Routledge, 1999), 85–98.

45. The Bible verse is cited from the King James Bible, Proverbs 5:3–8. Jenatsch's Bible was a 1566 Protestant version in Latin from Lyon, which apparently included a common heading for this passage (not found in the modern Catholic Latin Vulgate), "*Ne intenderis fallaciae mulieris*" ("Do not listen to the errors of a woman"). See Haffter, 412, and *Urkundenbuch*, 12. The actual Jenatsch Bible is currently in private possession.

46. Zinsli, 148–49.

47. Ibid. Also cited in Gartmann, 18, to whom I owe the suggestion about *carnaccio*.

48. Zinsli, 149.

49. From "Kurtz beschribne Pündtnerische Handlungen, deß 1618., 19. und 20. Jahrs." Attributed to Pompeius von Planta. Msc. copy by the copyist Heinrich Spätt, VAD 235.

50. Ibid., paragraphs 19 and 20.

51. Ibid., paragraph 20.

52. That republics often excluded women from the public sphere far more systematically than monarchies has been observed before, though a serious analysis is still lacking. See Melissa Matthes, *The Rape of Lucretia and the Founding of Republics: Readings in Livy, Machiavelli, and Rousseau* (University Park: Pennsylvania State University Press, 2000).

Chapter 6

1. Anhorn reports the story of the same axe in his 1639 obituary for Jenatsch (*Urkundenbuch*, 172); for later appearances of the axe, cf. Gartmann, 50.

2. *Urkundenbuch*, 169.

3. Pfister, 192.

4. The most astute analysis of this pairing is Hans Martin Schmid's study of Rohan in historiography: *Das Bild Herzog Heinrich Rohans in der bündnerischen und französischen Geschichtsschreibung* (Chur: Bischofsberger, 1966).

5. The main chronicles are all described, with publication history, in Edgar Bonjour and Richard Feller, *Geschichtsschreibung der Schweiz*, vol. 2, *Vom Spätmittelalter zur Neuzeit* (Basel: Benno Schwabe & Co. Verlag, 1962), 385–98.

6. Not until Andreas Wendland's 1995 study, *Der Nutzen der Pässe und die Gefährdung der Seelen: Spanien, Mailand und der Kampf ums Veltlin 1620–1641* (Zurich: Chronos, 1995), were the rich holdings in Spain fully brought into the picture.

7. The material in this collection up to 1629 is published as Anhorn, *Krieg*. The remaining material, covering from 1629 to the late 1630s, is preserved in manuscript form in Chur and St. Gallen. The obituary is reproduced in *Urkundenbuch*, 169–73.

8. Fortunat Sprecher [von Bernegg], *Pallas Raetica, armata et togata* (Basel: I. J. Genathius, 1617), and several later editions; Sprecher, *Historia motuum et bellorum, postremis hisce annis in Rhaetia excitatorum et gestorum* (Cologne: Petri Chouët, 1629); among several translations into German, the one published in the nineteenth century is the one cited in the abbreviations as Sprecher.

9. Ulisse de Salis, *Memorie del Maresciallo di campo Ulisse de Salis-Marschlins*, ed. Conrad Jecklin (Chur: F. Schuler, 1931).

10. Much of the biographical and fictional literature asserts that Jenatsch played a leading role in Thusis, an assertion not supported by the documents of the court itself. See StAGR AB 5/13, as well as the eighteenth-century copy of further documents in StAGR

B1592. This assertion rests largely on Juvalta's retrospective description, as well as a few comments in Sprecher, and is found in B[althasar] Reber, "Georg Jenatsch, Graubündtens Pfarrer und Held während des dreißigjährigen Kriegs," *Beiträge zur vaterländischen Geschichte herausgegeben von der historischen Gesellschaft in Basel* 7 (1860): 194n4, directly attributed to Juvalta. See also Gartmann, 21, who correctly describes Juvalta's discussion of Jenatsch at Thusis as "revenge."

11. For example, in nearly five hundred pages of Salis's memoir, which covers from the 1610s to the 1640s, Jenatsch is mentioned only thirty-one times.

12. The Latin poem (with Greek aphorisms) clearly comes from a clerical hand and is found today in the Zurich archives. *Urkundenbuch*, 127–33; cf. Gartmann, 24–29.

13. Gartmann, 37.

14. Ibid., 39.

15. See Ibid., 45–53, for examples of the scattered material from the late 1600s and 1700s.

16. Heinrich Ludwig Lehmann, *Die Republik Graubünden historisch-geographisch-statistisch dargestellt*, 2 vols. (Magdeburg and Brandenburg: Keil, 1797–1799); Heinrich Zschokke, *Die drey ewigen Bünde im hohen Rhätien: Historische Skizze* (Zurich: Orell, Gessner, & Füssli, 1798). Oddly enough, both Lehmann and Zschokke were German émigrés who settled in Graubünden, not local authors.

17. Louis Vulliemin, *Geschichte der Eidgenossen während des 16. und 17. Jahrhunderts*, 3 vols. (Zurich: Orell, Füßli, 1844). After brief mentions of Jenatsch's early career, Jenatsch plays an important role in vol. 2, pp. 634–43, which describe Henri de Rohan's campaigns and the Bündner expulsion of the French. The murder of Jenatsch gets two pages in vol. 2, on pp. 657–59.

18. Alfons Flugi, "Georg Jenatsch. Ein biographischer Versuch," *Bündnerisches Monatsblatt* 9, nos. 9 and 10 (1852).

19. For a full argument that the Three Leagues constituted a state, and even in certain meaningful ways a democratic state, see Randolph Head, *Early Modern Democracy in the Grisons* (Cambridge: Cambridge University Press, 1995). A critical response can be found in Thomas Maissen, "'Die Gemeinden und das Volck als höchste Gewalt unsers freyen democratischen Stands.' Die Erneuerung der politischen Sprache in Graubünden um 1700," *Jahrbuch der Historischen Gesellschaft von Graubünden* 131 (2001): 37–84.

20. The most accessible study that analyzes this debate is Olivier Zimmer, *A Contested Nation: History, Memory and Nationalism in Switzerland, 1761–1891* (Cambridge: Cambridge University Press, 2002).

21. As might be expected in Switzerland, the division was complicated by multiple crisscrossing identities, such as liberal Catholic French and Italian speakers, to mention only one further position. In Graubünden, moreover, even the ideological liberals tended to be democratic particularists, while language and religion cut across ideological lines in unpredictable ways. See in brief Joachim Remak, *A Very Civil War: The Swiss Sonderbund War of 1847* (Boulder, CO: Westview, 1993).

22. Benjamin Barber, *The Death of Communal Liberty: A History of Freedom in a Swiss Mountain Canton* (Princeton, NJ: Princeton University Press, 1974), analyzes the ideological struggle between community sovereignty and modern liberal politics in Graubünden with great sensitivity.

23. Peter Conradin von Planta, *Ritter Rudolf Planta: Ein Schauspiel* (Chur: n.p., 1849), discussed in Gartmann, 55–57.

24. Cited in Gartmann, 56.

25. Reber, "Georg Jenatsch," 299.

26. Meyer, 147–48.

27. Zschokke, *Die drei ewigen Bünde*, 2:186–87, cited in Reber, "Georg Jenatsch," 300.

28. Meyer, 197.

29. Rudolf Joho, *Jürg Jenatsch* (Elgg: Volksverlag Elgg, ca. 1955), 13. Joho depicts a charismatic Jenatsch superior to the European figures who seek to enlist him, such as Albrecht von Wallenstein and Cardinal Richelieu. His fatal flaw is his high opinion of his fellow citizens, whom he will not force to be their best (46). In contrast, Henri de Rohan is a stiff-necked perfectionist who insists on honor and keeping his word even when his actions play into the hands of cynical politicians like Richelieu (67). According to Joho, the endless conflicts will only end when one state dominates the world (75).

30. The term *Landamman* has overtones that are hard to convey in English. It has communal associations and connections with the myth of William Tell (in which one of the heroes is a *Landamman*) that set it apart from the overtly nationalistic terminology found in Germany in the 1930s. At the same time, it was not a conventional term for magistrates in Graubünden, but had been used for the national magistrate during the French-imposed Helvetic Republic of 1797–1803. In Joho's play, moreover, Jenatsch's adoption of the title is closely associated with his unilateral decision to seize personal power when the democratically assembled people fail either to elect him as their leader or to choose a sensible policy. In the later version of the play published after 1945, Joho changed the term from *Landamman* to *Landeshauptman*, closer to the historical terminology. Joho, *Jürg Jenatsch*, 50.

31. This version of the last speech comes from Rudolf Joho's manuscript of the 1930s, as cited in Gartmann, 131. The play seems to have been published privately and not circulated: *Jürg Jenatsch (Gewaltherrschaft?): Historisches Schauspiel in 5 Akten* (Hildesheim: Author, 1936). See also Rudolf Joho, *Schweizer Bühnenwerke: Berufstheater* (Elgg: Volksverlag Elgg, 1955), 89, which confirms the 1936 date of the original version. The staging in Chur in the spring of 2004 used Joho's postwar published version, whose final speech is altered considerably from the version cited above. See Joho, *Jürg Jenatsch*, 79.

32. See Melissa Matthes, *The Rape of Lucretia and the Founding of Republics: Readings in Livy, Machiavelli, and Rousseau* (University Park: Pennsylvania State University Press, 2000).

33. Heinrich Bullinger, *Lucretia-Dramen* (Leipzig: VEB Bibliographisches Institut, 1973), 16. Further discussion in Randolph Head, "William Tell and His Comrades: Association and Fraternity in the Propaganda of Fifteenth and Sixteenth Century Switzerland," *Journal of Modern History* 67, no. 3 (1995): 527–57.

34. For the earliest evidence of the new name, see Gartmann, 48–53; Haffter, 386.

35. Reber, "Georg Jenatsch," 293.

36. Theodor von Saussure, *Jenatsch, oder Graubünden während des dreissigjährigen Krieges* (Chur: Hitz und Hail, 1886), 87–90, in a translation of the 1868 French original. The placement of the murder at a ball, rather than in a tavern, goes back to eighteenth-century popular versions of the story. See Gartmann, 50.

37. Saussure, *Jenatsch*, 88.

38. See Hermann Bleuler, *Conrad Ferdinand Meyers "Jürg Jenatsch" im Verhältnis zu seinen Quellen* (Karlsruhe: n.p., 1920), 16–17, though Bleuler implausibly attributes this adjustment to Meyer's desire to make Jenatsch an exact contemporary of the narrator, Heinrich Waser. To make the childhood relationship possible, Meyer actually makes Jenatsch's father pastor of Scharans, rather than Jenatsch himself.

39. Meyer, 91.

40. In fact, Rohan died several months after Jenatsch, and the treaty with Spain was not completed until later in 1639.

41. Reber's characterization of Jenatsch as an "Egoist" even more than a patriot captures this view, while also echoing long-standing Protestant (and Christian) rhetoric about the hazards of self-love.

42. Meyer, 209.

43. See Gartmann, 115–17, including highly critical remarks about Voss's melodrama. A. Kenngott, "Jürg Jenatsch in Geschichte, Roman und Drama," *Washington University Studies* 2, pt. 2, no. 2 (1915): 177–220, consists of little more than a running attack on Voss, whose wild inventions are contrasted with the supposedly "historically grounded" narrative in Meyer.

44. Saussure, 88.

45. Hans von Mühlestein, *Der Diktator und der Tod: Die Tragödie Jörg Jenatschs. Bühnendichtung in 4 Akten* (Celerina: Author, 1933), 139. See also Gartmann, 132–34.

46. Published in his *Dramatisirte Geschichten* (Bern: n.p., 1885–1886); see also Gartmann, 58–59.

47. Quoted from http://www.amazon.de, in an anonymous reader review dated August 6, 2001 (accessed May 4, 2007): "Das Buch ist nicht nur für alle, die gerade Urlaub im Graubünden machen ein muss, sondern auch für alle, die gerne mal von einem Schweizer Helden etwas lesen wollen."

48. The theory, which puts improbable weight on the fact that Jenatsch had ordered some troops to be quartered in Haldenstein during the tumults, is worked out in Mathis Berger, "Die Ermordung Jörg Jenatschs," *Bündner Jahrbuch* (1960): 27–37, published the same year as Hans Mohler's novel, *Der Kampf mit dem Drachen: Ein Jenatsch-Roman* (Zurich: Buchklub Ex Libris, 1960); I quote Mohler from the 1988 reprint: *Georg Jenatsch: Roman* (Chur: Calven and Terra Grischuna, 1988).

49. Mohler, *Georg Jenatsch*, 527–28. In Hans von Mühlestein's 1933 play, the possibility that it had been too many years since Pompeius's murder for revenge to be a powerful motivation had already come up. Mühlestein has a character laugh at the idea that Rudolf von Planta (the murderer in Mühlestein's play) was raging for revenge: "Oh, Fausch! A little late for such anger, after eighteen years! No, no, the Spanish ambassador just made that hothead's head a little hotter" ("Hat dem Tollkopf seinen Kopf noch tollender gemacht") (Mühlestein, *Diktator*, 135).

50. To be clear, the "newsreel" is in fact part of the film made by Schmid. No film of the actual excavations of 1959 exists, nor was the archaeologist's name Tobler.

51. Daniel Schmid, *Jenatsch*, produced by Theres Scherrer and George Reinhardt (Zurich: Limbo Film, 1987).

52. Reto Hänny, "Guardati, Giorgio," afterword to *Jürg Jenatsch: Eine Bündnergeschichte, Mit einem Nachwort von Reto Hänny*, by Conrad Ferdinand Meyer (Berlin: Suhrkamp/Insel Verlag, 1988), 321–54 (quoting from 324–26). Thanks to the author for providing a revised typescript (1997).

53. Hänny, "Guardati, Giorgio," 340.

54. For a history of visual impressions by outsiders, see Bruno Weber, *Graubünden in alten Ansichten: Landschaftsporträts reisender Künstler vom 16. bis zum frühen 19. Jahrhundert* (Chur: Rätisches Museum, 1984).

55. See http://www.hotel-rates.com/switzerland/st-moritz/hotel-chesa-guardalej.html and www.chesa-guardalej.ch (accessed May 4, 2007). Several Hotels Jenatsch are scattered across Graubünden and Switzerland as well.

56. *Kathedrale Chur: Restaurierungsprojekt 2002–2007*, no. 6 (December 2005): 1.

57. Ibid.

58. The first plaque, labeled "Zum Staubigen Hüetli," describes Jenatsch as a man with many enemies and suggests that the Planta were involved in his murder, "probably the best known murder in the history of Graubünden." The second plaque, labeled "Die Tränen der Lucrecia," begins with the evocative line, "What William Tell is for Switzerland, Jörg Jenatsch is for Graubünden: an icon of liberty [*Freiheitsmythos*]." On this plaque, Lucretia, "whose real name was Katharina von Planta," is described as having brought about his murder. The nearby sculptural fountain by Christoph Haerle of Zurich (2006) is also titled *Die Tränen der Lucrecia*.

Epilogue

1. See Jon Mathieu, "33 Jahre nach Pfisters Jenatsch-Biographie: Neue Forschungsergebnisse und -perspektiven," in Pfister, 492n5.

2. Personal communication from the Archäologischer Dienst Graubünden (Dr. Manuel Janosa), September 26, 2007: "Bezüglich der Knochen ist mit ebenso grosser Wahrscheinlichkeit anzunehmen, dass sie 1961 wieder ins Grab zurückgelangten." For many years, the bones were simply thought to be lost. The Archäologischer Dienst investigated further during the renovations of the Chur cathedral between 2002 and 2007.

3. Jon Mathieu personally observed the trim in Hug's possession and identified by Hug during an interview on October 17, 1983. A representative of the Chur cathedral confirmed Hug's possession to Mathieu as well. Prof. Jon Mathieu, University of Lucerne, personal communication, October 10, 2007.

4. As Manuel Janosa notes, the exact location of Jenatsch's grave is, amazingly, still not entirely clear (personal communication, September 26, 2006): "Das Grab, übrigens, befand sich im Westen des nördlichen Seitenschiffes der Kathedrale. Wo ganz genau wird auch nach Studium der damaligen Zeitungsberichte . . . nicht richtig klar."

5. Personal communications, Jon Mathieu, on August 31, 2007 and October 10, 2007.

6. Most recently, Andreas Wendland, *Der Nutzen der Pässe und die Gefährdung der Seelen: Spanien, Mailand und der Kampf ums Veltlin 1620–1641* (Zurich: Chronos, 1995), clarified the situation between 1630 and 1639, when Jenatsch was at the height of his influence, by bringing the archives in Spain to bear for the first time; meanwhile, Silvio Färber, *Der bündnerische Herrenstand im 17. Jahrhundert: Politische, soziale, und wirtschaftliche Aspekte seiner Vorherrschaft* (Zurich: Zentralstelle der Studentenschaft, 1983), painstakingly assembled vast amounts of genealogical and political data to define the contours of Bündner factions in Jenatsch's time.

7. Personal communication, Jon Mathieu, University of Lucerne, August 31, 2007.

8. According to Mathieu's notes, the interview took place on October 17, 1983. Mathieu, personal communication, October 10, 2007.

9. The creation of this large facility, carved into a hillside near the baroque castle of Haldenstein, is a characteristically Swiss provision to protect "cultural goods" from any imaginable threat. See http://www.raetischesmuseum.gr.ch/de/node/11 (accessed October 10, 2007).

BIBLIOGRAPHY

Archival Material (signatures directly cited)

Archiv der Evangelischen Rhätischen Synode

 Msc. B 3

Kantonsbibliothek St. Gallen, Vadianische Sammlung

 Msc. 233, 235.

Staatsarchiv Graubünden (StAGR)

 A II Landesakten

 AB IV

 AB 5/13

 B 721

 B1592

 D II

Staatsarchiv Zürich (StAZH)

 E II 100–101

Published Sources

Amtliche Sammlung der älteren Eidgenössischen Abschiede. Various editors and publishers, 1856–1886.

Anhorn, Bartholomäus. *Graw-Pünter-Krieg, beschrieben von Barthol: Anhorn 1603–1629: Nach dem manuscript zum ersten Mal herausgegeben.* Edited by Conradin von Moor. Chur: Verlag der Antiquariatsbuchhandlung, 1873.

Bifrun, Jachiam Tütschett. *L'g Nuof Sainc Testamaint da Nos Signer Jesu Christi.* [Basel?]: Stevan Zorsch, 1560.

Blutige Sanfftmuet Der Caluinischen Predicanten: Wahrhaffte Relation auß einer Glaubwürdigen Person Sendschreiben. N.p., 1621. Microfilm in Flugschriftensammlung Gustav Freytag, #5139. Munich and New York: K. V. Sauer Verlag, 1980–1981.

"Das Grab des Jürg Jenatsch," *Neue Bündner Zeitung* (Chur, Switzerland), August 11, 1959.

"Das Grab des Jürg Jenatsch: Ergebnisse der wissenschaftlichen Untersuchung des Fundes," *Der Freie Rätier* (Chur, Switzerland), December 24, 1959.

"Die Grabmäler der Kathedrale," *Kathedrale Chur: Restaurierungsprojekt 2001–2007*, no. 6 (December 2005), http://bistum-chur.ch/Newsletter6.pdf (accessed May 4, 2007).

Flugi, Alfons. "George Jenatsch. Ein biographischer Versuch." *Bündnerisches Monatsblatt* 9, no. 9/10 (1852).

Grawpündtnerische Handlungen des MDCXVIII Jahrs, Darinnen klärlich unnd wahrhafftig angezeigt werden die rechtmeßigen unnd notzwingenden ursachen der zusammen kunfft deß gemeinen Landvolcks. N.p., 1618.

Guler, Johannes. *Raetia: Das ist Aussführliche und wahrhaffte Beschreibung der dreyen Loblichen Grawen Bündten uñ anderer Retischen völcker: Darinnen erklärt werden Dero aller begriff, härkommen thaaten.* Zurich: Joh. Rodolff Wolffen, 1616.

Haffter, Ernst, ed. *Georg Jenatsch: Urkundenbuch, enthaltend Exkurse und Beilagen.* Chur: n.p., 1895.

Hänny, Reto. "Guardati, Giorgio." Afterword to *Jürg Jenatsch: Eine Bündnergeschichte, Mit einem Nachwort von Reto Hänny*, by Conrad Ferdinand Meyer, 321–54. Berlin: Suhrkamp/Insel Verlag, 1988.

Jecklin, Fritz, ed. "Das Davoser Spendbuch vom Jahre 1562." *Jahresbericht der historisch-antiquarischen Gesellschaft von Graubünden* 54 (1924): 197–210.

———. *Materialien zur Standes- und Landesgeschichte Gem. III Bünde (Graubünden), 1464–1803.* 2 vols. Basel: Basler Buch- und Antiquariatshandlung, 1907–1909.

Joho, Rudolf. *Jürg Jenatsch.* Elgg: Volksverlag Elgg, ca. 1955.

———. *Jürg Jenatsch (Gewaltherrschaft?): Historisches Schauspiel in 5 Akten.* Hildesheim: Author, 1936.

"Jürg Jenatsch—ein großer Sohn Bündens," *Neue Bündner Zeitung* (Chur, Switzerland), August 15, 1959.

Juvalta, Fortunat von. *Denkwürdigkeiten des Fortunat von Juvalta, 1567–1649.* Edited by Conradin von Moor. Chur: O. Hitz, 1848.

Lehmann, Heinrich Ludwig. *Die Republik Graubünden historisch-geographisch-statistisch dargestellt.* 2 vols. Magdeburg and Brandenburg: Keil, 1797–1799.

Meyer, Conrad Ferdinand. *Jürg Jenatsch: Eine Bündnergeschichte.* Munich: Wilhelm Goldmann Verlag, 1984 (based on the 1885 Leipzig edition).

Mohler, Hans. *Der Kampf mit dem Drachen: Ein Jenatsch-Roman.* Zurich: Buchklub Ex Libris, 1960. Reprinted as *Georg Jenatsch: Roman.* Chur: Calven and Terra Grischuna, 1988.

Mühlestein, Hans von. *Der Diktator und der Tod: Die Tragödie Jörg Jenatschs. Bühnendichtung in 4 Akten.* Celerina: Author, 1933.

Padavino, Gian Battista. *Del Governo e Stato die Signori Svizzeri Relazione.* Edited by Victor Ceresole. Venice: Tipografia Antonelli, 1874.

Pascal, Charles. *Caroli Paschalii Regis in Sacro Consistorio Consilarii Legatio Rhaetica.* Paris: P. Chevalier, 1620.

Pfister, Alexander, ed. *Jörg Jenatsch: Briefe, 1614–1639.* Chur: Terra Grischuna Buchverlag, 1983.

Planta, Peter Conradin von. *Ritter Rudolf Planta: Ein Schauspiel.* Chur: n.p., 1849.

Salis, Hortensia von. *Glaubens-Rechenschaft; Conversations-Gespräche; Gebät.* Edited by Maya Widmer. Bern: Haupt, 2003.

Salis, Ulisse de. *Memorie del Maresciallo di campo Ulisse de Salis-Marschlins.* Edited by Conrad Jecklin. Chur: F. Schuler, 1931.

Saussure, Theodor de. *Jenatsch, oder Graubünden während des dreissigjährigen Krieges.* Chur: Hitz und Hail, 1886.

Schiess, Traugott, ed. *Bullingers Korrespondenz mit den Graubündnern.* Quellen zur Schweizer Geschichte, o.s. Vols. 23–25. Basel: Verlag der Basler Buch- und Antiquariatshandlung, 1904–1906. Reprint, Nieuwkoop: B. de Graaf, 1968.

Schmid, Daniel. *Jenatsch.* Motion picture produced by Theres Scherrer and George Reinhardt. Limbo Film, 1987.

Sprecher, Fortunat [von]. *Geschichte der bündnerischen Kriegen und Unruhen.* 2 vols. Edited and translated by Conradin von Mohr. Chur: Leonhard Hitz, 1856.

———. *Historia motuum et bellorum, postremis hisce annis in Rhaetia excitatorum et gestorum.* Cologne: Petri Chouët, 1629.

———. *Pallas Raetica, armata et togata.* Basel: I. J. Genathius, 1617.

Sprecher, Hans, ed. "Die gerächtigkeit, so ain gemaind uff Tavas zu ainem pfarrer hat." *Bündnerisches Monatsblatt,* n.S., 6, no.12 (1901): 253–58.

Tschudi, Aegidius. *Die uralt warhafftig Alpisch Rhetia / sampt dem Tract der anderen Alpgebirgen / nach Plinii / Ptolomei / Strabonis / auch anderen Welt und gschichtschribern warer anzeygung.* Basel: M. Isingren & J. Bebel, 1538.

Vulliemin, Louis. *Geschichte der Eidgenossen während des 16. und 17: Jahrhunderts.* 3 vols. Zurich: Orell, Füßli, 1844.

Zinsli, Philip, ed. "Politische Gedichte aus der Zeit der Bündner Wirren 1603–1639. Texte." *Jahresbericht der Historisch-antiquitarische Gesellschaft Graubündens* 40 (1911): 107–239, and 41 (1911): 23–120.

Zschokke, Heinrich. *Die drey ewigen Bünde im hohen Rhätien: Historische Skizze.* Zurich: Orell, Gessner, & Füssli, 1798.

"Zu den Ausgrabungen in der Kathedrale in Chur," *Der Freie Rätier* (Chur, Switzerland), August 12, 1959.

Secondary Literature

Anderson, Benedict. *Imagined Communities: Reflections on the Origin and Spread of Nationalism,* revised and extended edition. New York: Verso, 1991.

Armstrong, John. *Nations before Nationalism.* Chapel Hill: University of North Carolina Press, 1982.

Barber, Benjamin. *The Death of Communal Liberty: A History of Freedom in a Swiss Mountain Canton.* Princeton, NJ: Princeton University Press, 1974.

Baron, Hans. *The Crisis of the Early Italian Renaissance: Civic Humanism in an Age of Classicism and Tyranny.* Princeton, NJ: Princeton University Press, 1966.

Bellabarba, Marco. "Rituali, Leggi, e Disciplina del Duello: Italia e Germania fra Cinque e Settecento." In *Duelli, Faide e Rappacificazioni: Elaborazioni concettuali, esperienze storiche,* edited by Marco Cavina, 83–118. Milano: A. Giuffrè, 2001.

Bellow, Adam. *In Praise of Nepotism: A Natural History.* New York: Doubleday, 2003.

Berger, Mathis. "Die Ermordung Jörg Jenatschs." *Bündner Jahrbuch* (1960): 27–37.

Billigmeier, Robert H. *A Crisis in Swiss Pluralism: The Romansh and Their Relations with the German- and Italian-Swiss in the Perspective of a Millennium.* The Hague: Mouton, 1979.

Bisson, T. N. "The Military Origins of Medieval Representation." *American Historical Review* 71 (1966): 353–73.

Blattmann, Lynn. "Duell." *Historisches Lexicon der Schweiz,* http://www.hls-dhs-dss.ch/textes/d/D16330.php (accessed May 4, 2007).

Bleuler, Hermann. *Conrad Ferdinand Meyers "Jürg Jenatsch" im Verhältnis zu seinen Quellen.* Karlsruhe: n.p., 1920.

Bonjour, Edgar, and Richard Feller. *Geschichtsschreibung der Schweiz.* Vol. 2, *Vom Spätmittelalter zur Neuzeit.* Basel: Benno Schwabe & Co. Verlag, 1962.

Borchardt, Frank. *German Antiquity in Renaissance Myth.* Baltimore, MD: Johns Hopkins University Press, 1971.

Boringhieri, Paolo. "Pussaunza, richezza e poverted a Zuoz 1521–1801." *Annalas de la Società Retorumantscha* 102 (1988): 79–201.

Bornatico, Remo. *L'arte tipografica nelle Tre Leghe (1547–1803) e nei Grigioni (1803–1975).* 2nd. ed. Chur: Author, 1976.

Bossy, John. *Christianity in the West, 1400–1700.* Oxford: Oxford University Press, 1985.

Breuilly, John. *Nationalism and the State.* Manchester: Manchester University Press, 1982.

Brown, Horatio. "The Valtelline." In *Cambridge Modern History.* Vol. 4, *The Thirty Years' War,* edited by A. W. Ward et al., 35–63. Cambridge: Cambridge University Press, 1906.

Bundi, Martin. *Frühe Beziehungen zwischen Graubünden und Venedig.* Chur: Gasser, 1988.

Cameron, Euan. *The European Reformation.* Oxford: Clarendon, 1991.

Carrithers, Michael, et al., eds. *The Category of the Person: Anthropology, Philosophy, History.* Cambridge: Cambridge University Press, 1985.

Duby, Georges. *The Three Orders: Feudal Society Imagined.* Translated by Arthur Goldhammer. Chicago: University of Chicago Press, 1980.

Färber, Silvio. *Der bündnerische Herrenstand im 17. Jahrhundert: Politische, soziale, und wirtschaftliche Aspekte seiner Vorherrschaft.* Zurich: Zentralstelle der Studentenschaft, 1983.

Fontana, Giatgen. *Rechtshistorische Begriffsanalyse und das Paradigma der Freien: Ein methodischer und rechtssemantischer Begriffsbildungsversuch der mittelalterlicher Freiheit unter besonderer Bezugnahme auf die Historiographie Graubündens.* Zurich: Schulthess, 1987.

Friedeburg, Robert von. *"Patria" und "Patrioten" vor dem Patriotismus: Pflichten, Rechte, Glauben und die Rekonfigurierung europäischer Gemeinwesen im 17. Jahrhundert.* Wiesbaden: Harassowitz, 2005.

———."Why Did Seventeenth Century Estates Address the Jurisdictions of Their Princes as Fatherlands? War, Territorial Absolutism and Duties to the Fatherland in German Seventeenth Century Political Discourse." In *Orthodoxies and Heterodoxies in Early Modern German Culture: Order and Creativity 1550–1750,* edited by Randolph Head and Daniel Christensen. Leiden: Brill, 2007.

Fuchs, Esther. "Woman and the Discourse of Patriarchal Wisdom: A Study of Proverbs 1–9." In *Women in the Hebrew Bible: A Reader,* edited by Alice Bach, 85–98. New York: Routledge, 1999.

Furrer, Norbert. "Paroles de mercenaire: Aspects sociolinguistiques du service étranger." In *Gente ferocissima: Mercenariat et société en Suisse (XVe-XIXe siècle),* edited by Lucienne Hubler et al., 289–315. Lausanne and Zurich: Editions D'en Bas and Chronos Verlag, 1997.

Ganseuer, Frank. *Der Staat des "gemeinen Mannes": Gattungstypologie und Programmatik des politischen Schrifttums von Reformation und Bauernkrieg.* Frankfurt a.M.: Peter Lang, 1985.

Gartmann, Balzer. *Georg Jenatsch in der Literatur*. Disentis: Buchdruckerei Conradau, 1946.

Geary, Patrick. *The Myth of Nations: The Medieval Origins of Europe*. Princeton, NJ: Princeton University Press, 2002.

Gellner, Ernest. *Nations and Nationalism*. Oxford: Blackwell, 1983.

Grell, Ole Peter, and Bob Scribner, eds. *Tolerance and Intolerance in the European Reformation*. Cambridge: Cambridge University Press, 1996.

Grimm, Paul. *Die Anfänge der Bündner Aristokratie im 15. und 16. Jahrhundert*. Zurich: Juris, 1981.

Haffter, Ernst. *Georg Jenatsch: Ein Beitrag zur Geschichte der Bündner Wirren*. Davos: Hugo Richter, 1894.

Head, Randolph. "At the Frontiers of Theory: Confession Formation, Anti-Confessionalization and Religious Change in the Valtellina, 1520–1620." In *Konfessionalisierung und Konfessionskonflikt in Graubünden, 16.–18. Jahrhundert*, edited by Georg Jäger and Ulrich Pfister, 163–79. Zurich: Chronos, 2006.

———. "Catholics and Protestants in Graubünden: Confessional Discipline and Confessional Identities without an Early Modern State?" *German History* 17, no. 3 (1999): 321–45.

———. "'Cetera sunt politica et ad nos nihil': Social Power, Legitimacy and Struggles over the Clerical Voice in Post-Reformation Graubünden." In *Debatten über die Legitimation von Herrschaft. Politische Sprachen in der Frühen Neuzeit*, edited by Luise Schorn-Schutte and Sven Tode, 67–85. Berlin: Akademie-Verlag, 2006.

———. "Comunità di identità e comunità d'azione nei Grigione in età moderna: Le istituzioni politiche, confessionali e linguistiche di una repubblica alpina, 1470–1620." *Archivio Storico Ticinese*, no. 132 (2002): 167–82.

———. *Early Modern Democracy in the Grisons*. Cambridge: Cambridge University Press, 1995.

———. "'nit alß zwo Gmeinden, oder Partheyen, sonder ein Gmeind': Kommunalismus zwischen den Konfessionen in Graubünden, 1530–1620." In *Landgemeinde und Kirche im Zeitalter der Konfessionen*, edited by Beat Kümin and Peter Blickle, 21–57. Zurich: Chronos, 2004.

———. "A Plurilingual Family in the Sixteenth Century: Language Use and Linguistic Consciousness in the Salis Correspondence, 1580–1610." *Sixteenth Century Journal* 26, no. 3 (1995): 577–93.

———. "Rhaetian Ministers, from Shepherds to Citizens: Calvinism and Democracy in the Republic of the Three Leagues, 1550–1620." In *Later Calvinism: International Perspectives*, edited by W. Fred Graham. Kirksville, MO: Sixteenth Century Journal Publishers, 1994.

———. "William Tell and His Comrades: Association and Fraternity in the Propaganda of Fifteenth and Sixteenth Century Switzerland." *Journal of Modern History* 67, no. 3 (1995): 527–57.

Hexter, Jack. "The Myth of the Middle Class." In *Reappraisals in History*. 2nd ed., 71–115. 1961. Reprint, Chicago: University of Chicago Press, 1979.

Hsia, Ronnie Po-Chia. *Social Discipline in the Reformation: Central Europe, 1550–1750*. London: Routledge, 1989.

———. *The World of Catholic Renewal 1540–1770*. Cambridge: Cambridge University Press, 1998.

Israel, Jonathan. *Radical Enlightenment: Philosophy and the Making of Modernity 1650–1750*. Oxford: Oxford University Press, 2002.

Jecklin, C. "Das Duell G. Jenatschs mit Oberst J. von Ruinelli. 6/16 März 1627." *Jahres-bericht der Historisch-antiquarischen Gesellschaft Graubündens* 17 (1887): 55–72.

Jecklin, Fritz, and Michael Valèr, eds. "Die Ermordung Georg Jenatschs nach dem Churer Verhörprotokoll." *Zeitschrift für Schweizerische Geschichte* 4 (1924): 396–444.

Joho, Rudolf. *Schweizer Bühnenwerke: Berufstheater.* Elgg: Volksverlag Elgg, 1955.

Juergensmeyer, Mark. *Terror and the Mind of God: The Global Rise of Religious Violence.* Berkeley: University of California Press, 2000.

Karlebach, Elisheva. *Divided Souls: Converts from Judaism in Germany, 1500–1750.* New Haven, CT: Yale University Press, 2001.

Kenngott, A. "Jürg Jenatsch in Geschichte, Roman und Drama." *Washington University Studies* vol. 2, pt. 2, no. 2 (1915): 177–220.

Kent, Dale V. *The Rise of the Medici: Faction in Florence, 1426–1434.* Oxford: Oxford University Press, 1978.

Luther, Martin, "On the Freedom of a Christian," in Jaroslav Pelikan and Helmut T. Lehmann, eds., *Luther's Works,* 55 vols. (Saint Louis and Philadelphia: Concordia Press, 1955–1976), 31:327–78.

Maag, Karin. *Seminary or University?: The Genevan Academy and Reformed Higher Education, 1560–1620.* Aldershot: Ashgate, 1995.

Maissen, Felici. *Die Drei Bünde in der zweiten Hälfte des 17. Jahrhundert in politischer, kirchengeschichtlicher, und volkskundlicher Schau.* Vol. 1, 1647–1657. Aarau: Sauerländer, 1966.

Maissen, Thomas. "'Die Gemeinden und das Volck als höchste Gewalt unsers freyen democratischen Stands.' Die Erneuerung der politischen Sprache in Graubünden um 1700." *Jahrbuch der Historischen Gesellschaft von Graubünden* 131 (2001): 37–84.

Marchal, Guy. "Die Antwort der Bauern: Elemente und Schichtungen des eidgenössischen Geschichtsbewußtseins am Ausgang des Mittelalters." In *Geschichtsschreibung und Geschichtsbewusstsein im Späten Mittelalter,* edited by Hans Patze, 757–90. Sigmaringen: Jan Thorbecke, 1987.

Mathieu, Jon. *Bauern und Bären: Eine Geschichte des Unterengadins von 1650 bis 1800.* Chur: Octopus, 1987.

———. *Eine Agrargeschichte der Inneren Alpen.* Zurich: Juris, 1992.

———. *Geschichte der Alpen 1500–1900: Umwelt, Entwicklung, Gesellschaft.* Vienna: Böhlau, 1998.

———. "Eine Region am Rand: Das Unterengadin 1650–1800." PhD diss., University of Bern, 1983.

———. "In der Kirche schlafen. Eine sozialgeschichtliche Lektüre von Conradin Riolas 'Geistlicher Trompete' (Strada im Engadin, 1709)." *Schweizerisches Archiv für Volkskunde* 87, no. 3/4 (1991): 121–45.

———. "33 Jahre nach Pfisters Jenatsch-Biographie: Neue Forschungsergebnisse und perspektiven." In Pfister, *Georg Jenatsch,* 491–508. Chur: Verlag Bündner Monatsblatt, 1991.

Matthes, Melissa. *The Rape of Lucretia and the Founding of Republics: Readings in Livy, Machiavelli, and Rousseau.* University Park: Pennsylvania State University Press, 2000.

Medick, Hans, and David Sabean, eds. *Interest and Emotion: Essays on the study of Family and Kinship.* Cambridge and Paris: Cambridge University Press and Éditions de la Maison des sciences de l'homme, 1984.

Meyer von Knonau, G. "Das Album in Schola Tigurina." *Zürcher Taschenbuch,* n.F., no. 5 (1893): 147–57.

Moore, R. I. *The Formation of a Persecuting Society: Power and Deviance in Western Europe, 950–1250*. Oxford: Basil Blackwell, 1987.

Muir, Edward. *Mad Blood Stirring: Vendetta and Factions in Friuli during the Renaissance*. Baltimore, MD: Johns Hopkins University Press, 1993.

Neuschel, Kristin. *Word of Honor: Interpreting Noble Culture in Sixteenth-Century France*. Ithaca, NY: Cornell University Press, 1989.

Oexle, Otto Gerhard. "Die funktionale Dreiteilung als Deutungsschema der sozialen Wirklichkeit in der ständischen Gesellschaft des Mittelalters." In *Ständische Gesellschaft und soziale Mobilität*, edited by Winfried Schulze, 19–51. Munich: R. Oldenbourg, 1988.

Padrutt, Christian. *Staat und Krieg im Alten Bünden: Studien zur Beziehung zwischen Obrigkeit und Kriegertum in den Drei Bünden vornehmlich im 15. und 16. Jahrhundert*. Zurich: Fretz und Wasmuth, 1965.

Pagden, Anthony. *The Fall of Natural Man: The American Indian and the Origins of Comparative Ethnology*. Cambridge: Cambridge University Press, 1982.

Parker, Geoffrey. *The Army of Flanders and the Spanish Road, 1567–1659: The Logistics of Spanish Victory and Defeat in the Low Countries' Wars*. 2nd edition. Cambridge: Cambridge University Press, 2004.

———. "Success and Failure during the First Century of the Reformation." *Past & Present*, no. 136 (1992): 43–82.

Pennington, Kenneth. "Learned Law, Droit Savante, Gelehrtes Recht: The Tyranny of a Concept." *Syracuse International Journal of Law and Commerce* 20 (1994): 205–15.

Peyer, Hans Conrad. *Verfassungsgeschichte der alten Schweiz*. Zurich: Schulthess, 1978.

Pfister, Alexander. *Georg Jenatsch: Sein Leben und seine Zeit*. 5th ed. Chur: Verlag Bündner Monatsblatt, 1991.

———. "Partidas e combats ella Ligia Grischa, 1494–1794." *Annalas de la Società Retorumantscha* 40 (1926): 71–208.

Pfister, Christian. *Das Klima der Schweiz von 1525–1860 und seine Bedeutung in der Geschichte von Bevölkerung und Landwirtschaft*. Bern: Paul Haupt, 1984.

Planta, Peter Conradin von. *Die Planta im Spätmittelalter*. Chur: Historische Gesellschaft von Graubünden, 1996.

Plattner, Placidus. "Einführung." Introduction to *Die Raeteis: Schweizerisch-Deutscher Krieg von 1499: Epos in IX Gesängen*, by Simon Lemnius, i–xxxviii. Chur: Sprecher und Plattner, 1874.

Pocock, J. G. A. *The Machiavellian Moment: Florentine Political Thought and the Atlantic Republican Tradition*. Princeton, NJ: Princeton University Press, 1975.

Post, Gaines. "Medieval and Renaissance Ideas of Nation." *Dictionary of the History of Ideas*, 3: 318–24. Online at http://etext.virginia.edu/cgi-local/DHI/dhi.cgi?id=dv3-41 (accessed May 4, 2007).

Prada, Giovanni da. *L'Arciprete Nicolò Rusca e i cattolici del suo tempo*. Tirano: Tipografia Poletti, 1994.

Pufendorf, Samuel. *Severini de Monzambano Veronensis De statu Imperii Germanici ad Lealium fratrem, dominum Trezolani* (Geneva [i.e. Den Haag]: Petrus Columesius [i.e. Adrian Vlacq], 1667).

Reber, B[althasar]. "Georg Jenatsch, Graubündtens Pfarrer und Held während des dreißigjährigen Kriegs." *Beiträge zur vaterländischen Geschichte herausgegeben von der historischen Gesellschaft in Basel* 7 (1860): 177–300.

Redlich, Fritz. *The German Military Enterpriser and His Work Force: A Study in European Economic and Social History*. Vierteljahresschrift für Sozial und Wirtschaftsgeschichte, Beiheft 47. Wiesbaden: F. Steiner, 1964.

Remak, Joachim. *A Very Civil War: The Swiss Sonderbund War of 1847*. Boulder, CO: Westview, 1993.

Reynolds, Susan. *Fiefs and Vassals: The Medieval Evidence Reinterpreted*. Oxford: Oxford University Press, 1994.

Sabean, David. "Production of the Self in the Age of Confessionalism." *Central European History* 29, no. 1 (1996): 1–18.

Sahlins, Peter. *Boundaries: The Making of France and Spain in the Pyrenees*. Berkeley: University of California Press, 1989.

Sahr, Julius. *C. Ferd. Meyer: Jürg Jenatsch*. Berlin and Leipzig: B. G. Teubner, 1904.

Saulle Hippenmeyer, Immacolata. *Nachbarschaft, Pfarrei und Gemeinde in Grabünden 1400–1600*. Chur: Kommissionsverlag Bündner Monatsblatt/Desertina, 1997.

Scaramellini, Guglielmo. "Die Beziehungen zwischen den Drei Bünden und dem Veltlin, Chiavenna und Bormio." In *Handbuch der Bündner Geschichte*, edited by Jürg Simonett, vol. 2: 141–60. Chur: Verlag Bündner Monatsblatt, 2000.

Schalk Ellery. *From Valor to Pedigree: Ideas of Nobility in France in the Sixteenth and Seventeenth Centuries*. Princeton, NJ: Princeton University Press, 1986.

Schama, Simon. *The Embarrassment of Riches: An Interpretation of Dutch Culture in the Golden Age*. Berkeley: University of California Press, 1988.

Schilling, Heinz. "Confessional Europe." In *Handbook of European History 1400–1600*, edited by Thomas A. Brady, Heiko A. Oberman, and James D. Tracy, vol. 2: 640–70. Leiden: Brill, 1995.

Schmid, Hans Martin. *Das Bild Herzog Heinrich Rohans in der bündnerischen und französischen Geschichtsschreibung*. Chur: Bischofsberger, 1966.

Schulze, Winfried. *Reich und Türkengefahr im späten 16. Jahrhundert*. Munich: C. H. Beck, 1978.

Simonett, Jürg, ed. *Handbuch der Bündner Geschichte*. 4 vols. Chur: Verlag Bündner Monatsblatt, 2000.

Taylor, Charles. *Sources of the Self: The Making of the Modern Identity*. Cambridge, MA: Harvard University Press, 1989.

Thomas, Keith. *Religion and the Decline of Magic: Studies in Popular Beliefs in Sixteenth- and Seventeenth-Century England*. London: Weidenfeld and Nicholson, 1971.

Valèr, Michael. *Die Bestrafung von Staatsvergehen in der Republik der III Bünde: Ein Beitrag zur mittelalterlichen Rügegerichtsbarkeit und zur Geschichte der Demokratie in Graubünden*. Chur: Schuler, 1904.

Volkland, Frauke. *Konfession und Selbstverständnis: Reformierte Rituale in der gemischtkonfessionellen Kleinstadt Bischofszell im 17. Jahrhundert*. Göttingen: Vandenhoek & Ruprecht, 2005.

Vonrufs, Ulrich. *Die politische Führungsgruppe Zürichs zur Zeit von Hans Waldmann (1450–1489): Struktur, politische Networks und die sozialen Beziehungstypen Verwandschaft, Freundschaft und Patron-Klient-Beziehung*. Bern: Peter Lang, 2002.

Weber, Bruno. *Graubünden in alten Ansichten: Landschaftsporträts reisender Künstler vom 16. bis zum frühen 19. Jahrhundert*. Chur: Rätisches Museum, 1984.

Wedgewood, C. V. *The Thirty Years War*. 1938. Reprint, New York: New York Review of Books, 2005.

Weiss, Richard. *Das Alpwesen Graubündens: Wirtschaft, Sachkultur, Recht, Älplerarbeit und Älplerleben*. Zurich: E. Rentsch, 1942.

Wendland, Andreas. "Ai confini dell'eresia. Le frontiere religiose ed ecclesiastiche in Valtellina (1550–1640)." In *La Valtellina Crocevia dell'Europa: Politica e Religione nell'Età della Guerra dei Trent'Anni*, edited by Agostino Borromeo, 163–97. Milan: Monadori, 1998.

―――. *Der Nutzen der Pässe und die Gefährdung der Seelen. Spanien, Mailand und der Kampf ums Veltlin 1620–1641*. Zurich: Chronos, 1995.

―――. "Il missionario come politico–Il politico come missionario: Missionari cappucini e politica della controriforma in Valtellina e nel territorio delle Tre Leghe nel XVII secolo. Il programma di riconquista cattolica di Ignazio da Casnigo." *Archivio Storico Ticinese* 33 (1996): 199–218.

Wenneker, Erich. "Lemnius, Simon." *Biographisches-Bibliographisches Kirchenlexicon*, http://www.bautz.de/bbkl/1/Lemnius.shtml (accessed May 4, 2007).

Wiesner, Merry. *Women and Gender in Early Modern Europe*. 3rd ed. Cambridge: Cambridge University Press, 2008.

Zimmer, Olivier. *A Contested Nation: History, Memory and Nationalism in Switzerland, 1761–1891*. Cambridge: Cambridge University Press, 2002.

INDEX

CPSIA information can be obtained
at www.ICGtesting.com
Printed in the USA
FFHW021445200919
54964381-60663FF